Generative AI

Generative AI

Avery Kelly

Kruger Brentt
Publishers
2026

Kruger Brentt Publishers UK. LTD.
Company Number 9728962

Regd. Office: 68 St Margarets Road, Edgware, Middlesex HA8 9UU

ISBN: 978-1-78715-611-1

For information on all our publications visit our website at http://krugerbrentt.com/

Preface

Generative AI explores one of the most transformative areas of artificial intelligence, focusing on systems that can create new content, including text, images, audio, and video. Generative AI has rapidly evolved from a research concept to a powerful set of tools influencing industries such as healthcare, entertainment, design, education, and marketing. This book aims to provide students, researchers, and professionals with both foundational knowledge and practical understanding of generative AI technologies, their applications, and their implications for society.

The text begins by introducing the core principles of generative AI, including machine learning models, neural networks, and probabilistic methods. It then delves into popular generative models, such as Generative Adversarial Networks (GANs), Variational Autoencoders (VAEs), and large language models, explaining how these architectures function and how they are trained to produce high quality content.

A significant focus is placed on applications of generative AI across various domains, highlighting real-world examples such as content creation, drug discovery, synthetic data generation, and interactive AI systems. Ethical considerations, including bias, intellectual property, misinformation, and societal impact, are addressed throughout, emphasizing the responsibility of developers and users in deploying these technologies safely and equitably.

The book also explores emerging trends and future directions in generative AI, including multimodal generation, human-AI collaboration, and AI-driven creativity, providing readers with a forward-looking perspective on how these systems may reshape industries and daily life.

We hope that Generative AI will serve as a comprehensive guide for learners and professionals, equipping them with the knowledge and critical perspective necessary to understand, develop, and responsibly deploy generative AI technologies.

Avery Kelly

Contents

CHAPTER 1

Introduction to Generative AI

1.1 WHAT IS GENERATIVE AI?

Generative AI, short for generative artificial intelligence, refers to a branch of artificial intelligence that focuses on creating new content rather than simply analyzing or acting on existing data. This content can include text, images, music, video, and even code. Unlike traditional AI systems that classify or predict based on input data, generative AI models are designed to produce novel outputs that are similar to the data they were trained on. This transformative capability represents a significant shift in the function of artificial intelligence, moving from reactive systems to ones that simulate human creativity and problem-solving. Generative AI represents a paradigm shift in the capabilities of artificial intelligence, moving from analytical tasks to the realm of creation. It blurs the lines between human and machine creativity, offering powerful tools that can generate text, images, music, and more. While the potential of generative AI is immense, it also poses significant challenges related to ethics, bias, misinformation, and intellectual property. As we navigate these complexities, it is essential to foster a collaborative relationship between humans and AI, guided by responsible innovation and a commitment to the common good. The future of generative AI will be shaped not only by technological advancements but also by the values and choices of those who develop and use it.

1.1.1 The Foundation of Generative AI

At the core of generative AI are machine learning techniques, particularly deep learning models that are trained on large datasets. These models learn patterns, structures, and relationships within the data, enabling them to generate outputs that mimic those learned patterns. The most popular architectures behind generative AI include Generative Adversarial Networks (GANs), Variational Autoencoders (VAEs), and Transformer-based models such as GPT (Generative Pre-trained Transformer).

Each of these has its strengths and applications depending on the nature of the content to be generated. GANs operate through a dual-model system in which two neural networks—a generator and a discriminator—are trained simultaneously. The generator creates new data instances, while the discriminator evaluates their authenticity. Over time, the generator improves its outputs to the point that they are indistinguishable from real data. This technique has been widely used for image generation and enhancement. On the other hand, VAEs use a probabilistic approach to generate new data points by encoding input data into a latent space and then decoding it back into a new sample. Transformers, particularly the GPT series developed by OpenAI, have revolutionized natural language processing by generating coherent and contextually relevant text based on prompts.

1.1.2 Applications of Generative AI

The applications of generative AI are vast and continue to expand rapidly across industries. In the creative arts, it is being used to compose music, write poetry, generate artwork, and even produce scripts for films. In the business world, generative AI helps in drafting reports, generating marketing content, and automating customer service through chatbots capable of holding human-like conversations. In healthcare, it aids in drug discovery and medical imaging by generating molecular structures and enhancing diagnostic imagery. In engineering and design, it assists in creating prototypes and optimizing design models. Generative AI is also transforming education by enabling personalized learning experiences. Educational platforms are using AI to generate tailored content, quizzes, and explanations based on the learner's level and pace. In journalism and publishing, it assists writers by generating article drafts, summarizing information, or even writing complete reports, although editorial oversight remains critical to ensure factual accuracy and ethical standards.

1.1.3 Ethical Considerations and Challenges

While the promise of generative AI is vast, it also brings with it a host of ethical considerations and technical challenges. One of the primary concerns is the potential misuse of generative AI to create deepfakes—synthetic media that can convincingly impersonate individuals in audio, video, or image form. These can be used maliciously to spread misinformation, conduct fraud, or violate privacy. The ability of generative AI to produce highly realistic content has raised questions about authenticity and trust in digital media. Another challenge is the risk of bias in AI-generated outputs.

Since generative models learn from data that may reflect societal biases, they can unintentionally reproduce or even amplify these biases in their outputs. For example, a text generator trained on biased data may produce content that is discriminatory or offensive. Addressing this issue requires careful curation of training datasets and the implementation of fairness-aware algorithms.

Moreover, there is the concern of intellectual property. Since generative AI often trains on publicly available content, questions arise about the ownership of the generated outputs and whether they infringe on the rights of original creators. Legal frameworks around AI-generated content are still evolving, and there is an ongoing debate about how to fairly compensate creators whose work has contributed to the training of these models.

1.1.4 Human-AI Collaboration

Rather than replacing human creativity, generative AI is increasingly seen as a collaborative tool that can enhance human potential. Artists, writers, designers, and musicians are using AI to augment their creative processes, gain inspiration, and explore new possibilities. This human-AI collaboration allows for rapid prototyping, iterative experimentation, and the generation of ideas that might not have been considered otherwise. AI becomes a partner in creativity, handling the technical or repetitive aspects while leaving room for human intuition and emotional intelligence. In corporate settings, generative AI is being used to support decision-making by simulating scenarios, visualizing outcomes, and generating strategic insights. This enhances the ability of professionals to explore various options before making critical choices. By integrating generative AI into workflows, businesses are not only increasing efficiency but also unlocking new avenues for innovation.

1.1.5 The Future of Generative AI

As generative AI continues to evolve, its capabilities are expected to become even more sophisticated. Future models will likely be more efficient, requiring less data and computational power while delivering higher quality outputs. Multimodal AI, which can understand and generate content across different media types (e.g., text, images, video, audio), is an area of active research and development. This will enable the creation of more immersive and interactive experiences, such as AI-generated virtual environments or lifelike digital assistants. Another promising direction is the integration of generative AI with augmented reality (AR) and virtual reality (VR). This can lead to groundbreaking applications in entertainment, education, and training by enabling dynamic, real-time content creation. For instance, virtual classrooms can adapt in real-time to a student's learning style, or immersive storytelling experiences can evolve based on user interactions. At the same time, regulatory frameworks and ethical guidelines will need to keep pace with technological advancements. Policymakers, researchers, and industry leaders must work together to ensure that generative AI is developed and deployed responsibly. Transparency, accountability, and inclusivity will be key principles in building public trust and ensuring that the benefits of generative AI are equitably distributed.

1.2 HISTORY AND EVOLUTION OF GENERATIVE AI

The history and evolution of Generative AI is a compelling narrative that mirrors the broader trajectory of artificial intelligence itself. It is a story rooted in early theoretical work in computer science, matured through the steady progress of machine learning, and accelerated by exponential advances in data availability and computational power. Generative AI's primary aim—to create new data resembling existing data—has inspired decades of research, culminating in the powerful tools available today. The history and evolution of generative AI illustrate a journey from theoretical speculation to practical and transformative technology.

From early neural networks to sophisticated transformer-based systems, the field has progressed through decades of innovation, driven by breakthroughs in algorithm design, computational power, and data availability. Today's generative AI systems can compose music, write text, create images, and simulate human-like interactions. As we look to the future, the continued development of generative AI will undoubtedly shape our culture, economy, and society in profound ways, bringing both opportunity and responsibility in equal measure.

1.2.1 Early Foundations and Theoretical Origins

The conceptual foundation for generative artificial intelligence can be traced back to the mid-20th century when computer scientists and mathematicians began exploring the possibilities of machines mimicking human reasoning and creativity. Alan Turing, in his seminal 1950 paper "Computing Machinery and Intelligence," introduced the idea that machines could eventually simulate human cognitive processes. Though not explicitly about generative systems, Turing's ideas paved the way for the notion that machines could not only perform calculations but also exhibit creativity.

During the 1950s and 1960s, early AI researchers focused mainly on symbolic AI, which attempted to model intelligence using logical rules and symbolic representations. While symbolic AI laid important groundwork, it lacked the adaptability and learning capabilities necessary for generative tasks. Nonetheless, this period saw the development of early algorithms that could, in limited ways, generate language or solve simple puzzles, hinting at the creative potential of future systems.

1.2.2 The Emergence of Machine Learning

A significant turning point came in the 1980s and 1990s with the rise of machine learning, a subset of AI that emphasized learning patterns from data rather than programming explicit rules. This shift was critical to the eventual rise of generative models. The development of neural networks, which simulate the behavior of neurons in the human brain, enabled AI systems to process complex, high-dimensional data. During this era, researchers began experimenting with probabilistic models that could generate new data points. One of the early methods was the Hidden Markov Model (HMM), used extensively in speech recognition and other time-series applications. HMMs laid the foundation for understanding how sequences of data could be modeled and generated statistically. However, these models were still relatively limited in scope and complexity compared to what would come later.

1.2.3 Introduction of Generative Models

The real conceptual breakthrough in generative AI came with the introduction of more sophisticated generative models in the 2000s. Variational Autoencoders (VAEs), introduced in 2013, marked a significant advancement. VAEs are neural networks that learn to encode data into a compressed latent space and then decode that space back into new, similar data. This allowed for the generation of entirely new examples that captured the underlying features of the training data. VAEs were especially effective in image generation and laid the groundwork for further innovation. Another major leap occurred in 2014 with the invention of Generative Adversarial Networks (GANs) by Ian Goodfellow and his colleagues. GANs introduced a novel two-part system composed of a generator and a discriminator. The generator attempts to create fake data, while the discriminator tries to determine whether the input is real or generated. Through this adversarial training process, the generator becomes increasingly proficient at producing data that is indistinguishable from real examples. GANs rapidly gained popularity and were celebrated for their ability to generate high-resolution images, deepfake videos, and realistic artistic content.

1.2.4 The Rise of Natural Language Generation

While early generative models focused primarily on visual data, parallel developments were taking place in natural language processing (NLP). Recurrent Neural Networks (RNNs) and Long Short-Term Memory (LSTM) networks were among the first neural architectures capable of generating coherent text by learning the structure and syntax of language. These models were widely used in applications such as machine translation and text prediction. The real explosion in natural language generation came with the introduction of the Transformer architecture in 2017 by researchers at Google. The Transformer model, which abandoned recurrence in favor of attention mechanisms, proved to be both faster and more effective at handling long-range dependencies in text. This innovation led directly to the development of Generative Pre-trained Transformers (GPT), beginning with GPT in 2018 and evolving rapidly through GPT-2, GPT-3, and beyond. These models were trained on massive datasets using unsupervised learning and fine-tuned for specific tasks, achieving unprecedented fluency and coherence in text generation. GPT-3, released in 2020 by OpenAI, marked a watershed moment for generative AI in natural language. With 175 billion parameters, GPT-3 could generate human-like text responses that were contextually aware and stylistically diverse. Its ability to write essays, summarize content, translate languages, and even code, demonstrated the enormous potential of generative AI in everyday applications.

1.2.5 Multimodal Generative AI and Expanding Horizons

The 2020s have seen a rapid expansion of generative AI into multimodal domains—models that can handle multiple types of data simultaneously, such as text, images, and audio. OpenAI's DALL·E, for example, is a generative model capable of creating detailed images from textual descriptions. This marked a major leap in the ability of AI to understand and generate content across different sensory modalities. Similarly, CLIP, another OpenAI innovation, combined vision and language understanding, allowing AI to "see" and "read" in tandem. Multimodal models have enabled the creation of more immersive and interactive AI systems. These models can now produce videos, animations, and music compositions, widening the scope of generative AI to include entertainment, design, and education. The integration of text-to-speech, image generation, and video synthesis capabilities has led to new tools that can generate entire multimedia experiences based on simple prompts.

1.2.6 Challenges and Societal Impact

As generative AI has evolved, it has brought not only benefits but also significant challenges. The power of generative models to create convincing content has raised ethical questions around misinformation, deepfakes, and intellectual property. The potential for misuse of AI-generated content has prompted calls for regulation, transparency, and accountability in AI development. Bias in AI-generated outputs also remains a major concern. Because generative models are trained on large datasets sourced from the internet, they can inadvertently learn and reproduce harmful stereotypes or biased language. Efforts are underway to address these issues through dataset curation, algorithmic fairness, and human-in-the-loop systems that monitor and guide AI behavior. At the same time, generative AI has begun to reshape industries. In healthcare, it is being used to generate synthetic data for research, assist in medical imaging, and design new drugs. In education, it enables personalized learning content. In business, it enhances marketing, automates content creation, and supports customer engagement. As these applications grow, so too does the need for responsible innovation and public understanding.

1.2.7 Looking Ahead: The Future of Generative AI

The evolution of generative AI is far from complete. Ongoing research is focused on making models more efficient, interpretable, and aligned with human values. The next generation of generative models is likely to be more collaborative, working alongside humans to augment rather than replace their creativity and intelligence. The development of open-source models and community-driven innovation is also playing a crucial role in democratizing access to generative technologies.

Future advances may involve AI systems capable of reasoning, understanding context deeply, and engaging in multi-turn conversations across domains. As hardware capabilities improve and training techniques become more efficient, we can expect generative AI to become even more integrated into daily life, transforming how we work, learn, and create.

1.3 KEY CHARACTERISTICS OF GENERATIVE AI SYSTEMS

Generative AI systems represent a remarkable leap in the capabilities of artificial intelligence. Unlike traditional AI models that are primarily designed to classify, recognize, or retrieve information, generative AI systems are built to create. These systems can produce novel text, images, music, code, and even interactive environments, all from learned patterns in existing data. The fundamental characteristics that define generative AI are what distinguish it from other forms of AI and contribute to its transformative potential across industries and disciplines. The key characteristics of generative AI systems—creativity through learning, probabilistic generation, contextual sensitivity, generalization, scalability, multimodality, and ethical design—form the foundation of their growing impact across diverse fields.

These traits enable generative AI to produce content that is not only novel and coherent but also tailored to specific needs and contexts. As generative AI continues to evolve, these characteristics will become even more refined, empowering users to collaborate with machines in ways that were once thought impossible. Understanding these core attributes is essential not only for leveraging generative AI effectively but also for engaging with its broader implications in a thoughtful and responsible manner.

1.3.1 Creativity through Learning from Data

One of the most defining characteristics of generative AI systems is their ability to generate creative content by learning from data. These systems are trained on vast datasets, absorbing patterns, structures, and styles present in the data. For instance, a generative model trained on literature can write essays or poems, while one trained on artworks can create original paintings. The creativity displayed by these models is not conscious or intentional but emerges from statistical learning processes that replicate and remix features from the training data. What makes this characteristic particularly significant is that generative AI does not merely reproduce existing data. Instead, it synthesizes new content that is similar in style or structure but is often unique in its expression. This ability to generate new data points that fit within the learned distribution of the training data makes generative AI a tool for innovation and ideation in fields like art, design, and writing.

1.3.2 Probabilistic and Pattern-Based Generation

Generative AI systems operate on probabilistic principles, meaning they generate outputs based on learned probabilities rather than deterministic rules. This characteristic allows for a high degree of variation in the outputs. Every time a model like GPT-4 responds to a prompt, it evaluates a range of possible next words based on learned probabilities and selects one, often with an element of randomness or sampling involved. This process enables generative AI to produce diverse outputs from the same input, making it more dynamic and adaptable. Because of this probabilistic foundation, generative AI systems are adept at identifying and reproducing complex patterns in data. Whether the input is language, visual art, or sound, the system captures the nuanced relationships within the data. This pattern recognition enables it to maintain coherence, style, and logical progression in the content it generates. For example, in natural language generation, the model considers grammar, semantics, tone, and context to construct meaningful and fluid sentences.

1.3.3 Generalization across Domains

A powerful characteristic of modern generative AI systems is their capacity to generalize across tasks and domains. This means that a single model, once trained, can perform a variety of tasks without needing task-specific adjustments. A generative language model, for example, can summarize texts, answer questions, translate languages, write code, and compose poetry—all using the same underlying architecture. This generalization is made possible by training on large and diverse datasets that cover a wide spectrum of knowledge and linguistic contexts. This versatility makes generative AI especially valuable in real-world applications where the boundaries between tasks are often blurred. In creative industries, for instance, a single model might assist in writing advertising copy, generating social media content, and brainstorming marketing slogans. In healthcare, it can draft clinical notes, explain medical conditions, and even simulate diagnostic conversations. This adaptability significantly expands the range of potential use cases.

1.3.4 Contextual Awareness and Prompt Sensitivity

Generative AI systems are highly sensitive to context and input prompts. The same model can produce drastically different outputs depending on how a question or task is phrased. This sensitivity allows users to steer the model toward desired responses by carefully crafting their prompts. In practical terms, this characteristic enables interactive and responsive AI systems that can engage in human-like dialogues, adapt to user preferences, and tailor outputs to specific tones or formats. The ability to maintain context over long inputs is another key strength of advanced generative models. Earlier models struggled with long sequences or multi-step reasoning, but newer architectures like the Transformer have greatly enhanced the contextual capabilities of generative AI. As a result, these models can engage in complex conversations, follow narrative arcs, and remember earlier parts of a text to ensure coherence and consistency.

1.3.5 Scalability and Efficiency

Scalability is a foundational characteristic that underpins the success of generative AI systems. These models are typically built to scale with the availability of computational resources and data. Larger models tend to perform better, exhibiting more nuanced understanding and generation capabilities. This scalability means that, with sufficient training, a generative AI model can continually improve in fluency, accuracy, and complexity of output. Furthermore, once trained, generative AI systems are highly efficient in deployment. They can generate high-quality content within seconds, vastly outpacing human creators in terms of speed. This efficiency is valuable in business settings where large volumes of content must be produced quickly, such as in journalism, advertising, or customer service.

1.3.6 Autonomy with Guided Control

While generative AI systems operate autonomously during content generation, they can also be guided or fine-tuned to align with specific goals or constraints. This dual nature—autonomous yet controllable—is a key characteristic that enhances their utility. Developers and users can influence the model's behavior through techniques such as prompt engineering, fine-tuning, or reinforcement learning from human feedback. For example, a company might fine-tune a generative model on its proprietary documents to ensure that outputs reflect its brand voice or regulatory requirements. Alternatively, researchers might guide a generative model to produce scientifically accurate text by adjusting training data or providing structured prompts. This blend of autonomy and control allows generative AI to be customized for a wide variety of applications while still retaining its generative flexibility.

1.3.7 Multimodal Capabilities

As generative AI systems evolve, an increasingly important characteristic is their multimodal nature—the ability to handle and generate different types of data, such as text, images, audio, and video. Multimodal models are designed to understand the relationships between different forms of information and produce cohesive outputs that integrate these elements. For instance, a multimodal generative AI might generate a video complete with narration and visual elements based on a written script. This multimodal functionality opens new possibilities for cross-media storytelling, educational tools, design automation, and user interfaces. It also reflects a more human-like way of processing and expressing information, since people naturally integrate visual, auditory, and linguistic data in communication. As multimodal models become more advanced, they promise to redefine the boundaries of digital creativity and interactivity.

1.3.8 Ethical Awareness and Responsible Design

An emerging but crucial characteristic of modern generative AI systems is the inclusion of ethical awareness and responsible design considerations. Developers now strive to embed safety features such as content filtering, bias mitigation, and explainability into generative models. These features aim to prevent harmful outputs, protect user privacy, and ensure that the AI's behavior aligns with social and legal norms.

Ethical design also includes transparency in how models are trained and used. Users are increasingly being informed when they are interacting with AI-generated content, and developers are publishing documentation outlining the capabilities and limitations of their models. This focus on ethics is not just a technical challenge but a societal necessity, ensuring that the powerful capabilities of generative AI are used in a manner that respects human rights and promotes trust.

1.4 GENERATIVE AI VS. TRADITIONAL AI

The rapid advancements in artificial intelligence over the past few decades have led to the emergence of various AI models, each designed for specific purposes. Among these, Generative AI has gained particular attention for its ability to create new content, such as text, images, audio, and even code. This has sparked comparisons with what is commonly referred to as Traditional AI—systems designed primarily for analytical, rule-based, or predictive tasks.

While both types fall under the broad umbrella of artificial intelligence, they differ fundamentally in architecture, objectives, applications, and capabilities. Generative AI and Traditional AI represent two distinct yet complementary approaches to artificial intelligence. While traditional AI excels at structured, rule-based tasks with clear outcomes, generative AI shines in creative, open-ended tasks that require innovation and expression. Each has its own strengths, limitations, and ideal use cases.

Understanding their differences not only highlights the diversity within the field of AI but also empowers developers and users to choose the right tools for specific challenges. As AI continues to shape the future, the synergy between these two branches will play a critical role in defining how humans and machines collaborate in solving problems and creating new possibilities.

1.4.1 Definitional Distinctions

Traditional AI refers to a class of artificial intelligence systems focused on tasks that require classification, decision-making, pattern recognition, and problem-solving. These systems are often built with rule-based logic or statistical learning algorithms to perform specific, well-defined tasks. For example, traditional AI might be used in a spam filter that classifies emails as spam or not spam based on known characteristics, or in a recommendation engine that suggests products based on previous purchases.

Generative AI, on the other hand, is a subset of AI that focuses on the creation of new, original content. These systems are trained to understand patterns within large datasets and use that understanding to generate data that resembles the training material. Generative AI models can compose music, create artworks, write articles, generate human-like conversations, and more. Their goal is not merely to analyze or classify existing data but to produce novel outputs that mimic human creativity.

1.4.2 Architectural Differences

The architectural frameworks of Traditional AI and Generative AI differ significantly. Traditional AI systems are often constructed using decision trees, support vector machines, linear regression models, or expert systems that rely on predefined logic and rules. These models are relatively simple in structure and designed to perform narrowly defined tasks. Their operation is often transparent and interpretable, allowing users to understand how a specific output was reached. Generative AI systems, in contrast, are usually based on complex neural network architectures.

These include Variational Autoencoders (VAEs), Generative Adversarial Networks (GANs), and Transformer models like GPT (Generative Pre-trained Transformer). Such models are built to learn abstract representations of data through unsupervised or self-supervised learning, allowing them to generate outputs that exhibit creativity and variation. Their architecture is more opaque, often functioning as a "black box," which makes interpretability more challenging but enables a much broader range of outputs.

1.4.3 Learning and Data Requirements

Traditional AI typically relies on supervised learning, where the model is trained on labeled data. For example, an image recognition system might be trained on thousands of labeled images of cats and dogs to learn the distinguishing features of each. The model's performance improves with more labeled examples, but its scope is confined to the categories it was trained on. Generative AI, in contrast, often leverages unsupervised or self-supervised learning, which allows it to learn from vast amounts of unlabeled data. For instance, a generative language model like GPT is trained on massive corpora of text from books, websites, and articles, without needing labels for each word or sentence. This enables it to learn the syntax, semantics, and even stylistic nuances of language, allowing it to generate coherent and contextually appropriate text. Generative models usually require significantly more data and computational power than traditional models but offer much richer outputs as a result.

1.4.4 Objective and Functionality

The core objective of Traditional AI is to solve specific problems or make accurate predictions. Whether it is diagnosing diseases from medical scans, detecting fraud in financial transactions, or optimizing supply chains, traditional AI is focused on improving accuracy and efficiency in narrowly defined domains. The success of such systems is measured by metrics like precision, recall, and accuracy, which assess how well the model performs its taskGenerative AI, however, is not primarily concerned with accuracy in the conventional sense. Instead, its goal is to produce outputs that are realistic, coherent, and contextually appropriate. For a generative model creating art or poetry, the value lies in the quality and originality of the output, not whether it is "correct" by a specific standard. This creative function introduces a layer of subjectivity in evaluating generative AI, where human judgment and aesthetic appreciation often play a significant role.

1.4.5 Applications and Use Cases

Traditional AI has been successfully applied across many industries for routine, repetitive, or analytical tasks. In healthcare, it supports diagnostic systems and patient data analysis. In finance, it helps detect fraudulent activity and automate trading. In logistics, it powers route optimization and inventory forecasting. These applications benefit from the precision, reliability, and speed of traditional AI, especially when dealing with structured data and well-defined objectives. Generative AI, on the other hand, has carved out its space in more creative and dynamic domains. It is used to write content for blogs and advertisements, generate visual designs, create music compositions, simulate human speech, and even write software code. Generative AI is also being integrated into virtual assistants, chatbots, and video game development to produce interactive narratives and character dialogues. Its capacity to create rather than just analyze data makes it uniquely suited for tasks that require novelty and engagement.

1.4.6 Human Interaction and User Experience

Another important difference lies in how humans interact with these systems. Traditional AI is often embedded within software platforms where it functions in the background, providing recommendations, classifications, or optimizations without direct engagement from the user. The interaction is minimal and largely functional. Generative AI, however, invites a much more interactive and iterative user experience. Users engage with generative models through prompts, and the systems respond with creative outputs. This interaction can be refined over multiple turns, creating a conversational or collaborative dynamic between human and machine. This characteristic of generative AI has transformed how users perceive and use AI, making it a partner in creative tasks rather than a mere tool for automation.

1.4.7 Limitations and Risks

Both Traditional AI and Generative AI have limitations, but the nature of those limitations differs. Traditional AI can struggle with adaptability and transfer learning; a model trained for one task often cannot perform another without retraining. Its outputs are constrained by the scope of its programming and labeled training data. Generative AI faces different challenges, especially around bias, misinformation, and ethical considerations. Because generative models learn from vast, uncurated datasets, they may reproduce harmful stereotypes or generate false and misleading content. Their outputs can also be difficult to verify, which is problematic in domains where accuracy and truth are critical. The potential misuse of generative AI, such as in creating deepfakes or automated propaganda, has raised concerns among regulators, developers, and the public.

1.4.8 Future Prospects and Integration

Looking forward, both Traditional AI and Generative AI are likely to continue evolving and increasingly converging in practical applications. Hybrid systems that combine the analytical strength of traditional models with the creative capabilities of generative models are already emerging. For example, in healthcare, a system might use traditional AI to analyze patient data and generative AI to draft comprehensive medical reports. In education, traditional AI can assess learning outcomes, while generative AI can create personalized content and tutoring materials. As these technologies mature, the line between analysis and creation will continue to blur. This integration offers exciting possibilities but also requires thoughtful design and ethical oversight to ensure responsible use. Collaboration between engineers, domain experts, and policymakers will be essential in shaping the future landscape of AI in a way that leverages the best of both paradigms.

CHAPTER 2

Theoretical Foundations

2.1 PROBABILISTIC MODELS IN GENERATIVE AI

Generative AI has revolutionized how machines interact with and produce data, enabling them to create new content such as text, images, music, and video. At the heart of these innovations lie probabilistic models—mathematical frameworks that enable machines to reason under uncertainty and generate plausible outputs. Probabilistic models are essential to the functioning of generative AI because they allow systems to capture the complexities and variations of real-world data.

Rather than simply memorizing examples, probabilistic generative models learn to understand distributions and patterns, using this understanding to generate new samples that resemble the data they were trained on. Probabilistic models form the backbone of generative AI, enabling machines to learn from data and create new content that mimics human creativity. By modeling the uncertainty and variability inherent in real-world data, these models make it possible to generate diverse, plausible, and context-aware outputs across a wide range of domains.

Their applications are reshaping industries from media and design to healthcare and education. However, realizing their full potential requires addressing the technical, ethical, and computational challenges they present. As research in probabilistic modeling and generative AI continues to advance, we are likely to see even more powerful, expressive, and responsible systems that redefine how humans and machines collaborate in the act of creation.

2.1.1 Understanding Probabilistic Reasoning in AI

Probabilistic reasoning is the process by which machines model uncertainty and randomness. In real-world data, uncertainty is pervasive—language can be ambiguous, visual data can be noisy, and user behavior can be unpredictable. Probabilistic models use probability distributions to represent this uncertainty. Instead of assigning a single, fixed output to a given input, these models estimate a range of possible outcomes, each with an associated probability.

This allows the model to handle ambiguity, variability, and complexity more effectively than deterministic systems. In the context of generative AI, probabilistic models are used not just to analyze or classify data, but to generate new instances that are consistent with the patterns in the training data. These models do not produce exact copies of what they have seen. Instead, they generate new samples from the learned probability distribution, which governs the space of likely or valid outputs. This enables the creation of diverse and novel content, a key feature that distinguishes generative AI from more traditional forms of artificial intelligence.

2.1.2 The Role of Probability Distributions

Probability distributions are central to the operation of generative AI models. They define how likely different data points are, given the model's understanding of a particular dataset. For example, a probabilistic language model learns the likelihood of sequences of words based on their occurrence in a training corpus.

Given the word "artificial," the model might assign high probability to the next word being "intelligence" or "neural," based on learned patterns, while assigning low probability to unrelated words. Generative models use these distributions to sample new data points. In natural language processing, this might mean predicting the next word in a sentence. In image generation, it could involve producing pixel values that form a coherent visual pattern.

By using probability distributions in this way, generative AI systems maintain flexibility and creativity in their outputs, while still aligning with learned structures and meanings from the training data.

2.1.3 Types of Probabilistic Generative Models

There are several major types of probabilistic models used in generative AI, each with its own mechanisms and strengths. One of the earliest and most influential is the Bayesian network, a graphical model that represents conditional dependencies between variables.

Bayesian models have been widely used in AI for tasks involving reasoning and decision-making, and they laid the groundwork for more complex generative approaches. Another key class is the Hidden Markov Model (HMM), which has been extensively used in speech recognition and time-series prediction.

HMMs model systems where the observed data is generated by a sequence of hidden states, each following a probabilistic rule. Though now considered somewhat outdated, HMMs represent an important step in the evolution of probabilistic generative models.

More modern and powerful generative models include Variational Autoencoders (VAEs), Generative Adversarial Networks (GANs), and Autoregressive Models like GPT. VAEs combine deep learning with probabilistic inference, allowing for efficient encoding and decoding of complex data distributions.

They work by mapping inputs to a latent space that captures the distributional properties of the data, then sampling from this space to generate new outputs. GANs use a game-theoretic approach, where two networks—a generator and a discriminator—compete to produce and evaluate data, improving generation quality through adversarial feedback.

Autoregressive models like GPT use sequential probability modeling to predict each element in a sequence based on the preceding elements, allowing for highly coherent and context-aware generation of language.

2.1.4 Sampling and Inference in Generative AI

Sampling is a fundamental operation in probabilistic generative models. Once a model has learned the probability distribution of a dataset, it can sample from that distribution to generate new data points. This process involves drawing values from the distribution in a way that reflects the learned likelihoods. In language models, this might mean choosing the next word based on its conditional probability given the previous words.

In image models, it might involve selecting pixel intensities based on the learned relationships between visual features. Inference is the complementary process of estimating the hidden variables or latent structures that gave rise to observed data.

In models like VAEs, inference is used to map observed inputs to points in a latent space, which is then used for generation. Efficient inference is critical to making probabilistic models practical, as it enables both training and real-time generation.

Advanced probabilistic models often use techniques such as Markov Chain Monte Carlo (MCMC) or variational inference to perform sampling and inference more efficiently. These methods allow models to approximate complex distributions that would be intractable to compute exactly, enabling them to scale to large datasets and high-dimensional data.

2.1.5 Uncertainty and Diversity in Generation

One of the most significant advantages of probabilistic models in generative AI is their ability to represent and exploit uncertainty. This enables the generation of diverse outputs rather than deterministic, repetitive results.

For instance, a deterministic language model might always respond to a prompt with the same sentence, while a probabilistic model can produce multiple coherent and varied responses, each with a different style or emphasis. This diversity is crucial in creative and user-facing applications. In storytelling, design, or music, variation is often more valuable than repetition.

Probabilistic models allow generative AI systems to offer users a range of options, enhancing creativity and personalization. Furthermore, the ability to model uncertainty enables these systems to better handle ambiguous or incomplete inputs, making them more robust and flexible in real-world settings.

2.1.6 Applications across Domains

Probabilistic models have enabled generative AI to impact a wide range of industries and domains. In natural language processing, they power chatbots, content generators, and translation tools that produce fluent, context-aware text. In computer vision, they are used to create realistic images, perform style transfer, and fill in missing visual data.

In audio processing, probabilistic models can generate lifelike voices, music compositions, and sound effects. In healthcare, they are being used to simulate patient data, assist in diagnosis, and even design new drugs by modeling molecular interactions probabilistically. The strength of probabilistic generative models lies in their adaptability.

Because they model the underlying distribution of data, they can be applied to any domain where such distributions can be learned. This makes them especially valuable in fields where real-world data is complex, high-dimensional, and filled with uncertainty.

2.1.7 Challenges and Limitations

Despite their power, probabilistic generative models also face challenges. One major issue is the difficulty of accurately modeling extremely complex or high-dimensional distributions. Even with advanced techniques like deep learning, capturing all the nuances of human language or visual perception is a daunting task.

This can lead to outputs that are plausible on the surface but lack depth, coherence, or factual accuracy. Another challenge is computational cost. Training probabilistic generative models, especially those based on deep neural networks, requires significant processing power and large amounts of data. This can limit accessibility and raise environmental concerns due to high energy consumption.

Additionally, the probabilistic nature of these models can sometimes lead to unpredictable or inappropriate outputs, especially when dealing with open-ended prompts. Managing this risk requires careful training, testing, and deployment practices, as well as ongoing research into bias, safety, and interpretability.

2.2 BAYESIAN APPROACHES TO GENERATIVE MODELING

Bayesian approaches to generative modeling offer a powerful and mathematically grounded framework for understanding and generating data under conditions of uncertainty. Rooted in Bayes' theorem, these methods enable machines to not only make predictions but also estimate the degree of confidence in those predictions.

In the realm of generative modeling, Bayesian techniques provide a principled way to infer the underlying structure of data and to sample new instances that reflect the learned distribution. This makes Bayesian models particularly well-suited for applications where understanding uncertainty, incorporating prior knowledge, and handling sparse data are essential.

Bayesian approaches to generative modeling represent a robust, principled, and versatile methodology for learning from and generating data under uncertainty. By leveraging probabilistic reasoning, these models offer unique advantages in terms of uncertainty estimation, incorporation of prior knowledge, and adaptability to new data. From mixture models and VAEs to Bayesian neural networks, the Bayesian framework has significantly enriched the generative AI landscape, providing tools that are both mathematically rigorous and practically impactful.

While challenges remain in terms of computational cost and scalability, ongoing research continues to enhance the efficiency and applicability of Bayesian generative models. As AI systems increasingly require trust, interpretability, and adaptability, Bayesian approaches are likely to play an ever more important role in shaping the future of generative intelligence.

2.2.1 Understanding Bayes' Theorem and Its Role in Modeling

Bayes' theorem gives a mathematical rule for inverting conditional probabilities, allowing one to find the probability of a cause given its effect. For example, if the risk of developing health problems is known to increase with age, Bayes' theorem allows the risk to someone of a known age to be assessed more accurately by conditioning it relative to their age, rather than assuming that the person is typical of the population as a whole. Based on Bayes' law, both the prevalence of a disease in a given population and the error rate of an infectious disease test must be taken into account to evaluate the meaning of a positive test result and avoid the base-rate fallacy. One of Bayes' theorem's many applications is Bayesian inference, an approach to statistical inference, where it is used to invert the probability of observations given a model configuration (i.e., the likelihood function) to obtain the probability of the model configuration given the observations (i.e., the posterior probability).

History

Bayes' theorem is named after Thomas Bayes a minister, statistician, and philosopher. Bayes used conditional probability to provide an algorithm (his Proposition 9) that uses evidence to calculate limits on an unknown parameter. His work was published in 1763 as An Essay Towards Solving a Problem in the Doctrine of Chances. Bayes studied how to compute a distribution for the probability parameter of a binomial distribution (in modern terminology). After Bayes's death, his family gave his papers to a friend, the minister, philosopher, and mathematician Richard Price.

Price significantly edited the unpublished manuscript for two years before sending it to a friend who read it aloud at the Royal Society on 23 December 1763. Price edited Bayes's major work "An Essay Towards Solving a Problem in the Doctrine of Chances" (1763), which appeared in Philosophical Transactions, and contains Bayes' theorem. Price wrote an introduction to the paper that provides some of the philosophical basis of Bayesian statistics and chose one of the two solutions Bayes offered. In 1765, Price was elected a Fellow of the Royal Society in recognition of his work on Bayes's legacy. On 27 April, a letter sent to his friend Benjamin Franklin was read out at the Royal Society, and later published, in which Price applies this work to population and computing 'life-annuities'.

Independently of Bayes, Pierre-Simon Laplace used conditional probability to formulate the relation of an updated posterior probability from a prior probability, given evidence. He reproduced and extended Bayes's results in 1774, apparently unaware of Bayes's work, and summarized his results in Théorie analytique des probabilités (1812).

The Bayesian interpretation of probability was developed mainly by Laplace. About 200 years later, Sir Harold Jeffreys put Bayes's algorithm and Laplace's formulation on an axiomatic basis, writing in a 1973 book that Bayes' theorem "is to the theory of probability what the Pythagorean theorem is to geometry". Stephen Stigler used a Bayesian argument to conclude that Bayes' theorem was discovered by Nicholas Saunderson, a blind English mathematician, some time before Bayes, but that is disputed.

Martyn Hooper and Sharon McGrayne have argued that Richard Price's contribution was substantial:

- By modern standards, we should refer to the Bayes–Price rule. Price discovered Bayes's work, recognized its importance, corrected it, contributed to the article, and found a use for it. The modern convention of employing Bayes's name alone is unfair but so entrenched that anything else makes little sense.

F. Thomas Bruss reviewed Bayes' work "An essay towards solving a problem in the doctrine of chances" as communicated by Price. He agrees with Stigler's fine analysis in many points, but not as far as the question of priority is concerned. Bruss underlines the intuitive part of Bayes' formula and adds independent arguments of Bayes' probable motivation for his work. He concludes that, unless the contrary is really proven, we are entitled to be faithful to the name "Bayes' Theorem" or "Bayes' formula".

Statement of Theorem

Bayes' theorem is stated mathematically as the following equation:

$$P(A \mid B) = \frac{P(B \mid A)P(A)}{P(B)}$$

Proof

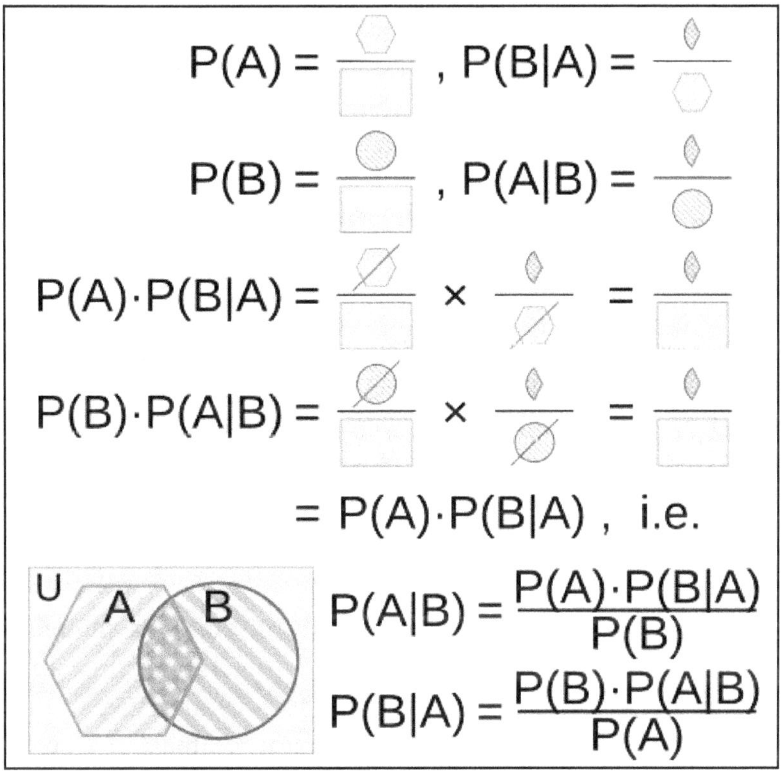

Fig: Visual Proof of Bayes' Theorem

For Events

Bayes' theorem may be derived from the definition of conditional probability:

$$P(A \mid B) = \frac{P(A \cap B)}{P(B)}, \text{ if } P(B) \neq 0,$$

where $P(A \cap B)$ is the probability of both A and B being true. Similarly,

$$P(B \mid A) = \frac{P(A \cap B)}{P(A)}, \text{ if } P(A) \neq 0.$$

Solving for $P(A \cap B)$ and substituting into the above expression for $P(A \mid B)$ yields Bayes' theorem:

$$P(A \mid B) = \frac{P(B \mid A)P(A)}{P(B)}, \text{ if } P(B) \neq 0.$$

For Continuous Random Variables

For two continuous random variables X and Y, Bayes' theorem may be analogously derived from the definition of conditional density:

$$f_{X|Y=y}(x) = \frac{f_{X,Y}(x,y)}{f_Y(y)}$$

$$f_{Y|X=x}(y) = \frac{f_{X,Y}(x,y)}{f_X(x)}$$

Therefore,

$$f_{X|Y=y}(x) = \frac{f_{Y|X=x}(y) f_X(x)}{f_Y(y)}.$$

2.2.2 Latent Variables and Bayesian Inference

Latent variables are unobserved variables that explain the structure or patterns in the observed data. In Bayesian generative models, latent variables are assigned prior distributions that reflect assumptions or prior knowledge about their nature. For example, in a simple Bayesian mixture model, each data point is assumed to be generated by one of several latent components, each governed by its own probability distribution. The model infers which component generated each data point, and how the components themselves are distributed, by using Bayesian inference. Bayesian inference involves computing the posterior distribution of latent variables given the observed data.

This is often analytically intractable, especially in complex models with high-dimensional data and intricate dependencies. To overcome this, approximation methods such as Markov Chain Monte Carlo (MCMC) and Variational Inference are employed. MCMC methods use sampling to approximate the posterior, while Variational Inference transforms the problem into an optimization task by approximating the posterior with a simpler, parameterized distribution. Both approaches have their strengths and weaknesses but are crucial in making Bayesian generative modeling computationally feasible.

2.2.3 Bayesian Mixture Models and Clustering

One of the earliest and most intuitive applications of Bayesian generative modeling is in clustering through mixture models. The Bayesian Gaussian Mixture Model (GMM) is a classic example. In this model, data is assumed to be generated from a mixture of several Gaussian distributions, each corresponding to a latent cluster. The model infers the parameters of these Gaussians and the probabilities that each data point belongs to a given cluster. A Bayesian approach to mixture modeling improves upon traditional methods by incorporating prior beliefs about the number and shape of clusters and by avoiding overfitting.

This is particularly useful when the number of clusters is unknown. The Dirichlet Process Mixture Model (DPMM) extends this idea by allowing for an infinite number of potential clusters, using a nonparametric Bayesian approach. This flexibility makes Bayesian mixture models highly effective for unsupervised learning and generative tasks where the underlying structure is complex and not well-defined in advance.

2.2.4 Variational Autoencoders and Bayesian Foundations

Variational Autoencoders (VAEs) are a popular class of generative models that explicitly incorporate Bayesian principles. A VAE is structured around the idea of learning a probabilistic encoder and decoder. The encoder maps input data to a distribution over latent variables, and the decoder maps samples from this distribution back to the data space. The training objective is to maximize a lower bound on the log-likelihood of the data, which includes a reconstruction term and a regularization term that enforces closeness between the learned latent distribution and a prior. This approach closely aligns with Bayesian inference. The regularization term in the VAE's objective is a Kullback-Leibler divergence that penalizes the difference between the approximate posterior (produced by the encoder) and the prior distribution. In this way, VAEs can be viewed as performing approximate Bayesian inference through variational methods. They offer a scalable and efficient way to perform Bayesian generative modeling on large and complex datasets, making them suitable for applications in image generation, speech synthesis, and anomaly detection.

2.2.5 Bayesian Neural Networks and Uncertainty Estimation

Bayesian Neural Networks (BNNs) extend the Bayesian approach to deep learning by treating the weights of the network as random variables with associated distributions, rather than fixed values. This allows the model to express uncertainty in its predictions and to regularize learning through the incorporation of prior knowledge. In generative contexts, BNNs can be used to model uncertainty in both the generation process and the underlying data distribution. For instance, a Bayesian generative model for time-series data might use a BNN to capture uncertainty in future values, allowing it to generate multiple plausible continuations of a sequence. This capacity to model uncertainty is particularly valuable in domains like finance, medicine, and autonomous systems, where the cost of overconfidence can be high. Training BNNs is computationally challenging due to the need to integrate over many possible weight configurations. However, advances in variational inference and Monte Carlo dropout have made it more practical to implement BNNs in large-scale systems. Their ability to generate data while quantifying confidence adds an important layer of interpretability and robustness to generative AI systems.

2.2.6 Advantages of Bayesian Generative Models

Bayesian approaches offer several key advantages in generative modeling. First, they provide a coherent framework for incorporating prior knowledge, which can be especially useful in data-scarce environments. Priors act as regularizers, preventing overfitting and guiding the model toward plausible solutions when data is limited or noisy. Second, Bayesian models naturally quantify uncertainty, offering probabilistic confidence intervals around their outputs. This is crucial in high-stakes applications such as healthcare or autonomous decision-making, where understanding the reliability of a generated output is just as important as the output itself. Third, Bayesian models are inherently adaptive. As new data becomes available, the model updates its beliefs rather than starting from scratch. This makes them well-suited for dynamic environments where data distributions may change over time. The ability to continuously learn and adapt is a distinguishing strength of the Bayesian paradigm.

2.2.7 Challenges and Limitations

Despite their strengths, Bayesian generative models face notable challenges. The most significant is computational complexity. Exact inference is often intractable, requiring approximation techniques that may be computationally intensive and sensitive to parameter choices. Even with modern hardware, training complex Bayesian models can be time-consuming and resource-demanding. Another challenge is model specification. Bayesian methods require the careful design of prior distributions and likelihood functions.

Poor choices can lead to biased or ineffective models. Moreover, interpreting the results of Bayesian models can be difficult, especially in high-dimensional settings where the posterior distributions are complex and multimodal. Scalability is another concern. While recent advancements have made it easier to scale Bayesian methods, they still lag behind some non-Bayesian deep learning models in terms of raw performance and speed, particularly in domains where vast amounts of data are available.

2.3 INFORMATION THEORY IN GENERATIVE SYSTEMS

Information theory plays a foundational role in modern generative systems by providing a mathematical framework for understanding, measuring, and optimizing information. At its core, information theory deals with the quantification of information, the limits of communication, and the efficiency of data encoding. When applied to generative models, this theory enables systems to learn patterns, compress knowledge, and produce new content that reflects the statistical properties of the training data.

The intersection of information theory and generative modeling allows for the design of systems that are not only capable of replicating human-like creativity but also operate efficiently and robustly in uncertain environments. Information theory provides a vital foundation for generative systems, offering mathematical tools to measure uncertainty, compress data, and optimize learning. Through concepts like entropy, mutual information, and the information bottleneck, generative models can better understand and recreate the structure of the data they are trained on. These insights lead to more efficient, flexible, and interpretable models, capable of generating high-quality outputs across a range of applications. As generative AI continues to evolve, the principles of information theory will remain indispensable in shaping its development and ensuring its responsible use.

2.3.1 The Basics of Information Theory

Information theory is the mathematical study of the quantification, storage, and communication of information. The field was established and formalized by Claude Shannon in the 1940s, though early contributions were made in the 1920s through the works of Harry Nyquist and Ralph Hartley. It is at the intersection of electronic engineering, mathematics, statistics, computer science, neurobiology, physics, and electrical engineering.

A key measure in information theory is entropy. Entropy quantifies the amount of uncertainty involved in the value of a random variable or the outcome of a random process. For example, identifying the outcome of a fair coin flip (which has two equally likely outcomes) provides less information (lower entropy, less uncertainty) than identifying the outcome from a roll of a die (which has six equally likely outcomes).

Some other important measures in information theory are mutual information, channel capacity, error exponents, and relative entropy. Important sub-fields of information theory include source coding, algorithmic complexity theory, algorithmic information theory and information-theoretic security.

Applications of fundamental topics of information theory include source coding/ data compression (e.g. for ZIP files), and channel coding/error detection and correction (e.g. for DSL). Its impact has been crucial to the success of the Voyager missions to deep space, the invention of the compact disc, the feasibility of mobile phones and the development of the Internet and artificial intelligence.

The theory has also found applications in other areas, including statistical inference, cryptography, neurobiology, perception, signal processing, linguistics, the evolution and function of molecular codes (bioinformatics), thermal physics, molecular dynamics, black holes, quantum computing, information retrieval, intelligence gathering, plagiarism detection, pattern recognition, anomaly detection, the analysis of music, art creation, imaging system design, study of outer space, the dimensionality of space, and epistemology.

Information theory studies the transmission, processing, extraction, and utilization of information. Abstractly, information can be thought of as the resolution of uncertainty. In the case of communication of information over a noisy channel, this abstract concept was formalized in 1948 by Claude Shannon in a paper entitled A Mathematical Theory of Communication, in which information is thought of as a set of possible messages, and the goal is to send these messages over a noisy channel, and to have the receiver reconstruct the message with low probability of error, in spite of the channel noise. Shannon's main result, the noisy-channel coding theorem, showed that, in the limit of many channel uses, the rate of information that is asymptotically achievable is equal to the channel capacity, a quantity dependent merely on the statistics of the channel over which the messages are sent.

Coding theory is concerned with finding explicit methods, called codes, for increasing the efficiency and reducing the error rate of data communication over noisy channels to near the channel capacity. These codes can be roughly subdivided into data compression (source coding) and error-correction (channel coding) techniques. In the latter case, it took many years to find the methods Shannon's work proved were possible. A third class of information theory codes are cryptographic algorithms (both codes and ciphers). Concepts, methods and results from coding theory and information theory are widely used in cryptography and cryptanalysis, such as the unit ban.

Historical Background

The landmark event establishing the discipline of information theory and bringing it to immediate worldwide attention was the publication of Claude E. Shannon's classic paper "A Mathematical Theory of Communication" in the Bell System Technical Journal in July and October 1948. Historian James Gleick rated the paper as the most important development of 1948, noting that the paper was "even more profound and more fundamental" than the transistor. He came to be known as the "father of information theory". Shannon outlined some of his initial ideas of information theory as early as 1939 in a letter to Vannevar Bush.

Prior to this paper, limited information-theoretic ideas had been developed at Bell Labs, all implicitly assuming events of equal probability. Harry Nyquist's 1924 paper, Certain Factors Affecting Telegraph Speed, contains a theoretical section quantifying "intelligence" and the "line speed" at which it can be transmitted by a communication system, giving the relation $W = K \log m$ (recalling the Boltzmann constant), where W is the speed of transmission of intelligence, m is the number of different voltage levels to choose from at each time step, and K is a constant.

Ralph Hartley's 1928 paper, Transmission of Information, uses the word information as a measurable quantity, reflecting the receiver's ability to distinguish one sequence of symbols from any other, thus quantifying information as H = log Sn = n log S, where S was the number of possible symbols, and n the number of symbols in a transmission. The unit of information was therefore the decimal digit, which since has sometimes been called the hartley in his honor as a unit or scale or measure of information. Alan Turing in 1940 used similar ideas as part of the statistical analysis of the breaking of the German second world war Enigma ciphers.

Much of the mathematics behind information theory with events of different probabilities were developed for the field of thermodynamics by Ludwig Boltzmann and J. Willard Gibbs. Connections between information-theoretic entropy and thermodynamic entropy, including the important contributions by Rolf Landauer in the 1960s, are explored in Entropy in thermodynamics and information theory.

In Shannon's revolutionary and groundbreaking paper, the work for which had been substantially completed at Bell Labs by the end of 1944, Shannon for the first time introduced the qualitative and quantitative model of communication as a statistical process underlying information theory, opening with the assertion:

- "The fundamental problem of communication is that of reproducing at one point, either exactly or approximately, a message selected at another point."

With it came the ideas of:

- The information entropy and redundancy of a source, and its relevance through the source coding theorem;
- The mutual information, and the channel capacity of a noisy channel, including the promise of perfect loss-free communication given by the noisy-channel coding theorem;
- The practical result of the Shannon–Hartley law for the channel capacity of a Gaussian channel; as well as
- The bit—a new way of seeing the most fundamental unit of information.

Quantities of Information

Information theory is based on probability theory and statistics, where quantified information is usually described in terms of bits. Information theory often concerns itself with measures of information of the distributions associated with random variables. One of the most important measures is called entropy, which forms the building block of many other measures. Entropy allows quantification of measure of information in a single random variable.

Another useful concept is mutual information defined on two random variables, which describes the measure of information in common between those variables, which can be used to describe their correlation. The former quantity is a property of the probability distribution of a random variable and gives a limit on the rate at which data generated by independent samples with the given distribution can be reliably compressed. The latter is a property of the joint distribution of two random variables, and is the maximum rate of reliable communication across a noisy channel in the limit of long block lengths, when the channel statistics are determined by the joint distribution.

The choice of logarithmic base in the following formulae determines the unit of information entropy that is used. A common unit of information is the bit or shannon, based on the binary logarithm. Other units include the nat, which is based on the natural logarithm, and the decimal digit, which is based on the common logarithm.

Entropy of an Information Source

Based on the probability mass function of each source symbol to be communicated, the Shannon entropy H, in units of bits (per symbol), is given by

$$H = -\sum_i p_i \log_2(p_i)$$

This equation gives the entropy in the units of "bits" (per symbol) because it uses a logarithm of base 2, and this base-2 measure of entropy has sometimes been called the shannon in his honor. Entropy is also commonly computed using the natural logarithm (base e, where e is Euler's number), which produces a measurement of entropy in nats per symbol and sometimes simplifies the analysis by avoiding the need to include extra constants in the formulas. Other bases are also possible, but less commonly used. For example, a logarithm of base 28 = 256 will produce a measurement in bytes per symbol, and a logarithm of base 10 will produce a measurement in decimal digits (or hartleys) per symbol.

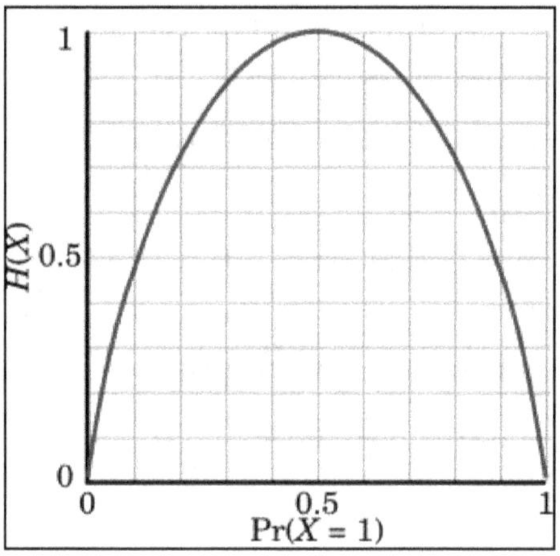

Fig: The Entropy of a Bernoulli Trial as a Function of Success Probability, Often Called The Binary Entropy Function, Hb(P). The Entropy is Maximized at 1 Bit Per Trial When The Two Possible Outcomes are Equally Probable, as in an Unbiased Coin Toss

Intuitively, the entropy HX of a discrete random variable X is a measure of the amount of uncertainty associated with the value of X when only its distribution is known. The entropy of a source that emits a sequence of N symbols that are independent and identically distributed (iid) is N · H bits (per message of N symbols). If the source data symbols are identically distributed but not independent, the entropy of a message of length N will be less than N · H.

If one transmits 1000 bits (0s and 1s), and the value of each of these bits is known to the receiver (has a specific value with certainty) ahead of transmission, it is clear that no information is transmitted. If, however, each bit is independently equally likely to be 0 or 1, 1000 shannons of information (more often called bits) have been transmitted. Between these two extremes, information can be quantified as follows. If $\mathbb{X}$ is the set of all messages {x1, ..., xn} that X could be, and p(x) is the probability of some $x \in \mathbb{X}$, then the entropy, H, of X is defined:

$$H(X) = \mathbb{E}_X[I(x)] = -\sum_{x \in \mathbb{X}} p(x) \log p(x).$$

(Here, I(x) is the self-information, which is the entropy contribution of an individual message, and $\mathbb{E}_X$ is the expected value.) A property of entropy is that it is maximized when all the messages in the message space are equiprobable p(x) = 1/n; i.e., most unpredictable, in which case H(X) = log n. The special case of information entropy for a random variable with two outcomes is the binary entropy function, usually taken to the logarithmic base 2, thus having the shannon as unit:

$$H_b(p) = -p \log_2 p - (1-p)\log_2(1-p).$$

Joint Entropy

The joint entropy of two discrete random variables X and Y is merely the entropy of their pairing: (X, Y). This implies that if X and Y are independent, then their joint entropy is the sum of their individual entropies.

For example, if (X, Y) represents the position of a chess piece—X the row and Y the column, then the joint entropy of the row of the piece and the column of the piece will be the entropy of the position of the piece.

$$H(X,Y) = \mathbb{E}_{X,Y}[-\log p(x,y)] = -\sum_{x,y} p(x,y) \log p(x,y)$$

Despite similar notation, joint entropy should not be confused with cross-entropy.

Conditional Entropy (Equivocation)

The conditional entropy or conditional uncertainty of X given random variable Y (also called the equivocation of X about Y) is the average conditional entropy over Y:

$$H(X \mid Y) = \mathbb{E}_Y[H(X \mid y)] = -\sum_{y \in Y} p(y) \sum_{x \in X} p(x \mid y) \log p(x \mid y) = -\sum_{x,y} p(x,y) \log p(x \mid y).$$

Because entropy can be conditioned on a random variable or on that random variable being a certain value, care should be taken not to confuse these two definitions of conditional entropy, the former of which is in more common use. A basic property of this form of conditional entropy is that:

$$H(X \mid Y) = H(X,Y) - H(Y).$$

Mutual Information (Transinformation)

Mutual information measures the amount of information that can be obtained about one random variable by observing another. It is important in communication where it can be used to maximize the amount of information shared between sent and received signals. The mutual information of X relative to Y is given by:

$$I(X;Y) = \mathbb{E}_{X,Y}[SI(x,y)] = \sum_{x,y} p(x,y)\log\frac{p(x,y)}{p(x)\,p(y)}$$

where SI (Specific mutual Information) is the pointwise mutual information. A basic property of the mutual information is that

$$I(X;Y) = H(X) - H(X \mid Y).$$

That is, knowing Y, we can save an average of I(X; Y) bits in encoding X compared to not knowing Y. Mutual information is symmetric:

$$I(X;Y) = I(Y;X) = H(X) + H(Y) - H(X,Y).$$

Mutual information can be expressed as the average Kullback-Leibler divergence (information gain) between the posterior probability distribution of X given the value of Y and the prior distribution on X:

$$I(X;Y) = \mathbb{E}_{p(y)}[D_{\mathrm{KL}}(p(X \mid Y = y) \,\|\, p(X))].$$

In other words, this is a measure of how much, on the average, the probability distribution on X will change if we are given the value of Y. This is often recalculated as the divergence from the product of the marginal distributions to the actual joint distribution:

$$I(X;Y) = D_{\mathrm{KL}}(p(X,Y) \,\|\, p(X)p(Y)).$$

Mutual information is closely related to the log-likelihood ratio test in the context of contingency tables and the multinomial distribution and to Pearson's $\chi 2$ test: mutual information can be considered a statistic for assessing independence between a pair of variables, and has a well-specified asymptotic distribution.

Kullback–Leibler Divergence (Information Gain)

The Kullback–Leibler divergence (or information divergence, information gain, or relative entropy) is a way of comparing two distributions: a "true" probability distribution $p(X)$, and an arbitrary probability distribution $q(X)$. If we compress data in a manner that assumes $q(X)$ is the distribution underlying some data, when, in reality, $p(X)$ is the correct distribution, the Kullback–Leibler divergence is the number of average additional bits per datum necessary for compression. It is thus defined

$$D_{KL}(p(X) \parallel q(X)) = \sum_{x \in X} -p(x) \log q(x) - \sum_{x \in X} -p(x) \log p(x) = \sum_{x \in X} p(x) \log \frac{p(x)}{q(x)}.$$

Although it is sometimes used as a 'distance metric', KL divergence is not a true metric since it is not symmetric and does not satisfy the triangle inequality (making it a semi-quasimetric).

Another interpretation of the KL divergence is the "unnecessary surprise" introduced by a prior from the truth: suppose a number X is about to be drawn randomly from a discrete set with probability distribution $p(x)$. If Alice knows the true distribution $p(x)$, while Bob believes (has a prior) that the distribution is $q(x)$, then Bob will be more surprised than Alice, on average, upon seeing the value of X.

The KL divergence is the (objective) expected value of Bob's (subjective) surprisal minus Alice's surprisal, measured in bits if the log is in base 2. In this way, the extent to which Bob's prior is "wrong" can be quantified in terms of how "unnecessarily surprised" it is expected to make him.

Coding Theory

Coding theory is one of the most important and direct applications of information theory. It can be subdivided into source coding theory and channel coding theory. Using a statistical description for data, information theory quantifies the number of bits needed to describe the data, which is the information entropy of the source.

- **Data Compression (Source Coding):** There are two formulations for the compression problem:
  - Lossless Data Compression: the data must be reconstructed exactly;
  - Lossy Data Compression: allocates bits needed to reconstruct the data, within a specified fidelity level measured by a distortion function. This subset of information theory is called rate–distortion theory.
- **Error-Correcting Codes (Channel Coding):** While data compression removes as much redundancy as possible, an error-correcting code adds just the right kind of redundancy (i.e., error correction) needed to transmit the data efficiently and faithfully across a noisy channel.

This division of coding theory into compression and transmission is justified by the information transmission theorems, or source channel separation theorems that justify the use of bits as the universal currency for information in many contexts. However, these theorems only hold in the situation where one transmitting user wishes to communicate to one receiving user. In scenarios with more than one transmitter (the multiple-access channel), more than one receiver (the broadcast channel) or intermediary "helpers" (the relay channel), or more general networks, compression followed by transmission may no longer be optimal.

Source Theory

Any process that generates successive messages can be considered a source of information. A memoryless source is one in which each message is an independent identically distributed random variable, whereas the properties of ergodicity and stationarity impose less restrictive constraints. All such sources are stochastic. These terms are well studied in their own right outside information theory.

Rate

Information rate is the average entropy per symbol. For memoryless sources, this is merely the entropy of each symbol, while, in the case of a stationary stochastic process, it is:

$$r = \lim_{n\to\infty} H(X_n \mid X_{n-1}, X_{n-2}, X_{n-3}, \ldots);$$

that is, the conditional entropy of a symbol given all the previous symbols generated. For the more general case of a process that is not necessarily stationary, the average rate is:

$$r = \lim_{n\to\infty} \frac{1}{n} H(X_1, X_2, \ldots X_n);$$

that is, the limit of the joint entropy per symbol. For stationary sources, these two expressions give the same result.

The information rate is defined as:

$$r = \lim_{n\to\infty} \frac{1}{n} I(X_1, X_2, \ldots X_n; Y_1, Y_2, \ldots Y_n);$$

It is common in information theory to speak of the "rate" or "entropy" of a language. This is appropriate, for example, when the source of information is English prose. The rate of a source of information is related to its redundancy and how well it can be compressed, the subject of source coding.

Channel Capacity

Communications over a channel is the primary motivation of information theory. However, channels often fail to produce exact reconstruction of a signal; noise, periods of silence, and other forms of signal corruption often degrade quality. Consider the communications process over a discrete channel. A simple model of the process is shown below:

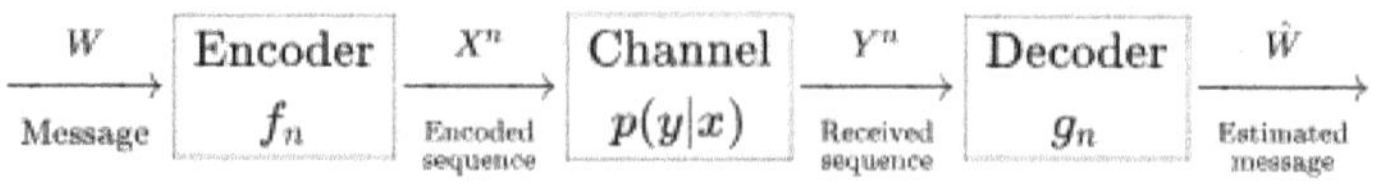

Here X represents the space of messages transmitted, and Y the space of messages received during a unit time over our channel. Let p(y|x) be the conditional probability distribution function of Y given X. We will consider p(y|x) to be an inherent fixed property of our communications channel (representing the nature of the noise of our channel). Then the joint distribution of X and Y is completely determined by our channel and by our choice of f(x), the marginal distribution of messages we choose to send over the channel. Under these constraints, we would like to maximize the rate of information, or the signal, we can communicate over the channel. The appropriate measure for this is the mutual information, and this maximum mutual information is called the channel capacity and is given by:

$$C = \max_f I(X;Y).$$

This capacity has the following property related to communicating at information rate R (where R is usually bits per symbol). For any information rate R < C and coding error ε > 0, for large enough N, there exists a code of length N and rate ≥ R and a decoding algorithm, such that the maximal probability of block error is ≤ ε; that is, it is always possible to transmit with arbitrarily small block error. In addition, for any rate R > C, it is impossible to transmit with arbitrarily small block error.

Channel coding is concerned with finding such nearly optimal codes that can be used to transmit data over a noisy channel with a small coding error at a rate near the channel capacity.

Capacity of Particular Channel Models

- A continuous-time analog communications channel subject to Gaussian noise.
- A binary symmetric channel (BSC) with crossover probability p is a binary input, binary output channel that flips the input bit with probability p. The BSC has a capacity of 1 - Hb(p) bits per channel use, where Hb is the binary entropy function to the base-2 logarithm:

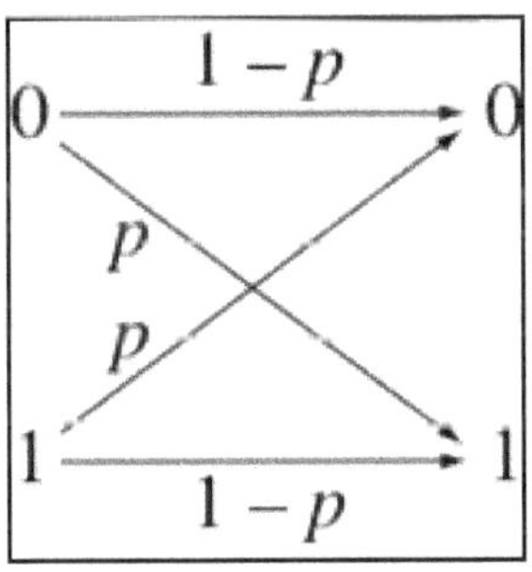

- A binary erasure channel (BEC) with erasure probability p is a binary input, ternary output channel. The possible channel outputs are 0,

1, and a third symbol 'e' called an erasure. The erasure represents complete loss of information about an input bit. The capacity of the BEC is 1 - p bits per channel use.

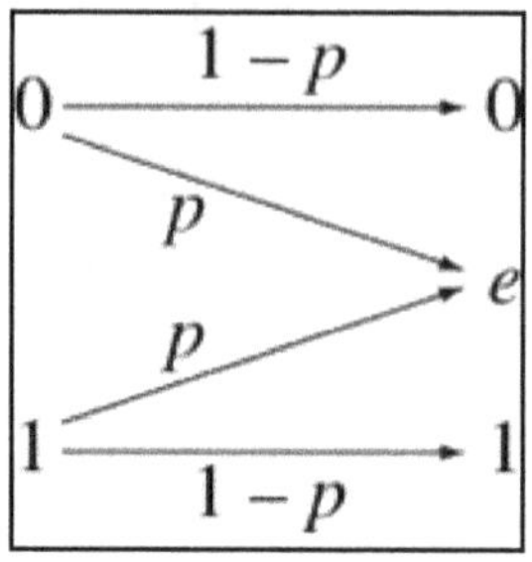

Applications to other Fields

Intelligence Uses and Secrecy Applications

Information theoretic concepts apply to cryptography and cryptanalysis. Turing's information unit, the ban, was used in the Ultra project, breaking the German Enigma machine code and hastening the end of World War II in Europe. Shannon himself defined an important concept now called the unicity distance. Based on the redundancy of the plaintext, it attempts to give a minimum amount of ciphertext necessary to ensure unique decipherability. Information theory leads us to believe it is much more difficult to keep secrets than it might first appear. A brute force attack can break systems based on asymmetric key algorithms or on most commonly used methods of symmetric key algorithms (sometimes called secret key algorithms), such as block ciphers. The security of all such methods comes from the assumption that no known attack can break them in a practical amount of time. Information theoretic security refers to methods such as the one-time pad that are not vulnerable to such brute force attacks. In such cases, the positive conditional mutual information between the plaintext and ciphertext (conditioned on the key) can ensure proper transmission, while the unconditional mutual information between the plaintext and ciphertext remains zero, resulting in absolutely secure communications. In other words, an eavesdropper would not be able to improve his or her guess of the plaintext by gaining knowledge of the ciphertext but not of the key. However, as in any other cryptographic system, care must be used to correctly apply even information-theoretically secure methods; the Venona project was able to crack the one-time pads of the Soviet Union due to their improper reuse of key material.

Pseudorandom Number Generation

Pseudorandom number generators are widely available in computer language libraries and application programs. They are, almost universally, unsuited to cryptographic use as they do not evade the deterministic nature of modern computer equipment and software. A class of improved random number generators is termed cryptographically secure pseudorandom number generators, but even they require random seeds external to the software to work as intended. These can be obtained via extractors, if done carefully.

The measure of sufficient randomness in extractors is min-entropy, a value related to Shannon entropy through Rényi entropy; Rényi entropy is also used in evaluating randomness in cryptographic systems. Although related, the distinctions among these measures mean that a random variable with high Shannon entropy is not necessarily satisfactory for use in an extractor and so for cryptography uses.

Seismic Exploration

One early commercial application of information theory was in the field of seismic oil exploration. Work in this field made it possible to strip off and separate the unwanted noise from the desired seismic signal. Information theory and digital signal processing offer a major improvement of resolution and image clarity over previous analog methods.

Semiotics

Semioticians Doede Nauta [nl] and Winfried Nöth both considered Charles Sanders Peirce as having created a theory of information in his works on semiotics. Nauta defined semiotic information theory as the study of "the internal processes of coding, filtering, and information processing." Concepts from information theory such as redundancy and code control have been used by semioticians such as Umberto Eco and Ferruccio Rossi-Landi [it] to explain ideology as a form of message transmission whereby a dominant social class emits its message by using signs that exhibit a high degree of redundancy such that only one message is decoded among a selection of competing ones.

Integrated Process Organization of Neural Information

Quantitative information theoretic methods have been applied in cognitive science to analyze the integrated process organization of neural information in the context of the binding problem in cognitive neuroscience. In this context, either an information-theoretical measure, such as functional clusters (Gerald Edelman and Giulio Tononi's functional clustering model and dynamic core hypothesis (DCH)) or effective information (Tononi's integrated information theory (IIT) of consciousness), is defined (on the basis of a reentrant process organization, i.e. the synchronization of neurophysiological activity between groups of neuronal populations), or the measure of the minimization of free energy on the basis of statistical methods (Karl J. Friston's free energy principle (FEP), an information-theoretical measure which states that every adaptive change in a self-organized system leads to a minimization of free energy, and the Bayesian brain hypothesis).

2.3.2 Entropy and Data Representation

Entropy is central to the design and evaluation of generative systems. When training a generative model, one of the goals is to approximate the probability distribution of the training data. If the model captures the data distribution accurately, it should generate outputs with entropy similar to that of the original data. A model that generates outputs with too little entropy may be overfitting, producing repetitive and uncreative outputs. Conversely, a model with excessively high entropy may be generating outputs that are too random or incoherent.

Generative models such as Variational Autoencoders (VAEs) and Generative Adversarial Networks (GANs) use entropy in various ways during training. In VAEs, for example, the objective function includes a Kullback-Leibler (KL) divergence term that measures the difference between the model's latent variable distribution and a prior distribution, effectively controlling the entropy of the latent space. This helps balance the trade-off between reconstruction accuracy and regularization, ensuring that the learned representations are both expressive and compact.

2.3.3 Mutual Information and Latent Representations

Mutual information is another powerful concept from information theory that has significant implications for generative modeling. In many generative systems, particularly those involving latent variables, the goal is to ensure that these variables meaningfully capture the underlying structure of the data. By maximizing the mutual information between latent variables and observed data, models can ensure that the latent space is informative and interpretable.

For instance, in InfoGAN, an extension of the GAN framework, mutual information is explicitly maximized between certain latent variables and the generated outputs. This encourages the model to use these latent dimensions to control interpretable aspects of the generation process, such as the shape, orientation, or style of objects in images. This application of mutual information facilitates disentanglement and makes the generative model more transparent and controllable.

2.3.4 Compression and Minimum Description Length Principle

One of the profound contributions of information theory to generative systems is the principle of data compression. According to Shannon's source coding theorem, any dataset can be compressed to a limit defined by its entropy. This insight has inspired the Minimum Description Length (MDL) principle, which states that the best model for a dataset is the one that compresses it most effectively. In other words, a good model should allow the data to be described using the fewest possible bits. Generative models inherently perform data compression when learning to replicate or generate data from a compact latent space. The VAE is a prime example where the encoder compresses the data into a low-dimensional latent representation, and the decoder reconstructs the data from this compressed form. The KL divergence term in the VAE objective can be interpreted as a penalty for the complexity of the latent encoding, encouraging the model to use fewer bits unless absolutely necessary. This principle aligns closely with Occam's razor, the idea that simpler explanations are preferable. By favoring models that compress data efficiently, generative systems can avoid overfitting and generalize better to unseen data. It also facilitates more interpretable representations, as more complex models must justify the additional bits they use.

2.3.5 Information Bottleneck and Regularization

The information bottleneck method is another concept from information theory that has found application in generative systems. It formalizes the trade-off between compressing the input data and preserving relevant information for a specific task. In this framework, the objective is to find a representation of the input that retains maximal mutual information with the output while minimizing mutual information with the input itself. Applied to generative modeling, the information bottleneck can serve as a form of regularization. It ensures that the model learns a compressed latent representation that still captures the essential features needed to reconstruct or generate data.

This technique helps prevent overfitting by discouraging the model from memorizing irrelevant details of the training data, thereby promoting more robust generalization. The idea of information bottlenecks is particularly relevant in deep learning, where networks with large capacity can easily overfit. By constraining the flow of information through the network, the information bottleneck approach helps enforce sparsity and abstraction, leading to more meaningful latent variables and better generative performance.

2.3.6 Evaluating Generative Models with Information Theory

Information-theoretic metrics provide valuable tools for evaluating the performance of generative models. Metrics such as entropy, cross-entropy, KL divergence, and mutual information are commonly used to assess how well a model captures the structure of the data and how diverse and plausible its outputs are. KL divergence, in particular, is widely used to measure the distance between the true data distribution and the model's learned distribution.

A lower KL divergence indicates that the model's outputs are more similar to the training data, suggesting better generative quality. However, KL divergence is asymmetric and sensitive to differences in the support of the distributions, so it is often used in conjunction with other metrics. Other evaluation methods include bits per dimension, which quantifies how many bits are needed to encode each data point under the model, and negative log-likelihood, which measures how well the model explains the observed data. These metrics are deeply rooted in information theory and provide a rigorous basis for comparing different generative systems.

2.3.7 Implications for Future Generative Systems

The integration of information theory into generative modeling has far-reaching implications for the future of artificial intelligence. As generative systems become more complex and widespread, the need for principled methods to measure, constrain, and guide their behavior becomes increasingly important. Information theory provides exactly such a toolkit. Future advances in generative AI are likely to continue leveraging information-theoretic concepts to improve efficiency, robustness, and interpretability. This includes developing models that can adaptively balance entropy and coherence, refine their latent representations using mutual information, and self-regularize using information bottlenecks.

Additionally, better evaluation metrics based on information theory can help ensure that generative systems meet high standards of quality, diversity, and fidelity. As generative models are deployed in critical applications—from creative industries to scientific discovery and beyond—the ability to understand and control their information flow will be essential. By grounding generative AI in the rigorous foundations of information theory, researchers and engineers can build systems that are not only powerful and expressive but also trustworthy and accountable.

2.4 GENERATIVE VS. DISCRIMINATIVE MODELS

In the domain of machine learning and artificial intelligence, two broad categories of models are employed to analyze, learn from, and make predictions based on data: generative models and discriminative models. These categories differ fundamentally in their objectives, learning strategies, and applications. Understanding the distinction between generative and discriminative models is crucial for selecting the appropriate approach for a given task. While both types of models serve valuable roles in AI systems, they operate with differing philosophies. Generative models aim to understand how data is generated by modeling the joint probability distribution of inputs and outputs, whereas discriminative models focus on learning the decision boundary between different classes by modeling the conditional probability of outputs given inputs.

Generative and discriminative models represent two fundamental paradigms in machine learning, each with distinct strengths and limitations. Discriminative models are typically more accurate and efficient for classification tasks, focusing on learning the boundary between classes. Generative models, on the other hand, offer greater flexibility, can learn from less labeled data, and are capable of generating new samples. The choice between them depends on the specific requirements of the task at hand, including the availability of data, the need for interpretability, and the desired outcomes. As AI continues to evolve, the integration of these two approaches into hybrid models is likely to play a key role in creating more intelligent, adaptable, and human-like systems.

2.4.1 Foundations of Generative Models

Generative models attempt to learn the underlying structure of the data by modeling the joint probability distribution P(x, y), where x represents the input data and y the corresponding labels or outcomes. In essence, these models aim to capture how the data is generated and use that understanding to generate new data points, predict labels, or even fill in missing data. By understanding both the input and output spaces, generative models can sample from the distribution to produce entirely new examples that resemble the training data. Examples of generative models include Naïve Bayes classifiers, Hidden Markov Models, Gaussian Mixture Models, Variational Autoencoders (VAEs), and Generative Adversarial Networks (GANs). These models not only enable classification tasks but also support more complex objectives such as data synthesis, anomaly detection, and semi-supervised learning. One of the key strengths of generative models is their versatility and ability to perform a wide range of tasks that go beyond simple classification.

2.4.2 Core Principles of Discriminative Models

In contrast to generative models, discriminative models learn the conditional probability distribution P(y | x), which describes the probability of a label y given an input x. Instead of modeling how the data is generated, discriminative models concentrate on the boundary that separates different classes in the input space. Their primary objective is to make accurate predictions, focusing solely on distinguishing among classes based on input features. Discriminative models include Logistic Regression, Support Vector Machines (SVMs), Decision Trees, Random Forests, and most deep learning architectures such as Convolutional Neural Networks (CNNs) and Recurrent Neural Networks (RNNs) when used for classification tasks. These models typically outperform generative models on pure classification tasks due to their ability to focus exclusively on the decision boundary without the additional burden of modeling the data distribution.

2.4.3 Comparative Learning Approaches

The learning approach of generative models is often more complex because they require estimating both the distribution of inputs and outputs. For instance, a generative model trained on image data must understand not only which labels correspond to which images but also how images of each class are distributed in pixel space. This involves a higher-dimensional estimation problem and typically requires more data and computational resources. Discriminative models simplify this process by ignoring the distribution of inputs and focusing directly on learning the mapping from inputs to outputs. This makes them easier to train, especially when the goal is straightforward classification or regression. As a result, discriminative models often converge faster and achieve higher accuracy in supervised tasks with ample labeled data.

2.4.4 Performance in Classification Tasks

When it comes to classification, discriminative models generally achieve superior performance because they directly optimize for predictive accuracy. They are specifically designed to distinguish between classes and thus often yield better results on benchmark datasets where the primary goal is correct classification. This makes them the preferred choice for many real-world applications such as image recognition, speech detection, and medical diagnostics. Generative models, while capable of classification, typically do not match the raw predictive power of discriminative models on these tasks. However, they offer benefits in situations where labeled data is scarce or when the model needs to perform multiple tasks beyond classification. Because generative models can learn from both labeled and unlabeled data, they are especially useful in semi-supervised learning scenarios, where their understanding of the data distribution provides additional leverage.

2.4.5 Ability to Generate New Data

A defining feature of generative models is their ability to create new data samples that resemble those in the training set. This ability stems from their foundational goal of modeling the joint distribution of inputs and outputs. In practice, this means a generative model trained on handwritten digits can produce new digit images that look authentic. Similarly, a generative model trained on human speech can produce synthetic voice samples. Discriminative models lack this capability because they do not model the data distribution itself. They cannot generate new samples because their learning process involves only decision boundaries, not the process that produces the data. This distinction is crucial in applications such as creative AI, simulation, and data augmentation, where the ability to generate realistic and diverse samples is essential.

2.4.6 Interpretability and Flexibility

Generative models often offer greater interpretability, particularly in settings where understanding the data generation process is important. Because these models describe how data is generated, they can provide insights into the underlying mechanisms of the system being modeled. This makes them valuable in fields such as natural sciences and social sciences, where interpretability is as important as prediction accuracy. Discriminative models, particularly deep learning models, are often seen as black boxes. While they excel at prediction, they can be more difficult to interpret. Efforts such as feature importance analysis and saliency maps have been developed to improve the transparency of these models, but they still fall short of the natural interpretability provided by some generative approaches.

2.4.7 Handling Missing or Incomplete Data

Another area where generative models shine is in handling missing or incomplete data. Because they model the full joint distribution of variables, they can infer the missing values by leveraging the relationships between variables. This is particularly useful in medical, financial, and survey data, where missing entries are common. Discriminative models struggle with missing data unless preprocessing steps such as imputation are performed. Since they do not model the input distribution, they cannot naturally account for missing variables. This limits their applicability in some real-world scenarios where data is often noisy or incomplete.

2.4.8 Application Domains and Use Cases

Generative and discriminative models are each suited to different types of problems. Discriminative models dominate in areas such as image classification, object detection, spam filtering, and fraud detection, where the main goal is accurate prediction. These models are preferred when large labeled datasets are available and interpretability is less critical. Generative models are more prevalent in tasks such as text generation, music composition, image synthesis, style transfer, and data denoising. They are also crucial in fields like reinforcement learning, where models need to simulate environments, and in healthcare, where generating synthetic data can help preserve privacy while supporting model training.

2.4.9 Hybrid Models and the Future

The strict division between generative and discriminative models is beginning to blur as researchers develop hybrid models that combine the strengths of both approaches. For example, semi-supervised learning frameworks often use generative models to enhance the performance of discriminative models when labeled data is limited. Generative adversarial networks (GANs), although primarily generative, can be trained to support discriminative tasks by improving data quality through augmentation. Another promising direction is the use of energy-based models and contrastive learning techniques that incorporate principles from both generative and discriminative paradigms. These hybrid approaches seek to maximize data efficiency, generalization, and interpretability, and they represent a growing trend in the development of more robust and versatile AI systems.

CHAPTER

3 Generative AI Techniques

3.1 GENERATIVE ADVERSARIAL NETWORKS (GANS)

3.1.1 Architecture of GANs

A generative adversarial network (GAN) is a class of machine learning frameworks and a prominent framework for approaching generative artificial intelligence. The concept was initially developed by Ian Goodfellow and his colleagues in June 2014. In a GAN, two neural networks compete with each other in the form of a zero-sum game, where one agent's gain is another agent's loss. Given a training set, this technique learns to generate new data with the same statistics as the training set. For example, a GAN trained on photographs can generate new photographs that look at least superficially authentic to human observers, having many realistic characteristics. Though originally proposed as a form of generative model for unsupervised learning, GANs have also proved useful for semi-supervised learning, fully supervised learning, and reinforcement learning. The core idea of a GAN is based on the "indirect" training through the discriminator, another neural network that can tell how "realistic" the input seems, which itself is also being updated dynamically. This means that the generator is not trained to minimize the distance to a specific image, but rather to fool the discriminator. This enables the model to learn in an unsupervised manner. GANs are similar to mimicry in evolutionary biology, with an evolutionary arms race between both networks.

Definition

In Practice

The generative network generates candidates while the discriminative network evaluates them. The contest operates in terms of data distributions. Typically, the generative network learns to map from a latent space to a data distribution of interest, while the discriminative network distinguishes candidates produced by the generator from the true data distribution. The generative network's training objective is to increase the error rate of the discriminative network (i.e., "fool" the discriminator network by producing novel candidates that the discriminator thinks are not synthesized (are part of the true data distribution)). A known dataset serves as the initial training data for the discriminator. Training involves presenting it with samples from the training dataset until it achieves acceptable accuracy. The generator is trained based on whether it succeeds in fooling the discriminator. Typically, the generator is seeded with randomized input that is sampled from a predefined latent space (e.g. a multivariate normal distribution).

Thereafter, candidates synthesized by the generator are evaluated by the discriminator. Independent backpropagation procedures are applied to both networks so that the generator produces better samples, while the discriminator becomes more skilled at flagging synthetic samples. When used for image generation, the generator is typically a deconvolutional neural network, and the discriminator is a convolutional neural network.

Relation to other Statistical Machine Learning Methods

GANs are implicit generative models, which means that they do not explicitly model the likelihood function nor provide a means for finding the latent variable corresponding to a given sample, unlike alternatives such as flow-based generative model.

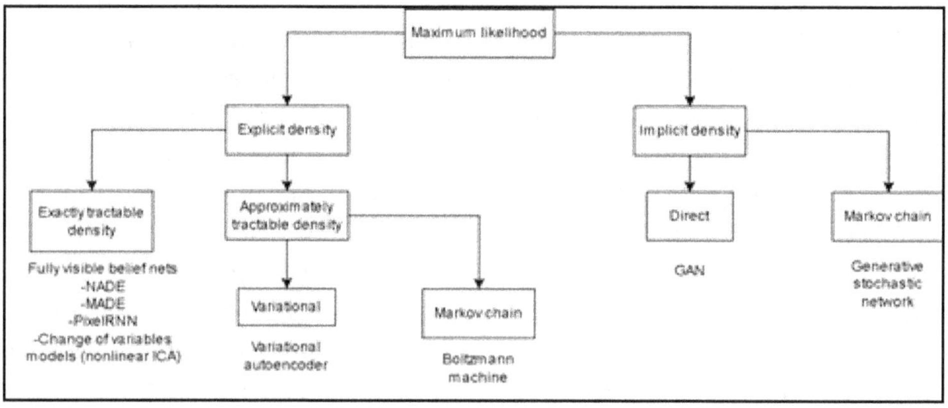

Fig: Main Types of Deep Generative Models that Perform Maximum Likelihood Estimation

Compared to fully visible belief networks such as WaveNet and PixelRNN and autoregressive models in general, GANs can generate one complete sample in one pass, rather than multiple passes through the network.

Compared to Boltzmann machines and linear ICA, there is no restriction on the type of function used by the network. Since neural networks are universal approximators, GANs are asymptotically consistent. Variational autoencoders might be universal approximators, but it is not proven as of 2017.

3.1.2 Types of GANs (e.g., StyleGAN, CycleGAN, BigGAN)

StyleGAN

The StyleGAN family is a series of architectures published by Nvidia's research division.

Progressive GAN

Progressive GAN is a method for training GAN for large-scale image generation stably, by growing a GAN generator from small to large scale in a pyramidal fashion. Like SinGAN, it decomposes the generator as $G = G_1 \circ G_2 \circ \cdots \circ G_N$, and the discriminator as $D = D_1 \circ D_2 \circ \cdots \circ D_N$. During training, at first only G_N, D_N are used in a GAN game to generate 4x4 images. Then G_{N-1}, D_{N-1} are added to reach the second stage of GAN game, to generate 8x8 images, and so on, until we reach a GAN game to generate 1024x1024 images. To avoid shock between stages of the GAN game, each new layer is "blended in" (Figure 2 of the paper). For example, this is how the second stage GAN game starts:

- Just before, the GAN game consists of the pair G_N, D_N generating and discriminating 4x4 images.
- Just after, the GAN game consists of the pair

$$((1-\alpha)+\alpha \cdot G_{N-1}) \circ u \circ G_N, D_N \circ d \circ ((1-\alpha)+\alpha \cdot D_{N-1})$$

generating and discriminat-ing 8x8 images. Here, the functions u, d are image up- and down-sampling functions, and α is a blend-in factor (much like an alpha in image composing) that smoothly glides from 0 to 1.

StyleGAN-1

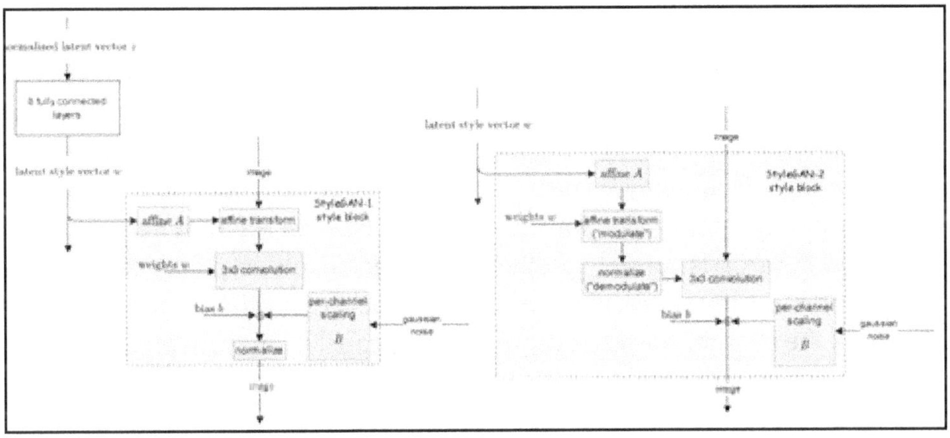

Fig: The Main Architecture of StyleGAN-1 and StyleGAN-2

StyleGAN-1 is designed as a combination of Progressive GAN with neural style transfer. The key architectural choice of StyleGAN-1 is a progressive growth mechanism, similar to Progressive GAN. Each generated image starts as a constant $4 \times 4 \times 512$ array, and repeatedly passed through style blocks. Each style block applies a "style latent vector" via affine transform ("adaptive instance normalization"), similar to how neural style transfer uses Gramian matrix. It then adds noise, and normalize (subtract the mean, then divide by the variance).

At training time, usually only one style latent vector is used per image generated, but sometimes two ("mixing regularization") in order to encourage each style block to independently perform its stylization without expecting help from other style blocks (since they might receive an entirely different style latent vector).

After training, multiple style latent vectors can be fed into each style block. Those fed to the lower layers control the large-scale styles, and those fed to the higher layers control the fine-detail styles. Style-mixing between two images x, x' can be performed as well. First, run a gradient descent to find z, z' such that $G(z) \approx x, G(z') \approx x'$. This is called "projecting an image back to style latent space". Then, z can be fed to the lower style blocks, and z' to the higher style blocks, to generate a composite image that has the large-scale style of x, and the fine-detail style of x'. Multiple images can also be composed this way.

StyleGAN-2

StyleGAN-2 improves upon StyleGAN-1, by using the style latent vector to transform the convolution layer's weights instead, thus solving the "blob" problem. This was updated by the StyleGAN-2-ADA ("ADA" stands for "adaptive"), which uses invertible data augmentation. It also tunes the amount of data augmentation applied by starting at zero, and gradually increasing it until an "overfitting heuristic" reaches a target level, thus the name "adaptive".

StyleGAN-3

StyleGAN-3 improves upon StyleGAN-2 by solving the "texture sticking" problem, which can be seen in the official videos. They analyzed the problem by the Nyquist–Shannon sampling theorem, and argued that the layers in the generator learned to exploit the high-frequency signal in the pixels they operate upon. To solve this, they proposed imposing strict lowpass filters between each generator's layers, so that the generator is forced to operate on the pixels in a way faithful to the continuous signals they represent, rather than operate on them as merely discrete signals. They further imposed rotational and translational invariance by using more signal filters. The resulting StyleGAN-3 is able to solve the texture sticking problem, as well as generating images that rotate and translate smoothly.

CycleGAN

CycleGAN is an architecture for performing translations between two domains, such as between photos of horses and photos of zebras, or photos of night cities and photos of day cities.

The CycleGAN game is defined as follows:

There are two probability spaces $(\Omega_X, \mu_X), (\Omega_Y, \mu_Y)$, corresponding to the two domains needed for translations fore-and-back.

There are 4 players in 2 teams: generators $G_X : \Omega_X \to \Omega_Y, G_Y : \Omega_Y \to \Omega_X$, and discriminators $D_X : \Omega_X \to [0,1], D_Y : \Omega_Y \to [0,1]$.

The objective function is $L(G_X, G_Y, D_X, D_Y) = L_{GAN}(G_X, D_X) + L_{GAN}(G_Y, D_Y) + \lambda L_{cycle}(G_X, G_Y)$ where

- λ is a positive adjustable parameter,
- L_{GAN} is the GAN game objective,
- L_{cycle} is the cycle consistency loss:
  $L_{cycle}(G_X, G_Y) = E_{x \sim \mu_X} \| G_X(G_Y(x)) - x \| + E_{y \sim \mu_Y} \| G_Y(G_X(y)) - y \|$
- The generators aim to minimize the objective, and
- the discriminators aim to maximize it $\min_{G_X, G_Y} \max_{D_X, D_Y} L(G_X, G_Y, D_X, D_Y)$

Unlike previous work like pix2pix, which requires paired training data, cycleGAN requires no paired data. For example, to train a pix2pix model to turn a summer scenery photo to winter scenery photo and back, the dataset must contain pairs of the same place in summer and winter, shot at the same angle; cycleGAN would only need a set of summer scenery photos, and an unrelated set of winter scenery photos.

BigGAN

The standard GAN generator is a function of type $G : \Omega_Z \to \Omega_X$, that is, it is a mapping from a latent space Ω_Z to the image space $z \in \Omega_Z$. This can be understood as a "decoding" process, whereby every latent vector $z \in \Omega_Z$ is a code for an image $x \in \Omega_X$, and the generator performs the decoding. This naturally leads to the idea of training another network that performs "encoding", creating an autoencoder out of the encoder-generator pair.

Already in the original paper, the authors noted that "Learned approximate inference can be performed by training an auxiliary network to predict $z\ given\ x$ ". The bidirectional GAN architecture performs exactly this.

The BiGAN is defined as follows:

Two probability spaces define a BiGAN game:

- (Ω_X, μ_X), the space of reference images.
- (Ω_Z, μ_Z), the latent space.

There are 3 players in 2 teams: generator, encoder, and discriminator. The generator and encoder are on one team, and the discriminator on the other team.

The generator's strategies are functions $G:\Omega_Z \to \Omega_X$, and the encoder's strategies are functions $E:\Omega_X \to \Omega_Z$. The discriminator's strategies are functions $D:\Omega_X \to [0,1]$.

The objective function is $L(G,E,D) = \mathbb{E}_{x\sim\mu_X}[\ln D(x,E(x))] + \mathbb{E}_{z\sim\mu_Z}[\ln(1-D(G(z),z))]$

Generator-encoder team aims to minimize the objective, and discriminator aims to maximize it: $\min_{G,E}\max_D L(G,E,D)$

They gave a more abstract definition of the objective as:

$$L(G,E,D) = \mathbb{E}_{(x,z)\sim\mu_{E,X}}[\ln D(x,z)] + \mathbb{E}_{(x,z)\sim\mu_{G,Z}}[\ln(1-D(x,z))]$$

3.1.3 Applications of GANs

Science

- Iteratively reconstruct astronomical images
- Simulate gravitational lensing for dark matter research.
- Model the distribution of dark matter in a particular direction in space and to predict the gravitational lensing that will occur.
- Model high energy jet formation and showers through calorimeters of high-energy physics experiments.
- Approximate bottlenecks in computationally expensive simulations of particle physics experiments. Applications in the context of present and proposed CERN experiments have demonstrated the potential of these methods for accelerating simulation and/or improving simulation fidelity.
- Reconstruct velocity and scalar fields in turbulent flows.

Medical

One of the major concerns in medical imaging is preserving patient privacy. Due to these reasons, researchers often face difficulties in obtaining medical images for their research purposes. GAN has been used for generating synthetic medical images, such as MRI and PET images to address this challenge. GAN can be used to detect glaucomatous images helping the early diagnosis which is essential to avoid partial or total loss of vision. GANs have been used to create forensic facial reconstructions of deceased historical figures.

Malicious

Concerns have been raised about the potential use of GAN-based human image synthesis for sinister purposes, e.g., to produce fake, possibly incriminating, photographs and videos. GANs can be used to generate unique, realistic profile photos of people who do not exist, in order to automate creation of fake social media profiles. In 2019 the state of California considered and passed on October 3, 2019, the bill AB-602, which bans the use of human image synthesis technologies to make fake pornography without the consent of the people depicted, and bill AB-730, which prohibits distribution of manipulated videos of a political candidate within 60 days of an election. Both bills were authored by Assembly member Marc Berman and signed by Governor Gavin Newsom. The laws went into effect in 2020. DARPA's Media Forensics program studies ways to counteract fake media, including fake media produced using GANs.

Fashion, Art and Advertising

GANs can be used to generate art; The Verge wrote in March 2019 that "The images created by GANs have become the defining look of contemporary AI art." GANs can also be used to

- Inpaint photographs
- Generate fashion models, shadows, photorealistic renders of interior design, industrial design, shoes, etc. Such networks were reported to be used by Facebook.

Some have worked with using GAN for artistic creativity, as "creative adversarial network". A GAN, trained on a set of 15,000 portraits from WikiArt from the 14th to the 19th century, created the 2018 painting Edmond de Belamy, which sold for US$432,500. GANs were used by the video game modding community to up-scale low-resolution 2D textures in old video games by recreating them in 4k or higher resolutions via image training, and then down-sampling them to fit the game's native resolution (resembling supersampling anti-aliasing).

In 2020, Artbreeder was used to create the main antagonist in the sequel to the psychological web horror series Ben Drowned. The author would later go on to praise GAN applications for their ability to help generate assets for independent artists who are short on budget and manpower. In May 2020, Nvidia researchers taught an AI system (termed "GameGAN") to recreate the game of Pac-Man simply by watching it being played. In August 2019, a large dataset consisting of 12,197 MIDI songs each with paired lyrics and melody alignment was created for neural melody generation from lyrics using conditional GAN-LSTM (refer to sources at GitHub AI Melody Generation from Lyrics).

Miscellaneous

GANs have been used to

- Show how an individual's appearance might change with age.
- Reconstruct 3D models of objects from images,
- Generate novel objects as 3D point clouds,

- Model patterns of motion in video.
- Inpaint missing features in maps, transfer map styles in cartography or augment street view imagery.
- Use feedback to generate images and replace image search systems.
- Visualize the effect that climate change will have on specific houses.
- Reconstruct an image of a person's face after listening to their voice.
- Produces videos of a person speaking, given only a single photo of that person.
- Recurrent sequence generation.

3.2 VARIATIONAL AUTOENCODERS (VAES)

3.2.1 Overview of VAEs

In machine learning, a variational autoencoder (VAE) is an artificial neural network architecture introduced by Diederik P. Kingma and Max Welling. It is part of the families of probabilistic graphical models and variational Bayesian methods. In addition to being seen as an autoencoder neural network architecture, variational autoencoders can also be studied within the mathematical formulation of variational Bayesian methods, connecting a neural encoder network to its decoder through a probabilistic latent space (for example, as a multivariate Gaussian distribution) that corresponds to the parameters of a variational distribution.

Thus, the encoder maps each point (such as an image) from a large complex dataset into a distribution within the latent space, rather than to a single point in that space. The decoder has the opposite function, which is to map from the latent space to the input space, again according to a distribution (although in practice, noise is rarely added during the decoding stage).

By mapping a point to a distribution instead of a single point, the network can avoid overfitting the training data. Both networks are typically trained together with the usage of the reparameterization trick, although the variance of the noise model can be learned separately. Although this type of model was initially designed for unsupervised learning, its effectiveness has been proven for semi-supervised learning and supervised learning.

Architecture and Operation

A variational autoencoder is a generative model with a prior and noise distribution respectively. Usually such models are trained using the expectation-maximization meta-algorithm (e.g. probabilistic PCA, (spike & slab) sparse coding). Such a scheme optimizes a lower bound of the data likelihood, which is usually computationally intractable, and in doing so requires the discovery of q-distributions, or variational posteriors. These q-distributions are normally parameterized for each individual data point in a separate optimization process. However, variational autoencoders use a neural network as an amortized approach to jointly optimize across data points. In that way, the same parameters are reused for multiple data points, which can result in massive memory savings. The first neural network takes as input the data points themselves, and outputs parameters for the variational distribution. As it maps from a known input space to the low-dimensional latent space, it is called the encoder.

The decoder is the second neural network of this model. It is a function that maps from the latent space to the input space, e.g. as the means of the noise distribution. It is possible to use another neural network that maps to the variance, however this can be omitted for simplicity. In such a case, the variance can be optimized with gradient descent.

To optimize this model, one needs to know two terms: the "reconstruction error", and the Kullback–Leibler divergence (KL-D). Both terms are derived from the free energy expression of the probabilistic model, and therefore differ depending on the noise distribution and the assumed prior of the data, here referred to as p-distribution. For example, a standard VAE task such as IMAGENET is typically assumed to have a gaussianly distributed noise; however, tasks such as binarized MNIST require a Bernoulli noise.

The KL-D from the free energy expression maximizes the probability mass of the q-distribution that overlaps with the p-distribution, which unfortunately can result in mode-seeking behaviour. The "reconstruction" term is the remainder of the free energy expression, and requires a sampling approximation to compute its expectation value.

Variations

Many variational autoencoders applications and extensions have been used to adapt the architecture to other domains and improve its performance.

β-VAE is an implementation with a weighted Kullback–Leibler divergence term to automatically discover and interpret factorised latent representations. With this implementation, it is possible to force manifold disentanglement for β values greater than one. This architecture can discover disentangled latent factors without supervision.

The conditional VAE (CVAE), inserts label information in the latent space to force a deterministic constrained representation of the learned data. Some structures directly deal with the quality of the generated samples or implement more than one latent space to further improve the representation learning. Some architectures mix VAE and generative adversarial networks to obtain hybrid models. It is not necessary to use gradients to update the encoder. In fact, the encoder is not necessary for the generative model.

3.2.2 VAE vs. Traditional Autoencoders

Autoencoders are a class of neural network architectures used for learning efficient representations of input data in an unsupervised manner. They function by encoding the input into a lower-dimensional latent representation and then decoding it back to reconstruct the original input. Traditional autoencoders are widely used in tasks such as dimensionality reduction, denoising, and feature learning. However, they lack a probabilistic foundation and often fail to generate new, diverse data samples.

To overcome these limitations, Variational Autoencoders (VAEs) were introduced as a more powerful and mathematically grounded extension. VAEs integrate principles from probabilistic graphical models and deep learning, allowing for both effective representation learning and data generation. The distinction between VAEs and traditional autoencoders lies in their architectures, training objectives, theoretical foundations, and practical applications, making it essential to understand their comparative strengths and limitations. The evolution from traditional autoencoders to Variational Autoencoders represents a significant advancement in representation learning and generative modeling. While both models share the core concept of encoding and decoding data, they diverge in their objectives, capabilities, and mathematical foundations.

Traditional autoencoders offer simplicity and effectiveness in tasks focused on reconstruction and compression, but they fall short in generative applications. VAEs introduce a probabilistic framework that enables structured latent spaces, smooth interpolation, and data generation, making them powerful tools for modern machine learning. Understanding the distinctions between these models allows practitioners to choose the most appropriate approach based on the nature of the task and the desired outcomes.

Fundamental Architecture of Traditional Autoencoders

Traditional autoencoders consist of two main components: an encoder and a decoder. The encoder compresses the input data into a fixed-size latent vector, often referred to as the "bottleneck," which captures the most important features of the input. The decoder then reconstructs the input data from this latent vector, aiming to reproduce the original as closely as possible.

The training objective of a traditional autoencoder is to minimize the reconstruction error, which is typically measured using mean squared error (MSE) or binary cross-entropy, depending on the data type. This architecture encourages the model to learn meaningful and compact representations of the input data. However, traditional autoencoders treat the latent space as deterministic, meaning each input maps to a single point in the latent space. While this is effective for compression and denoising, it does not allow for smooth interpolation or generative sampling, as there is no well-defined distribution over the latent space.

The Probabilistic Framework of Variational Autoencoders

Variational Autoencoders extend the traditional architecture by introducing a probabilistic approach to the latent space. Instead of mapping each input to a single point, the encoder in a VAE maps the input to a distribution, typically a Gaussian. This distribution is defined by a mean and a standard deviation, from which the model samples latent vectors. The decoder then reconstructs the input from these sampled latent vectors.

The key innovation of the VAE lies in its objective function, which combines two components: the reconstruction loss and the Kullback-Leibler (KL) divergence. The reconstruction loss ensures that the decoder can accurately reconstruct the input, similar to a traditional autoencoder. The KL divergence, on the other hand, regularizes the learned latent distribution to be close to a standard normal distribution. This regularization is essential for ensuring that the latent space is continuous and structured, enabling smooth interpolation and effective sampling.

Latent Space Characteristics and Structure

The latent space in a traditional autoencoder lacks a coherent structure, as there is no constraint on how the encoder organizes latent representations. This often results in irregular or disconnected regions in the latent space, making interpolation between latent vectors unreliable and generated outputs unrealistic. Furthermore, since traditional autoencoders do not impose any prior distribution on the latent space, sampling from it arbitrarily is unlikely to yield meaningful data. In contrast, the VAE enforces a structured latent space by encouraging all latent representations to follow a standard normal distribution. This has several important implications. First, it ensures that any point sampled from the latent space is likely to produce a plausible output. Second, it allows for smooth and meaningful interpolation between points in the latent space, leading to continuous transformations in the generated outputs. Third, it facilitates better generalization and prevents overfitting, as the model is not allowed to memorize the training data.

Training Objectives and Optimization

Training a traditional autoencoder involves minimizing the reconstruction loss between the input and the output. This objective directly encourages the network to capture the most salient features of the data but does not account for the structure or distribution of the latent space. As a result, the model may learn arbitrary and overfitted mappings that do not generalize well to new data. In the case of VAEs, the training objective is derived from variational inference, a method for approximating complex probability distributions. The VAE maximizes a lower bound on the marginal likelihood of the data, known as the Evidence Lower Bound (ELBO). This objective comprises the reconstruction term, which encourages accurate reconstructions, and the KL divergence term, which ensures that the learned latent distribution approximates the prior. The use of the reparameterization trick—a technique that allows gradients to flow through stochastic nodes—enables efficient optimization using backpropagation.

Generative Capabilities and Applications

One of the most significant advantages of VAEs over traditional autoencoders is their generative capability. Because the VAE learns a smooth, continuous latent space, it can generate new data samples by sampling from the prior distribution and decoding the resulting latent vectors. This makes VAEs particularly useful in tasks such as image synthesis, text generation, and data augmentation. The structured latent space also allows for controlled generation, where specific attributes of the generated data can be manipulated by adjusting corresponding dimensions in the latent vector.

Traditional autoencoders, while capable of compressing and reconstructing data, do not possess this generative ability. Since their latent space is not governed by a known distribution, randomly sampling latent vectors and decoding them typically yields nonsensical or noisy outputs. Consequently, traditional autoencoders are more suited to tasks such as denoising, anomaly detection, and representation learning, rather than data generation.

Model Complexity and Training Challenges

The added complexity of the VAE architecture and training process introduces new challenges. Training a VAE requires careful tuning of the balance between the reconstruction loss and the KL divergence. If the KL divergence dominates, the model may ignore the latent variables altogether, leading to a phenomenon known as "posterior collapse." Conversely, if the reconstruction loss dominates, the latent space may become irregular and fail to support meaningful sampling. Traditional autoencoders, being simpler in design and training, are often easier to implement and optimize. They do not suffer from issues like posterior collapse, and their objectives are straightforward to monitor. However, this simplicity comes at the cost of reduced flexibility and generalization, particularly in tasks that require generative modeling.

Interpretability and Control

VAEs also offer greater potential for interpretability and control over the generative process. Since the latent space is regularized to follow a standard distribution, specific dimensions in the latent vector can correspond to interpretable features of the data. For instance, in a VAE trained on facial images, certain dimensions may encode attributes like age, gender, or expression. By manipulating these dimensions, users can generate variations of the input data with desired characteristics. Traditional autoencoders lack this level of control and interpretability. Their latent representations are not constrained or disentangled, making it difficult to understand or manipulate individual features. This limits their utility in applications where explainability or attribute-specific generation is important.

Suitability for Different Use Cases

In practice, the choice between a VAE and a traditional autoencoder depends on the specific requirements of the application. For tasks that prioritize data compression, denoising, or feature extraction, traditional autoencoders may be sufficient and more efficient. Their simpler training process and deterministic nature make them well-suited for use in real-time systems and resource-constrained environments. VAEs, on the other hand, are better suited to applications that require generative modeling, semi-supervised learning, or interpretable latent representations. Their ability to generate high-quality, diverse samples and explore the latent space makes them ideal for creative tasks, synthetic data generation, and scientific modeling. However, they require more computational resources and careful tuning to achieve optimal performance.

3.3 DIFFUSION MODELS

3.3.1 Fundamentals of Diffusion Processes

Diffusion processes are fundamental concepts in both natural and artificial systems, describing how substances, particles, or information spread over time and space. Originating in physics and chemistry to explain the movement of molecules, diffusion has found relevance in a wide array of disciplines including biology, finance, and more recently, machine learning. At its core, diffusion refers to the process by which particles move from regions of higher concentration to regions of lower concentration, driven by the tendency toward equilibrium.

This movement is inherently stochastic, shaped by random fluctuations and interactions within the medium. In mathematical modeling, diffusion processes are used to represent the dynamics of systems that evolve with some degree of randomness and uncertainty. These processes are especially critical in understanding and modeling real-world phenomena where deterministic models fall short due to the complexity and variability of nature. The fundamentals of diffusion processes encompass a rich blend of empirical observations, mathematical formulations, and theoretical insights. Originating in the physical sciences, diffusion has evolved into a versatile and widely applicable concept that informs diverse fields ranging from biology and chemistry to finance and machine learning. Whether modeled deterministically through partial differential equations or stochastically through Brownian motion and random walks, diffusion provides a powerful lens through which to understand the dynamic behavior of complex systems. As our ability to model, simulate, and leverage diffusion processes grows, their relevance continues to expand, shaping the future of both scientific research and technological innovation.

Historical Foundations and Physical Intuition

The study of diffusion began in the 19th century with the work of scientists such as Robert Brown, Adolf Fick, and Albert Einstein. Brown observed the erratic movement of pollen grains in water, later termed Brownian motion, which laid the empirical foundation for understanding microscopic particle behavior. Fick formalized the diffusion process with his laws of diffusion, which mathematically describe how the rate of diffusion is proportional to the gradient of concentration. Einstein built upon this with his theoretical model linking Brownian motion to diffusion, providing a bridge between macroscopic observations and microscopic mechanisms. These early developments established diffusion as a central phenomenon governed by probabilistic laws, deeply rooted in thermodynamics and statistical mechanics.

Mathematical Formulation and Fick's Laws

The mathematical treatment of diffusion begins with Fick's first law, which states that the flux of particles is proportional to the negative gradient of concentration. This law expresses the idea that particles move from areas of higher concentration to lower concentration at a rate proportional to the steepness of the gradient. Fick's second law, derived from the first, describes how the concentration of a diffusing substance changes over time. It takes the form of a partial differential equation known as the diffusion equation or heat equation.

This equation models how the concentration field evolves, taking into account both the spatial and temporal dynamics of diffusion. These laws provide a deterministic approximation of an inherently stochastic process and are widely used in engineering and physics to model heat transfer, mass transport, and other similar phenomena.

Stochastic Interpretation and Brownian Motion

While Fick's laws offer a macroscopic view, the stochastic interpretation of diffusion provides a more granular understanding. Brownian motion serves as the foundational model for the random movement of particles. In this view, a diffusing particle undergoes a series of random steps in different directions, resulting in an unpredictable trajectory. This randomness can be modeled using probability distributions, leading to the concept of a Wiener process, a continuous-time stochastic process with stationary, independent increments. Brownian motion is a central model in stochastic calculus and underpins various applications in finance, biology, and physics. The mean squared displacement of a particle undergoing Brownian motion increases linearly with time, a key signature of diffusive behavior. This random walk approach provides powerful tools for modeling systems where uncertainty plays a significant role.

Diffusion in Multi-Dimensional Systems

In real-world scenarios, diffusion often occurs in more than one dimension. The extension of diffusion models to two or three dimensions introduces complexity but also provides a more accurate representation of natural systems. In multiple dimensions, the diffusion equation accounts for spatial variability across different axes, capturing the anisotropic nature of many diffusion processes. For example, diffusion in biological tissues or porous media may vary depending on the structure and orientation of the medium.

These multi-dimensional models are essential for simulating phenomena such as chemical dispersion in the environment, neural signal transmission, or molecular transport within cells. The solutions to multi-dimensional diffusion equations often involve advanced mathematical techniques, including Fourier and Laplace transforms, to address the complexity introduced by higher degrees of freedom.

Thermodynamic and Statistical Mechanics Perspectives

From a thermodynamic standpoint, diffusion can be understood as a system's tendency to move toward equilibrium. When a concentration gradient exists, the system is in a state of disequilibrium. Diffusion acts as a mechanism for redistributing particles until a uniform concentration is achieved, thereby increasing entropy. This process aligns with the second law of thermodynamics, which states that systems evolve toward states of higher disorder. Statistical mechanics provides a microscopic explanation by considering the ensemble behavior of a large number of particles. Each particle moves randomly due to thermal energy, and the collective effect results in the observable diffusion behavior. These thermodynamic insights not only validate the empirical observations but also offer a framework for deriving the fundamental equations governing diffusion from first principles.

Applications in Biology and Chemistry

Diffusion plays a critical role in biological and chemical systems. In biology, diffusion is essential for processes such as nutrient uptake, gas exchange, and signal transduction. For instance, oxygen diffuses across cell membranes to reach mitochondria, where it is used in cellular respiration. Similarly, neurotransmitters diffuse across synaptic gaps to transmit signals between neurons. In chemistry, diffusion governs the mixing of reactants and the rate of chemical reactions. Reaction-diffusion systems, which couple chemical kinetics with diffusion, can model pattern formation in natural systems, such as animal coat patterns or the spread of chemical waves. Understanding diffusion in these contexts is crucial for developing medical treatments, designing drug delivery systems, and studying ecological dynamics.

Diffusion in Modern Machine Learning

In recent years, diffusion processes have gained prominence in machine learning, particularly in the field of generative modeling. Diffusion models in machine learning simulate the gradual addition of noise to data and then learn to reverse this process, effectively denoising the data to generate new samples. This concept, inspired by physical diffusion, allows for the training of highly expressive generative models capable of producing realistic images, audio, and text.

These models, such as Denoising Diffusion Probabilistic Models (DDPMs), operate by modeling the distribution of data as a stochastic process that evolves over time. During training, the model learns the trajectory of data degradation and uses this knowledge to reconstruct high-fidelity samples from random noise. The success of diffusion models in machine learning underscores the versatility of diffusion as a conceptual tool that extends far beyond its physical origins.

Connection to Partial Differential Equations

Diffusion processes are inherently connected to partial differential equations (PDEs), particularly the diffusion or heat equation. Solving these equations provides insights into the behavior of diffusing systems under various initial and boundary conditions. Analytical solutions to these equations exist for simple geometries and conditions, while numerical methods are employed for more complex scenarios. Techniques such as finite difference methods, finite element methods, and spectral methods allow researchers and engineers to approximate the behavior of diffusion in intricate systems. The ability to solve diffusion equations efficiently and accurately is crucial in designing systems ranging from chemical reactors to climate models. This mathematical framework bridges theoretical understanding with practical application, making diffusion a cornerstone of scientific modeling.

Advanced Topics and Nonlinear Diffusion

While classical diffusion assumes a linear relationship between flux and concentration gradient, many real-world systems exhibit nonlinear diffusion behavior. Nonlinear diffusion arises when the diffusion coefficient depends on the concentration or other dynamic variables, leading to more complex and often more accurate models. These models can describe phenomena such as crowd dynamics, heat transfer in reactive media, and the spread of diseases. Nonlinear diffusion equations often require sophisticated mathematical tools for analysis and simulation but offer richer insights into system behavior. Additionally, anomalous diffusion, which deviates from the standard linear time-dependence of mean squared displacement, occurs in systems with memory or long-range interactions. Modeling such processes involves fractional calculus and generalized stochastic models, expanding the frontiers of diffusion theory.

3.3.2 State-of-the-Art Diffusion Models

Diffusion models have emerged as one of the most powerful and versatile frameworks in machine learning, particularly in the domain of generative modeling. Rooted in the principles of stochastic processes and inspired by physical diffusion phenomena, these models have revolutionized the way machines generate data such as images, audio, and text. Unlike traditional generative models like Generative Adversarial Networks (GANs) or Variational Autoencoders (VAEs), diffusion models exhibit remarkable stability during training and produce samples of unprecedented quality and diversity. The recent surge of interest and rapid advancements in this field highlight their importance and potential in a wide array of applications. State-of-the-art diffusion models represent a transformative leap in generative modeling, combining elegant theoretical foundations with practical architectural innovations. Their unique approach of reversing a stochastic noising process enables stable training, high-quality sample generation, and versatile applications. From image and audio synthesis to scientific modeling, diffusion models are reshaping the capabilities of artificial intelligence. Continued research aimed at improving efficiency, interpretability, and ethical deployment promises to unlock even greater potential, making diffusion models a cornerstone of future machine learning advancements.

Theoretical Foundations of Diffusion Models

At their core, diffusion models are probabilistic generative models that model the data generation process as the reverse of a gradual noising process. The forward process gradually corrupts the data by adding small amounts of noise over many time steps, transforming structured data into pure noise. The reverse process, learned by the model, attempts to denoise this noisy data step-by-step until it reconstructs the original data distribution. This approach is mathematically formalized through stochastic differential equations (SDEs) or discrete Markov chains, which describe the continuous or discrete evolution of the data distribution over time. The strength of diffusion models lies in this carefully designed two-phase approach. By decomposing generation into a series of incremental denoising steps, the model avoids the instability problems commonly encountered in other frameworks. The training objective typically involves learning to predict the noise added at each step, which can be optimized efficiently with gradient-based methods. The theoretical guarantee of likelihood maximization further grounds diffusion models in solid probabilistic foundations, distinguishing them from other generative models that often rely on adversarial or heuristic losses.

Denoising Diffusion Probabilistic Models (DDPMs)

A pivotal milestone in the diffusion model literature is the introduction of Denoising Diffusion Probabilistic Models (DDPMs). These models popularized the discrete-time diffusion framework, which simulates a Markov chain of forward noising steps and learns a reverse chain to reconstruct data. The DDPM architecture typically employs deep neural networks, such as U-Nets, to predict noise at each time step conditioned on the noisy input.

DDPMs demonstrated that it is possible to generate high-fidelity images competitive with GANs, but without the mode collapse and training instability issues GANs often suffer. Their ability to model complex multimodal data distributions has opened new pathways for applications in image synthesis, inpainting, and super-resolution. The training process in DDPMs is relatively straightforward, consisting of minimizing a simplified variational bound on the negative log-likelihood, making them accessible and reproducible by the research community.

Continuous-Time Diffusion Models and Score-Based Generative Modeling

Building on the discrete-time framework, continuous-time diffusion models represent the forward and reverse diffusion as stochastic differential equations. This perspective enables the use of continuous score matching techniques, where the model learns to estimate the gradient (score) of the log probability density function of the data at varying noise levels. Score-based generative models, a prominent class within continuous-time diffusion, leverage this technique to produce data by simulating the reverse-time SDE starting from pure noise. These models use neural networks trained with score matching objectives, which ensure the learned score functions accurately represent the underlying data manifold. This approach has shown superior flexibility, enabling the design of advanced sampling algorithms such as predictor-corrector methods that improve generation quality and speed. The continuous formulation also allows for better theoretical understanding and connections to other probabilistic models, bridging gaps between different machine learning paradigms. Moreover, it facilitates the use of adaptive solvers during sampling, which can dynamically adjust the number of denoising steps based on desired quality or computational constraints.

Architectural Innovations in Diffusion Models

While the core principle of diffusion remains consistent, state-of-the-art models incorporate several architectural innovations to enhance performance. Neural network backbones such as U-Nets have become the standard choice due to their ability to capture multi-scale features and context effectively. These networks use encoder-decoder structures with skip connections, enabling them to retain spatial information while processing noisy inputs at different resolutions. Attention mechanisms have also been integrated into diffusion models to improve the modeling of long-range dependencies, particularly in high-resolution images and complex data domains like natural language.

Transformer-based architectures and hybrid models combining convolutional layers with attention blocks have demonstrated significant improvements in sample quality and diversity. Conditioning mechanisms have further extended the applicability of diffusion models. By conditioning on class labels, text prompts, or other modalities, diffusion models can perform conditional generation, enabling applications such as text-to-image synthesis and guided image editing. These conditioning signals are incorporated into the model through techniques like cross-attention layers or adaptive normalization, allowing precise control over the generated content.

Sampling Efficiency and Speed Improvements

Despite their impressive results, a notable challenge of diffusion models has been their relatively slow sampling speed. Generating a single data sample typically requires hundreds to thousands of iterative denoising steps, which is computationally intensive and limits real-time applications. Recent advances have focused on accelerating the sampling process without sacrificing quality.

Techniques such as knowledge distillation, which trains smaller models to approximate the output of full diffusion processes, have been proposed to reduce the number of required steps. Other approaches involve designing specialized solvers for the reverse diffusion SDE that take larger, adaptive steps while maintaining stability. Moreover, hybrid models combining diffusion with other generative frameworks seek to leverage the strengths of each.

For example, integrating diffusion with GANs has been explored to combine the high-quality sample generation of GANs with the stability and diversity of diffusion. These developments point toward more practical deployment of diffusion models in resource-constrained or latency-sensitive environments.

Applications and Impact

The impact of state-of-the-art diffusion models extends across multiple domains. In computer vision, they have become a dominant approach for image synthesis, offering unprecedented fidelity and fine-grained control. Diffusion models excel in tasks like inpainting, super-resolution, style transfer, and image-to-image translation. Their ability to generate diverse samples mitigates issues like mode collapse, common in GANs, making them highly valuable for creative industries and content generation. Beyond vision, diffusion models have been adapted for audio generation, including speech synthesis and music creation, demonstrating their versatility in handling different data modalities.

Natural language processing has also benefited, with diffusion-inspired techniques being explored for text generation and language modeling. Furthermore, the interpretability and probabilistic nature of diffusion models make them suitable for scientific simulations and uncertainty quantification. Their ability to model complex distributions with clear likelihood objectives supports applications in physics, chemistry, and healthcare, where understanding data uncertainty is crucial.

Challenges and Future Directions

Despite remarkable progress, diffusion models face several challenges. The computational cost of training and sampling remains significant, necessitating further research into efficiency improvements. Model interpretability and understanding the latent representations learned by diffusion models are active areas of investigation, aiming to make these systems more transparent and controllable.

Another frontier is the exploration of diffusion models in multimodal and structured data domains, such as 3D modeling, video generation, and reinforcement learning. Integrating diffusion processes with domain knowledge and constraints poses both challenges and opportunities for more powerful and specialized models. Ethical considerations also arise, especially concerning the potential misuse of highly realistic synthetic data. Responsible development and deployment practices are critical to mitigate risks related to misinformation, privacy, and security.

3.4 TRANSFORMER MODELS IN GENERATIVE AI

3.4.1 GPT Series and Large Language Models

GPT Series

A generative pre-trained transformer (GPT) is a type of large language model (LLM) and a prominent framework for generative artificial intelligence. It is an artificial neural network that is used in natural language processing by machines. It is based on the transformer deep learning architecture, pre-trained on large data sets of unlabeled text, and able to generate novel human-like content.

As of 2023, most LLMs had these characteristics and are sometimes referred to broadly as GPTs. The first GPT was introduced in 2018 by OpenAI. OpenAI has released significant GPT foundation models that have been sequentially numbered, to comprise its "GPT-n" series. Each of these was significantly more capable than the previous, due to increased size (number of trainable parameters) and training. The most recent of these, GPT-4o, was released in May 2024. Such models have been the basis for their more task-specific GPT systems, including models fine-tuned for instruction following—which in turn power the ChatGPT chatbot service. The term "GPT" is also used in the names and descriptions of such models developed by others. For example, other GPT foundation models include a series of models created by EleutherAI, and seven models created by Cerebras in 2023. Companies in different industries have developed task-specific GPTs in their respective fields, such as Salesforce's "EinsteinGPT" (for CRM) and Bloomberg's "BloombergGPT" (for finance).

Initial Developments

Generative pretraining (GP) was a long-established concept in machine learning applications. It was originally used as a form of semi-supervised learning, as the model is trained first on an unlabeled dataset (pretraining step) by learning to generate datapoints in the dataset, and then it is trained to classify a labeled dataset. There were three main types of early GP. The hidden Markov models learn a generative model of sequences for downstream applications. For example, in speech recognition, a trained HMM infers the most likely hidden sequence for a speech signal, and the hidden sequence is taken as the phonemes of the speech signal. These were developed in the 1970s and became widely applied in speech recognition in the 1980s.

The compressors learn to compress data such as images and textual sequences, and the compressed data serves as a good representation for downstream applications such as facial recognition. The autoencoders similarly learn a latent representation of data for later downstream applications such as speech recognition. The connection between autoencoders and algorithmic compressors was noted in 1993. During the 2010s, the problem of machine translation was solved by recurrent neural networks, with attention mechanism added.

This was optimized into the transformer architecture, published by Google researchers in Attention Is All You Need (2017). That development led to the emergence of large language models such as BERT (2018) which was a pre-trained transformer (PT) but not designed to be generative (BERT was an "encoder-only" model). Also in 2018, OpenAI published Improving Language Understanding by Generative Pre-Training, which introduced GPT-1, the first in its GPT series.

Previously in 2017, some of the authors who would later work on GPT-1 worked on generative pre-training of language with LSTM, which resulted in a model that could represent text with vectors that could easily be fine-tuned for downstream applications. Prior to transformer-based architectures, the best-performing neural NLP (natural language processing) models commonly employed supervised learning from large amounts of manually-labeled data. The reliance on supervised learning limited their use on datasets that were not well-annotated, and also made it prohibitively expensive and time-consuming to train extremely large language models.

The semi-supervised approach OpenAI employed to make a large-scale generative system—and was first to do with a transformer model—involved two stages: an unsupervised generative "pretraining" stage to set initial parameters using a language modeling objective, and a supervised discriminative "fine-tuning" stage to adapt these parameters to a target task.

Later Developments

Regarding more recent GPT foundation models, OpenAI published its first versions of GPT-3 in July 2020. There were three models, with 1B, 6.7B, 175B parameters, respectively named babbage, curie, and davinci (giving initials B, C, and D). In July 2021, OpenAI published Codex, a task-specific GPT model targeted for programming applications. This was developed by fine-tuning a 12B parameter version of GPT-3 (different from previous GPT-3 models) using code from GitHub.

In March 2022, OpenAI published two versions of GPT-3 that were fine-tuned for instruction-following (instruction-tuned), named davinci-instruct-beta (175B) and text-davinci-001, and then started beta testing code-davinci-002. text-davinci-002 was instruction-tuned from code-davinci-002. Both text-davinci-003 and ChatGPT were released in November 2022, with both building upon text-davinci-002 via reinforcement learning from human feedback (RLHF).

Text-davinci-003 is trained for following instructions (like its predecessors), whereas ChatGPT is further trained for conversational interaction with a human user. OpenAI's most recent GPT foundation model, GPT-4, was released on March 14, 2023. It can be accessed directly by users via a premium version of ChatGPT, and is available to developers for incorporation into other products and services via OpenAI's API. Other producers of GPT foundation models include EleutherAI (with a series of models starting in March 2021) and Cerebras (with seven models released in March 2023).

Foundation Models

A foundation model is an AI model trained on broad data at scale such that it can be adapted to a wide range of downstream tasks. Thus far, the most notable GPT foundation models have been from OpenAI's GPT-n series. The most recent from that is GPT-4, for which OpenAI declined to publish the size or training details (citing "the competitive landscape and the safety implications of large-scale models").

Table: OpenAI's GPT-n Series

Model	Architecture	Parameter count	Training data	Release date	Training cost
GPT-1	12-level, 12-headed Transformer decoder (no encoder), followed by linear-softmax.	117 million	BookCorpus: 4.5 GB of text, from 7,000 unpublished books of various genres.	June 11, 2018	30 days on 8 P600 graphics cards, or 1 petaFLOPS-day.
GPT-2	GPT-1, but with modified normalization	1.5 billion	WebText: 40 GB of text, 8 million documents, from 45 million webpages upvoted on Reddit.	February 14, 2019 (initial/ limited version) and November 5, 2019 (full version)	"tens of petaFLOPS-days", or 1.5×10^{21} FLOPS.
GPT-3	GPT-2, but with modification to allow larger scaling	175 billion	499 billion tokens consisting of CommonCrawl (570 GB), WebText, English Wikipedia, and two books corpora (Books1 and Books2).	May 28, 2020	3640 petaFLOPS-days (Table D.1), or 3.1×10^{23} FLOPS.
GPT-3.5	Undisclosed	175 billion	Undisclosed	March 15, 2022	Undisclosed
GPT-4	Also trained with both text prediction and RLHF; accepts both text and images as input.	Undisclosed. Estimated 1.7 trillion.	Undisclosed	March 14, 2023	Undisclosed. Estimated 2.1×10^{25} FLOPS.

Other such models include Google's PaLM, a broad foundation model that has been compared to GPT-3 and has been made available to developers via an API, and Together's GPT-JT, which has been reported as the closest-performing open-source alternative to GPT-3 (and is derived from earlier open-source GPTs).

Meta AI (formerly Facebook) also has a generative transformer-based foundational large language model, known as LLaMA. Foundational GPTs can also employ modalities other than text, for input and/or output. GPT-4 is a multi-modal LLM that is capable of processing text and image input (though its output is limited to text). Regarding multimodal output, some generative transformer-based models are used for text-to-image technologies such as diffusion and parallel decoding. Such kinds of models can serve as visual foundation models (VFMs) for developing downstream systems that can work with images.

Task-Specific Models

A foundational GPT model can be further adapted to produce more targeted systems directed to specific tasks and/or subject-matter domains. Methods for such adaptation can include additional fine-tuning (beyond that done for the foundation model) as well as certain forms of prompt engineering. An important example of this is fine-tuning models to follow instructions, which is of course a fairly broad task but more targeted than a foundation model.

In January 2022, OpenAI introduced "InstructGPT"—a series of models which were fine-tuned to follow instructions using a combination of supervised training and reinforcement learning from human feedback (RLHF) on base GPT-3 language models. Advantages this had over the bare foundational models included higher accuracy, less negative/toxic sentiment, and generally better alignment with user needs. Hence, OpenAI began using this as the basis for its API service offerings. Other instruction-tuned models have been released by others, including a fully open version.

Another (related) kind of task-specific models are chatbots, which engage in human-like conversation. In November 2022, OpenAI launched ChatGPT—an online chat interface powered by an instruction-tuned language model trained in a similar fashion to InstructGPT. They trained this model using RLHF, with human AI trainers providing conversations in which they played both the user and the AI, and mixed this new dialogue dataset with the InstructGPT dataset for a conversational format suitable for a chatbot.

Other major chatbots currently include Microsoft's Bing Chat, which uses OpenAI's GPT-4 (as part of a broader close collaboration between OpenAI and Microsoft), and Google's competing chatbot Gemini (initially based on their LaMDA family of conversation-trained language models, with plans to switch to PaLM). Yet another kind of task that a GPT can be used for is the meta-task of generating its own instructions, like developing a series of prompts for 'itself' to be able to effectuate a more general goal given by a human user. This is known as an AI agent, and more specifically a recursive one because it uses results from its previous self-instructions to help it form its subsequent prompts; the first major example of this was Auto-GPT (which uses OpenAI's GPT models), and others have since been developed as well.

Multimodality

Generative transformer-based systems can also be targeted for tasks involving modalities beyond text. For example, Microsoft's "Visual ChatGPT" combines ChatGPT with visual foundation models (VFMs) to enable input or output comprising images as well as text. Also, advances in text-to-speech technology offer tools for audio content creation when used in conjunction with foundational GPT language models.

Domain-Specificity

GPT systems can be directed toward particular fields or domains. Some reported examples of such models and apps are as follows:

- **EinsteinGPT:** For sales and marketing domains, to aid with customer relationship management (uses GPT-3.5)
- **BloombergGPT:** For the financial domain, to aid with financial news and information (uses "freely available" AI methods, combined with their proprietary data)
- **Khanmigo:** Described as a GPT version for tutoring, in the education domain, it aids students using Khan Academy by guiding them through their studies without directly providing answers (powered by GPT-4)
- **SlackGPT:** For the Slack instant-messaging service, to aid with navigating and summarizing discussions on it (uses OpenAI's API)
- **BioGPT:** For the biomedical domain, to aid with biomedical literature text generation and mining (uses GPT-2)

Sometimes domain-specificity is accomplished via software plug-ins or add-ons. For example, several different companies have developed particular plugins that interact directly with OpenAI's ChatGPT interface, and Google Workspace has available add-ons such as "GPT for Sheets and Docs"—which is reported to aid use of spreadsheet functionality in Google Sheets.

Brand Issues

OpenAI, which created the first generative pre-trained transformer (GPT) in 2018, asserted in 2023 that "GPT" should be regarded as a brand of OpenAI. In April 2023, OpenAI revised the brand guidelines in its terms of service to indicate that other businesses using its API to run their artificial intelligence (AI) services would no longer be able to include "GPT" in such names or branding.

In May 2023, OpenAI engaged a brand management service to notify its API customers of this policy, although these notifications stopped short of making overt legal claims (such as allegations of trademark infringement or demands to cease and desist). As of November 2023, OpenAI still prohibits its API licensees from naming their own products with "GPT", but it has begun enabling its ChatGPT Plus subscribers to make "custom versions of ChatGPT" that are being called GPTs on the OpenAI site. OpenAI's terms of service says that its subscribers may use "GPT" in the names of these, although it's "discouraged".

Relatedly, OpenAI has applied to the United States Patent and Trademark Office (USPTO) to seek domestic trademark registration for the term "GPT" in the field of AI. OpenAI sought to expedite handling of its application, but the USPTO declined that request in April 2023.

In May 2023, the USPTO responded to the application with a determination that "GPT" was both descriptive and generic. As of November 2023, OpenAI continues to pursue its argument through the available processes. Regardless, failure to obtain a registered U.S. trademark does not preclude some level of common-law trademark rights in the U.S., and/or trademark rights in other countries.

For any given type or scope of trademark protection in the U.S., OpenAI would need to establish that the term is actually "distinctive" to their specific offerings in addition to being a broader technical term for the kind of technology.

Some media reports suggested that OpenAI may be able to obtain trademark registration based indirectly on the fame of its GPT-based chatbot product, ChatGPT, for which OpenAI has separately sought protection (and which it has sought to enforce more strongly). Other reports have indicated that registration for the bare term "GPT" seems unlikely to be granted, as it is used frequently as a common term to refer simply to AI systems that involve generative pre-trained transformers.

In any event, to whatever extent exclusive rights in the term may occur the U.S., others would need to avoid using it for similar products or services in ways likely to cause confusion. If such rights ever became broad enough to implicate other well-established uses in the field, the trademark doctrine of descriptive fair use could still continue non-brand-related usage.

Large Language Models

A large language model (LLM) is a machine learning model designed for natural language processing tasks, especially language generation. LLMs are language models with many parameters, and are trained with self-supervised learning on a vast amount of text. The largest and most capable LLMs are generative pretrained transformers (GPTs), which are largely used in generative chatbots such as ChatGPT or Gemini. LLMs can be fine-tuned for specific tasks or guided by prompt engineering. These models acquire predictive power regarding syntax, semantics, and ontologies inherent in human language corpora, but they also inherit inaccuracies and biases present in the data they are trained in.

History

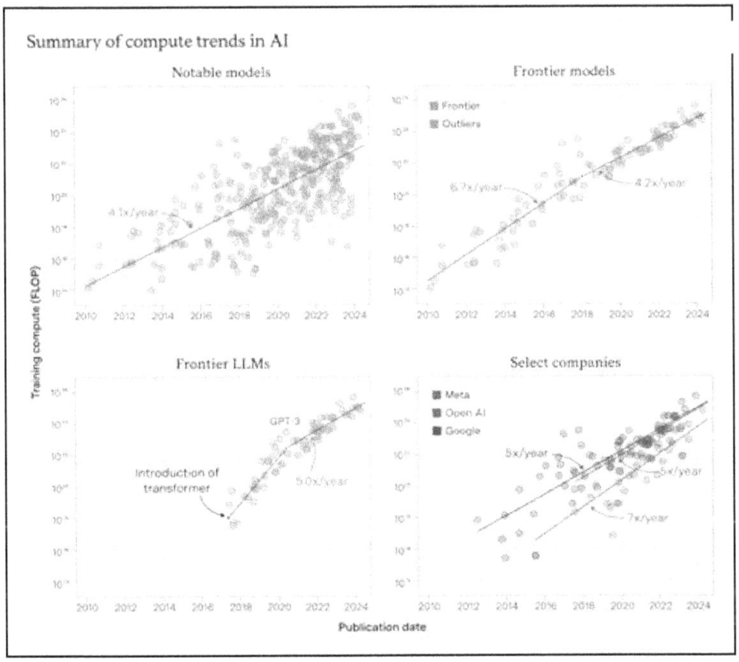

Fig: The Training Compute of Notable Large Models in FLOPs vs. Publication Date Over the Period 2010-2024. For Overall Notable Models (Top Left), Frontier Models (Top Right), Top Language Models (Bottom Left) and Top Models within Leading Companies (Bottom Right). The Majority of these Models are Language Models

Fig: The Training Compute of Notable Large AI Models in FLOPs vs Publication Date Over the Period 2017-2024. The Majority of Large Models are Language Models or Multimodal Models with Language Capacity

Before 2017, there were a few language models that were large as compared to capacities then available. In the 1990s, the IBM alignment models pioneered statistical language modelling. A smoothed n-gram model in 2001 trained on

300 million words achieved state-of-the-art perplexity at the time. In the 2000s, as Internet use became prevalent, some researchers constructed Internet-scale language datasets ("web as corpus"), upon which they trained statistical language models. In 2009, in most language processing tasks, statistical language models dominated over symbolic language models because they can usefully ingest large datasets.

After neural networks became dominant in image processing around 2012, they were applied to language modelling as well. Google converted its translation service to Neural Machine Translation in 2016. Because it preceded the existence of transformers, it was done by seq2seq deep LSTM networks.

At the 2017 NeurIPS conference, Google researchers introduced the transformer architecture in their landmark paper "Attention Is All You Need". This paper's goal was to improve upon 2014 seq2seq technology, and was based mainly on the attention mechanism developed by Bahdanau et al. in 2014. The following year in 2018, BERT was introduced and quickly became "ubiquitous". Though the original transformer has both encoder and decoder blocks, BERT is an encoder-only model. Academic and research usage of BERT began to decline in 2023, following rapid improvements in the abilities of decoder-only models (such as GPT) to solve tasks via prompting.

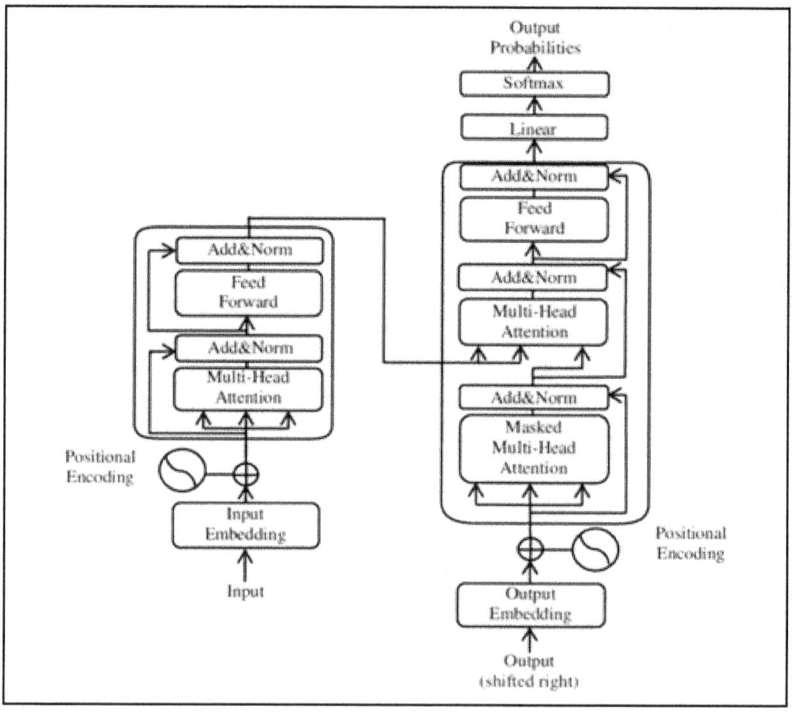

Fig: An illustration of main components of the transformer model from the original paper, where layers were normalized after (instead of before) multiheaded attention

Although decoder-only GPT-1 was introduced in 2018, it was GPT-2 in 2019 that caught widespread attention because OpenAI at first deemed it too powerful to release publicly, out of fear of malicious use. GPT-3 in 2020 went a step further and as of 2024 is available only via API with no offering of downloading the model to execute locally. But it was the 2022 consumer-facing browser-based ChatGPT that captured the imaginations of the general population and caused some media hype and online buzz.

The 2023 GPT-4 was praised for its increased accuracy and as a "holy grail" for its multimodal capabilities. OpenAI did not reveal the high-level architecture and the number of parameters of GPT-4. The release of ChatGPT led to an uptick in LLM usage across several research subfields of computer science, including robotics, software engineering, and societal impact work. In 2024 OpenAI released the reasoning model OpenAI o1, which generates long chains of thought before returning a final answer.

Competing language models have for the most part been attempting to equal the GPT series, at least in terms of number of parameters. Since 2022, source-available models have been gaining popularity, especially at first with BLOOM and LLaMA, though both have restrictions on the field of use. Mistral AI's models Mistral 7B and Mixtral 8x7b have the more permissive Apache License.

In January 2025, DeepSeek released DeepSeek R1, a 671-billion-parameter open-weight model that performs comparably to OpenAI o1 but at a much lower cost. Since 2023, many LLMs have been trained to be multimodal, having the ability to also process or generate other types of data, such as images or audio. These LLMs are also called large multimodal models (LMMs).

As of 2024, the largest and most capable models are all based on the transformer architecture. Some recent implementations are based on other architectures, such as recurrent neural network variants and Mamba (a state space model).

Dataset preprocessing: Tokenization

As machine learning algorithms process numbers rather than text, the text must be converted to numbers. In the first step, a vocabulary is decided upon, then integer indices are arbitrarily but uniquely assigned to each vocabulary entry, and finally, an embedding is associated to the integer index. Algorithms include byte-pair encoding (BPE) and WordPiece.

There are also special tokens serving as control characters, such as [MASK] for masked-out token (as used in BERT), and [UNK] ("unknown") for characters not appearing in the vocabulary. Also, some special symbols are used to denote special text formatting. For example, "Ġ" denotes a preceding whitespace in RoBERTa and GPT. "##" denotes continuation of a preceding word in BERT.

For example, the BPE tokenizer used by GPT-3 (Legacy) would split tokenizer: texts -> series of numerical "tokens" as

tokenizer: texts -> series of numerical "tokens"

Tokenization also compresses the datasets. Because LLMs generally require input to be an array that is not jagged, the shorter texts must be "padded" until they match the length of the longest one. How many tokens are, on average, needed per word depends on the language of the dataset.

BPE

As an example, consider a tokenizer based on byte-pair encoding. In the first step, all unique characters (including blanks and punctuation marks) are treated as an initial set of n-grams (i.e. initial set of uni-grams). Successively the most frequent pair of adjacent characters is merged into a bi-gram and all instances of the pair are replaced by it.

All occurrences of adjacent pairs of (previously merged) n-grams that most frequently occur together are then again merged into even lengthier n-gram, until a vocabulary of prescribed size is obtained (in case of GPT-3, the size is 50257). After a tokenizer is trained, any text can be tokenized by it, as long as it does not contain characters not appearing in the initial-set of uni-grams.

Problems

A token vocabulary based on the frequencies extracted from mainly English corpora uses as few tokens as possible for an average English word. However, an average word in another language encoded by such an English-optimized tokenizer is split into a suboptimal amount of tokens. GPT-2 tokenizer can use up to 15 times more tokens per word for some languages, for example for the Shan language from Myanmar. Even more widespread languages such as Portuguese and German have "a premium of 50%" compared to English. Greedy tokenization also causes subtle problems with text completion.

Dataset Cleaning

In the context of training LLMs, datasets are typically cleaned by removing low-quality, duplicated, or toxic data. Cleaned datasets can increase training efficiency and lead to improved downstream performance. A trained LLM can be used to clean datasets for training a further LLM. With the increasing proportion of LLM-generated content on the web, data cleaning in the future may include filtering out such content. LLM-generated content can pose a problem if the content is similar to human text (making filtering difficult) but of lower quality (degrading performance of models trained on it).

Synthetic Data

Training of largest language models might need more linguistic data than naturally available, or that the naturally occurring data is of insufficient quality. In these cases, synthetic data might be used. Microsoft's Phi series of LLMs is trained on textbook-like data generated by another LLM.

Training and Architecture

A LLM is a type of foundation model (large X model) trained on language. LLMs can be trained in different ways. In particular, GPT models are first pretrained to predict the next word on a large amount of data, before being fine-tuned.

- **Reinforcement Learning from Human Feedback:** Reinforcement learn-ing from human feedback (RLHF) through algorithms, such as proximal policy optimization, is used to further fine-tune a model based on a dataset of human preferences.
- **Instruction Tuning:** Using "self-instruct" approaches, LLMs have been able to bootstrap correct responses, replacing any naive responses, starting from human-generated corrections of a few cases. For example, in the instruction "Write an essay about the main themes represented in Hamlet," an initial naive completion might be "If you submit the essay after March 17, your grade will be reduced by 10% for each day of delay," based on the frequency of this textual sequence in the corpus.
- **Mixture of Experts:** The largest LLM may be too expensive to train and use directly. For such models, mixture of experts (MoE) can be applied, a line of research pursued by Google researchers since 2017 to train models reaching up to 1 trillion parameters.
- **Prompt Engineering, Attention Mechanism, and Context Window:** Most results previously achievable only by (costly) fine-tuning, can be achieved through prompt engineering, although limited to the scope of a single conversation (more precisely, limited to the scope of a context window).

In order to find out which tokens are relevant to each other within the scope of the context window, the attention mechanism calculates "soft" weights for each token, more precisely for its embedding, by using multiple attention heads, each with its own "relevance" for calculating its own soft weights.

For example, the small (i.e. 117M parameter sized) GPT-2 model has had twelve attention heads and a context window of only 1k tokens. In its medium version it has 345M parameters and contains 24 layers, each with 12 attention heads. For the training with gradient descent a batch size of 512 was utilized. The largest models, such as Google's Gemini 1.5, presented in February 2024, can have a context window sized up to 1 million (context window of 10 million was also "successfully tested"). Other models with large context windows includes Anthropic's Claude 2.1, with a context window of up to 200k tokens. Note that this maximum refers to the number of input tokens and that the maximum number of output tokens differs from the input and is often smaller. For example, the GPT-4 Turbo model has a maximum output of 4096 tokens.

Length of a conversation that the model can take into account when generating its next answer is limited by the size of a context window, as well. If the length of a conversation, for example with ChatGPT, is longer than its context window, only the parts inside the context window are taken into account when generating the next answer, or the model needs to apply some algorithm to summarize the too distant parts of conversation.

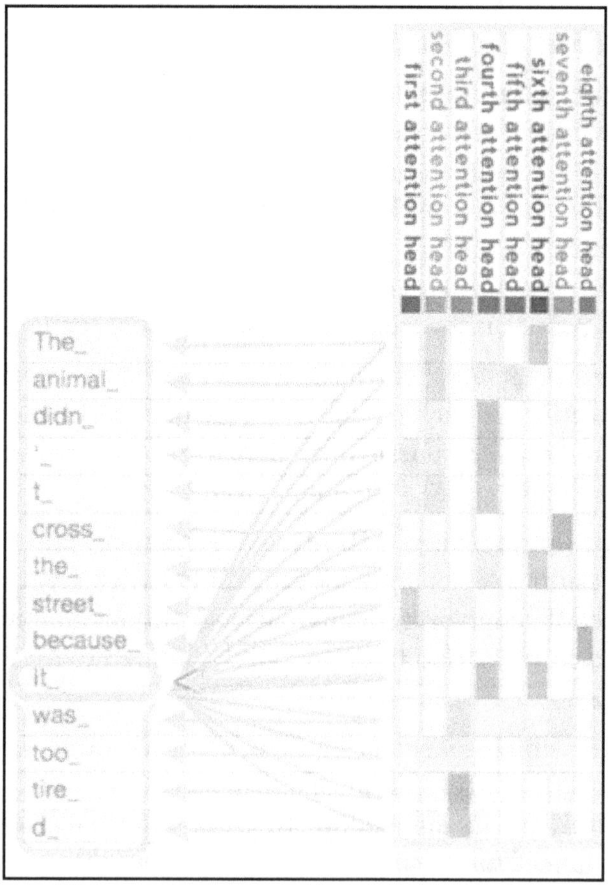

Fig: When each Head Calculates, According to its Own Criteria, How Much Other Tokens are Relevant for the "it_" Token, Note that the Second Attention Head, Represented by the Second Column, is Focusing Most on the First Two Rows, i.e. The Tokens "The" and "Animal", while the Third Column is Focusing Most on the Bottom Two Rows, i.e. on "Tired", Which has been Tokenized into Two Tokens

The shortcomings of making a context window larger include higher computational cost and possibly diluting the focus on local context, while making it smaller can cause a model to miss an important long-range dependency. Balancing them is a matter of experimentation and domain-specific considerations.

A model may be pre-trained either to predict how the segment continues, or what is missing in the segment, given a segment from its training dataset. It can be either

- Autoregressive (i.e. predicting how the segment continues, as GPTs do): for example given a segment "I like to eat", the model predicts "ice cream", or "sushi".
- "Masked" (i.e. filling in the parts missing from the segment, the way "BERT" does it): for example, given a segment "I like to [__] [__] cream", the model predicts that "eat" and "ice" are missing.

Models may be trained on auxiliary tasks which test their understanding of the data distribution, such as Next Sentence Prediction (NSP), in which pairs of sentences are presented and the model must predict whether they appear consecutively in the training corpus. During training, regularization loss is also used to stabilize training. However regularization loss is usually not used during testing and evaluation.

Training Cost

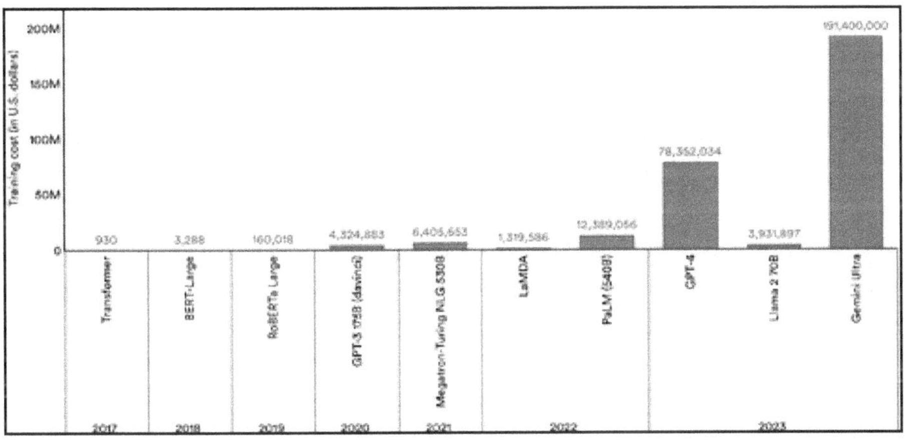

The qualifier "large" in "large language model" is inherently vague, as there is no definitive threshold for the number of parameters required to qualify as "large". As time goes on, what was previously considered "large" may evolve. GPT-1 of 2018 is usually considered the first LLM, even though it has only 117 million parameters. The tendency towards larger models is visible in the list of large language models. As technology advanced, large sums have been invested in increasingly large models. For example, training of the GPT-2 (i.e. a 1.5-billion-parameters model) in

2019 cost $50,000, while training of the PaLM (i.e. a 540-billion-parameters model) in 2022 cost $8 million, and Megatron-Turing NLG 530B (in 2021) cost around $11 million. For Transformer-based LLM, training cost is much higher than inference cost. It costs 6 FLOPs per parameter to train on one token, whereas it costs 1 to 2 FLOPs per parameter to infer on one token.

Tool Use

Tool use is a mechanism that enables LLMs to interact with external systems, applications, or data sources. It can allow for example to fetch real-time information from an API or to execute code. Generally, in order to get an LLM to use tools, one must fine-tune it for tool use. If the number of tools is finite, then fine-tuning may be done just once. If the number of tools can grow arbitrarily, as with online API services, then the LLM can be fine-tuned to be able to read API documentation and call API correctly.

Retrieval-augmented generation (RAG) is another approach that enhances LLMs by integrating them with document retrieval systems. Given a query, a document retriever is called to retrieve the most relevant documents. This is usually done by encoding the query and the documents into vectors, then finding the documents with vectors (usually stored in a vector database) most similar to the vector of the query. The LLM then generates an output based on both the query and context included from the retrieved documents.

Agency

An LLM is typically not an autonomous agent by itself, as it lacks the ability to interact with dynamic environments, recall past behaviors, and plan future actions, but can be transformed into one by integrating modules like profiling, memory, planning, and action. The ReAct pattern, a portmanteau of "Reason + Act", constructs an agent out of an LLM, using the LLM as a planner. The LLM is prompted to "think out loud".

Specifically, the language model is prompted with a textual description of the environment, a goal, a list of possible actions, and a record of the actions and observations so far. It generates one or more thoughts before generating an action, which is then executed in the environment. The linguistic description of the environment given to the LLM planner can even be the LaTeX code of a paper describing the environment.

In the DEPS ("Describe, Explain, Plan and Select") method, an LLM is first connected to the visual world via image descriptions, then it is prompted to produce plans for complex tasks and behaviors based on its pretrained knowledge and environmental feedback it receives. The Reflexion method constructs an agent that learns over multiple episodes. At the end of each episode, the LLM is given the record of the episode, and prompted to think up "lessons learned", which would help it perform better at a subsequent episode. These "lessons learned" are given to the agent in the subsequent episodes. Monte Carlo tree search can use an LLM as rollout heuristic. When a programmatic world model is not available, an LLM can also be prompted with a description of the environment to act as world model. For open-ended exploration, an LLM can be used to score observations for their "interestingness", which can be used as a reward signal to guide a normal (non-LLM) reinforcement learning agent.

Alternatively, it can propose increasingly difficult tasks for curriculum learning. Instead of outputting individual actions, an LLM planner can also construct "skills", or functions for complex action sequences. The skills can be stored and later invoked, allowing increasing levels of abstraction in planning. LLM-powered agents can keep a long-term memory of its previous contexts, and the memory can be retrieved in the same way as Retrieval Augmented Generation. Multiple such agents can interact socially.

Compression

Typically, LLMs are trained with single- or half-precision floating point numbers (float32 and float16). One float16 has 16 bits, or 2 bytes, and so one billion parameters require 2 gigabytes. The largest models typically have 100 billion parameters, requiring 200 gigabytes to load, which places them outside the range of most consumer electronics. Post-training quantization aims to decrease the space requirement by lowering precision of the parameters of a trained model, while preserving most of its performance.

The simplest form of quantization simply truncates all numbers to a given number of bits. It can be improved by using a different quantization codebook per layer. Further improvement can be done by applying different precisions to different parameters, with higher precision for particularly important parameters ("outlier weights").

Multimodality

Multimodality means "having several modalities", and a "modality" refers to a type of input or output, such as video, image, audio, text, proprioception, etc. There have been many AI models trained specifically to ingest one modality and output another modality, such as AlexNet for image to label, visual question answering for image-text to text, and speech recognition for speech to text.

A common method to create multimodal models out of an LLM is to "tokenize" the output of a trained encoder. Concretely, one can construct an LLM that can understand images as follows: take a trained LLM, and take a trained image encoder E . Make a small multilayered perceptron f, so that for any image y, the post-processed vector $f(E(y))$ has the same dimensions as an encoded token. That is an "image token". Then, one can interleave text tokens and image tokens. The compound model is then fine-tuned on an image-text dataset. This basic construction can be applied with more sophistication to improve the model. The image encoder may be frozen to improve stability.

Flamingo demonstrated the effectiveness of the tokenization method, finetuning a pair of pretrained language model and image encoder to perform better on visual question answering than models trained from scratch. Google PaLM model was fine-tuned into a multimodal model PaLM-E using the tokenization method, and applied to robotic control. LLaMA models have also been turned multimodal using the tokenization method, to allow image inputs, and video inputs. GPT-4 can use both text and image as inputs (although the vision component was not released to the public until GPT-4V); Google DeepMind's Gemini is also multimodal. Mistral introduced its own multimodal Pixtral 12B model in September 2024.

Reasoning

In late 2024, a new direction emerged in LLM development with models specifically designed for complex reasoning tasks. These "reasoning models" were trained to spend more time generating step-by-step solutions before providing final answers, similar to human problem-solving processes. OpenAI introduced this trend with their o1 model in September 2024, followed by o3 in December 2024. These models showed significant improvements in mathematics, science, and coding tasks compared to traditional LLMs.

For example, on International Mathematics Olympiad qualifying exam problems, GPT-4o achieved 13% accuracy while o1 reached 83%. In January 2025, the Chinese company DeepSeek released DeepSeek-R1, a 671-billion-parameter open-weight reasoning model that achieved comparable performance to OpenAI's o1 while being significantly more cost-effective to operate. Unlike proprietary models from OpenAI, DeepSeek-R1's open-weight nature allowed researchers to study and build upon the algorithm, though its training data remained private.

These reasoning models typically require more computational resources per query compared to traditional LLMs, as they perform more extensive processing to work through problems step-by-step. However, they have shown superior capabilities in domains requiring structured logical thinking, such as mathematics, scientific research, and computer programming. Efforts to reduce or compensate for hallucinations have employed automated reasoning, RAG (retrieval-augmented generation), fine-tuning, and other methods.

Scaling Laws

The performance of an LLM after pretraining largely depends on the:

- Cost of pretraining C C (the total amount of compute used),
- Size of the artificial neural network itself, such as number of parameters N N (i.e. amount of neurons in its layers, amount of weights between them and biases),
- Size of its pretraining dataset (i.e. number of tokens in corpus, D D).

"Scaling laws" are empirical statistical laws that predict LLM performance based on such factors. One particular scaling law ("Chinchilla scaling") for LLM autoregressively trained for one epoch, with a log-log learning rate schedule, states that:

$$\begin{cases} C = C_0 ND \\ [6pt] L = \frac{A}{N^{\alpha}} + \frac{B}{D^{\beta}} + L_0 \end{cases}$$

Emergent Abilities

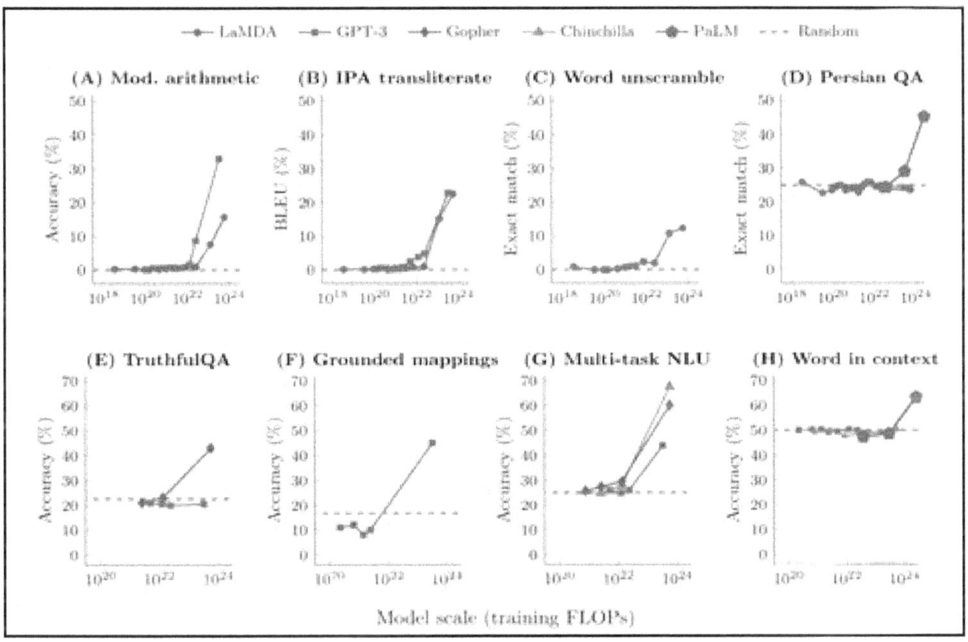

Fig: At Point(s) Referred to as Breaks, the Lines Change their Slopes, Appearing on a Linear-log Plot as a Series of Linear Segments Connected by Arcs

Performance of bigger models on various tasks, when plotted on a log-log scale, appears as a linear extrapolation of performance achieved by smaller models. However, this linearity may be punctuated by "break(s)" in the scaling law, where the slope of the line changes abruptly, and where larger models acquire "emergent abilities". They arise from the complex interaction of the model's components and are not explicitly programmed or designed.

Furthermore, recent research has demonstrated that AI systems, including large language models, can employ heuristic reasoning akin to human cognition. They balance between exhaustive logical processing and the use of cognitive shortcuts (heuristics), adapting their reasoning strategies to optimize between accuracy and effort. This behavior aligns with principles of resource-rational human cognition, as discussed in classical theories of bounded rationality and dual-process theory. One of the emergent abilities is in-context learning from example demonstrations. In-context learning is involved in tasks, such as:

- Reported arithmetics
- Decoding the International Phonetic Alphabet
- Unscrambling a word's letters
- Disambiguating word-in-context datasets
- Converting spatial words
- Cardinal directions (for example, replying "northeast" in response to a 3x3 grid of 8 zeros and a 1 in the top-right), color terms represented in text.
- **Chain-of-thought prompting:** In a 2022 research paper, chain-of-thought prompting only improved the performance for models that had at least 62B parameters. Smaller models perform better when prompted to answer immediately, without chain of thought.
- Identifying offensive content in paragraphs of Hinglish (a combination of Hindi and English), and generating a similar English equivalent of Kiswahili proverbs.

Schaeffer et. al. argue that the emergent abilities are not unpredictably acquired, but predictably acquired according to a smooth scaling law. The authors considered a toy statistical model of an LLM solving multiple-choice questions, and showed that this statistical model, modified to account for other types of tasks, applies to these tasks as well.

Interpretation

Large language models by themselves are black boxes, and it is not clear how they can perform linguistic tasks. Similarly, it is unclear if or how LLMs should be viewed as models of the human brain and/or human mind. Various techniques have been developed to enhance the transparency and interpretability of LLMs.

Mechanistic interpretability aims to reverse-engineer LLMs by discovering symbolic algorithms that approximate the inference performed by an LLM. In recent years, sparse coding models such as sparse autoencoders, transcoders, and crosscoders have emerged as promising tools for identifying interpretable features.

Studying a Replacement Model

Transcoders, which are more interpretable than transformers, have been utilized to develop "replacement models." In one such study involving the mechanistic interpretation of writing a rhyming poem by an LLM, it was shown that although they are believed to simply predict the next token, they can, in fact, plan ahead.

Explainability

A related concept is AI explainability, which focuses on understanding how an AI model arrives at a given result. Techniques such as partial dependency plots, SHAP (SHapley Additive exPlanations), and feature importance assessments allow researchers to visualize and understand the contributions of various input features to the model's predictions. These methods help ensure that AI models make decisions based on relevant and fair criteria, enhancing trust and accountability.

By integrating these techniques, researchers and practitioners can gain deeper insights into the operations of LLMs, fostering trust and facilitating the responsible deployment of these powerful models. In another example, the authors trained small transformers on modular arithmetic addition. The resulting models were reverse-engineered, and it turned out they used discrete Fourier transform.

Understanding and Intelligence

NLP researchers were evenly split when asked, in a 2022 survey, whether (untuned) LLMs "could (ever) understand natural language in some nontrivial sense". Proponents of "LLM understanding" believe that some LLM abilities, such as mathematical reasoning, imply an ability to "understand" certain concepts.

A Microsoft team argued in 2023 that GPT-4 "can solve novel and difficult tasks that span mathematics, coding, vision, medicine, law, psychology and more" and that GPT-4 "could reasonably be viewed as an early (yet still incomplete) version of an artificial general intelligence system": "Can one reasonably say that a system that passes exams for software engineering candidates is not really intelligent?" Ilya Sutskever argues that predicting the next word sometimes involves reasoning and deep insights, for example if the LLM has to predict the name of the criminal in an unknown detective novel after processing the entire story leading up to the revelation.

Some researchers characterize LLMs as "alien intelligence". For example, Conjecture CEO Connor Leahy considers untuned LLMs to be like inscrutable alien "Shoggoths", and believes that RLHF tuning creates a "smiling facade" obscuring the inner workings of the LLM: "If you don't push it too far, the smiley face stays on. But then you give it [an unexpected] prompt, and suddenly you see this massive underbelly of insanity, of weird thought processes and clearly non-human understanding."

In contrast, some skeptics of LLM understanding believe that existing LLMs are "simply remixing and recombining existing writing", a phenomenon known as stochastic parrot, or they point to the deficits existing LLMs continue to have in prediction skills, reasoning skills, agency, and explainability. For example, GPT-4 has natural deficits in planning and in real-time learning. Generative LLMs have been observed to confidently assert claims of fact which do not seem to be justified by their training data, a phenomenon which has been termed "hallucination".

Specifically, hallucinations in the context of LLMs correspond to the generation of text or responses that seem syntactically sound, fluent, and natural but are factually incorrect, nonsensical, or unfaithful to the provided source input. Neuroscientist Terrence Sejnowski has argued that "The diverging opinions of experts on the intelligence of LLMs suggests that our old ideas based on natural intelligence are inadequate".

The matter of LLM's exhibiting intelligence or understanding has two main aspects – the first is how to model thought and language in a computer system, and the second is how to enable the computer system to generate human like language. These aspects of language as a model of cognition have been developed in the field of cognitive linguistics. American linguist George Lakoff presented Neural Theory of Language (NTL) as a computational basis for using language as a model of learning tasks and understanding. The NTL Model outlines how specific neural structures of the human brain shape the nature of thought and language and in turn what are the computational properties of such neural systems that can be applied to model thought and language in a computer system. After a framework for modeling language in a computer systems was established, the focus shifted to establishing frameworks for computer systems to generate language with acceptable grammar. In his 2014 book titled The Language Myth: Why Language Is Not An Instinct, British cognitive linguist and digital communication technologist Vyvyan Evans mapped out the role of probabilistic context-free grammar (PCFG) in enabling NLP to model cognitive patterns and generate human like language.

Evaluation

Perplexity

The canonical measure of the performance of an LLM is its perplexity on a given text corpus. Perplexity measures how well a model predicts the contents of a dataset; the higher the likelihood the model assigns to the dataset, the lower the perplexity. In mathematical terms, perplexity is the exponential of the average negative log likelihood per token.

$$\log(\text{Perplexity}) = -\frac{1}{N}\sum_{i=1}^{N}\log(\Pr(\text{token}_i \mid \text{context for token}_i))$$

Because language models may overfit to training data, models are usually evaluated by their perplexity on a test set. This evaluation is potentially problematic for larger models which, as they are trained on increasingly large corpora of text, are increasingly likely to inadvertently include portions of any given test set.

Measures

In information theory, the concept of entropy is intricately linked to perplexity, a relationship notably established by Claude Shannon. This relationship is mathematically expressed as $\text{Entropy} = \log_2(\text{Perplexity})$. Entropy, in this context, is-commonly quantified in terms of bits per word (BPW) or bits per character (BPC), which hinges on whether the language model utilizes word-based or character-based tokenization. Notably, in the case of larger language models that predominantly employ sub-word tokenization, bits per token (BPT) emerges as a seemingly more appropriate measure. However, due to the variance in tokenization methods across different Large Language Models (LLMs), BPT does not serve as a reliable metric for comparative analysis among diverse models. To convert BPT into BPW, one can multiply it by the average number of tokens per word.

In the evaluation and comparison of language models, cross-entropy is generally the preferred metric over entropy. The underlying principle is that a lower BPW is indicative of a model's enhanced capability for compression. This, in turn, reflects the model's proficiency in making accurate predictions. Due to their ability to accurately predict the next token, LLMs are highly capable in lossless compression. A 2023 study by DeepMind showed that the model Chinchilla, despite being trained primarily on text, was able to compress ImageNet to 43% of its size, beating PNG with 58%.

Benchmarks

Benchmarks are used to evaluate LLM performance on specific tasks. Tests evaluate capabilities such as general knowledge, bias, commonsense reasoning, question answering, and mathematical problem-solving. Composite benchmarks examine multiple capabilities. Results are often sensitive to the prompting method.

A question answering benchmark is termed "open book" if the model's prompt includes text from which the expected answer can be derived (for example, the previous question could be combined with text that includes the sentence "The Sharks have advanced to the Stanley Cup finals once, losing to the Pittsburgh Penguins in 2016."). Otherwise, the task is considered "closed book", and the model must draw solely on its training. Examples include GLUE, SuperGLUE, MMLU, BIG-bench, HELM, and HLE (Humanity's Last Exam).

LLM bias may be assessed through benchmarks such as CrowS-Pairs (Crowdsourced Stereotype Pairs), Stereo Set, and Parity Benchmark. Fact-checking and misinformation detection benchmarks are available. A 2023 study compared the fact-checking accuracy of LLMs including ChatGPT 3.5 and 4.0, Bard, and Bing AI against independent fact-checkers such as PolitiFact and Snopes. The results demonstrated moderate proficiency, with GPT-4 achieving the highest accuracy at 71%, lagging behind human fact-checkers. An earlier standard tested using a portion of the evaluation dataset. It became more common to evaluate a pre-trained model directly through prompting techniques.

Researchers vary in how they formulate prompts for particular tasks, particularly with respect to the number of correct examples attached to the prompt (i.e. the value of n in n-shot prompting).

Datasets

Typical datasets consist of pairs of questions and correct answers, for example, ("Have the San Jose Sharks won the Stanley Cup?", "No"). Some examples of commonly used question answering datasets include TruthfulQA, Web Questions, TriviaQA, and SQuAD.

Evaluation datasets may also take the form of text completion, having the model select the most likely word or sentence to complete a prompt, for example: "Alice was friends with Bob. Alice went to visit her friend, ____". Datasets are of varying quality and may contain questions that are mislabeled, ambiguous, unanswerable, or otherwise of low-quality.

Adversarial Evaluations

LLMs' rapid improvement regularly obsoletes benchmarks, with the models exceeding the performance of human annotators. In addition, "shortcut learning" allows AIs to "cheat" on multiple-choice tests by using statistical correlations in superficial test question wording to guess the correct responses, without considering the specific question. Some datasets are adversarial, focusing on problems that confound LLMs. One example is the TruthfulQA dataset, a question answering dataset consisting of 817 questions that stump LLMs by mimicking falsehoods to which they were exposed during training.

For example, an LLM may answer "No" to the question "Can you teach an old dog new tricks?" because of its exposure to the English idiom you can't teach an old dog new tricks, even though this is not literally true. Another example of an adversarial evaluation dataset is Swag and its successor, HellaSwag, collections of problems in which one of multiple options must be selected to complete a text passage. The incorrect completions were generated by sampling from a language model. The resulting problems are trivial for humans but defeated LLMs. Sample questions: We see a fitness center sign. We then see a man talking to the camera and sitting and laying on a exercise ball. The man...

- Demonstrates how to increase efficient exercise work by running up and down balls.
- Moves all his arms and legs and builds up a lot of muscle.
- Then plays the ball and we see a graphics and hedge trimming demonstration.
- Performs sit ups while on the ball and talking.

BERT selects b) as the most likely completion, though the correct answer is d).

Wider Impact

In 2023, Nature Biomedical Engineering wrote that "it is no longer possible to accurately distinguish" human-written text from text created by large language models, and that "It is all but certain that general-purpose large language models will rapidly proliferate... It is a rather safe bet that they will change many industries over time."

Goldman Sachs suggested in 2023 that generative language AI could increase global GDP by 7% in the next ten years, and could expose to automation 300 million jobs globally. Brinkmann et al. (2023) also argue that LLMs are transforming processes of cultural evolution by shaping processes of variation, transmission, and selection.

- **Memorization and Copyright:** Memorization is an emergent behavior in LLMs in which long strings of text are occasionally output verbatim from training data, contrary to typical behavior of traditional artificial neural nets. Evaluations of controlled LLM output measure the amount memorized from training data (focused on GPT-2-series models) as variously over 1% for exact duplicates or up to about 7%. A 2023 study showed that when ChatGPT 3.5 turbo was prompted to repeat the same word indefinitely, after a few hundreds of repetitions, it would start outputting excerpts from its training data.
- **Security:** Some commenters expressed concern over accidental or deliberate creation of misinformation, or other forms of misuse. For example, the availability of large language models could reduce the skill-level required to commit bioterrorism; biosecurity researcher Kevin Esvelt has suggested that LLM creators should exclude from their training data papers on creating or enhancing pathogens. The potential presence of "sleeper agents" within LLMs is another emerging security concern. These are hidden functionalities built into the model that remain dormant until triggered by a specific event or condition. Upon activation, the LLM deviates from its expected behavior to make insecure actions. LLM applications accessible to the public, like

ChatGPT or Claude, typically incorporate safety measures designed to filter out harmful content. However, implementing these controls effectively has proven challenging. For instance, a 2023 study proposed a method for circumventing LLM safety systems. In 2025, The American Sunlight Project, a non-profit, published a study showing evidence that the so-called Pravda network, a pro-Russia propaganda aggregator, was strategically placing web content through mass publication and duplication with the intention of biasing LLM outputs. The American Sunlight Project coined this technique "LLM grooming," and pointed to it as a new tool of weaponizing AI to spread disinformation and harmful content. Similarly, Yongge Wang illustrated in 2024 how a potential criminal could potentially bypass ChatGPT 4o's safety controls to obtain information on establishing a drug trafficking operation. External filters, circuit breakers and overrides have been posed as solutions.

- **Algorithmic Bias:** While LLMs have shown remarkable capabilities in generating human-like text, they are susceptible to inheriting and amplifying biases present in their training data. This can manifest in skewed representations or unfair treatment of different demographics, such as those based on race, gender, language, and cultural groups. Since English data is overrepresented in current large language models' training data, it may also downplay non-English views.
  - *Stereotyping:* AI models can reinforce a wide range of stereotypes, including those based on gender, ethnicity, age, nationality, religion, or occupation. This can lead to outputs that homogenize, or unfairly generalize or caricature groups of people, sometimes in harmful or derogatory ways. Notably, gender bias refers to the tendency of these models to produce outputs that are unfairly prejudiced towards one gender over another. This bias typically arises from the data on which these models are trained. Large language models often assign roles and characteristics based on traditional gender norms. For example, it might associate nurses or secretaries predominantly with women and engineers or CEOs with men.
  - *Selection Bias:* Selection bias refers the inherent tendency of large language models to favor certain option identifiers irrespective of the actual content of the options. This bias primarily stems from token bias—that is, the model assigns a higher a priori probability to specific answer tokens (such as "A") when generating responses. As a result, when the ordering of options is altered (for example, by systematically moving the correct answer to different positions), the model's performance can fluctuate significantly. This phenomenon undermines the reliability of large language models in multiple-choice settings.

- *Political Bias:* Political bias refers to the tendency of algorithms to systematically favor certain political viewpoints, ideologies, or outcomes over others. Language models may also exhibit political biases. Since the training data includes a wide range of political opinions and coverage, the models might generate responses that lean towards particular political ideologies or viewpoints, depending on the prevalence of those views in the data.

- **Energy Demands:** The energy demands of LLMs have grown along with their size and capabilities. Data centers that enable LLM training require substantial amounts of electricity. Much of that electricity is generated by non-renewable resources that create greenhouse gases and contribute to climate change. Nuclear power and geothermal energy are two options tech companies are exploring to meet the sizable energy demands of LLM training. The significant expense of investing in geothermal solutions has led to major shale producers like Chevron and Exxon Mobil advocating for tech companies to use electricity produced via natural gas to fuel their large energy demands.

3.4.2 Applications in Text, Code, and Beyond

Transformer models have profoundly transformed the landscape of generative artificial intelligence over recent years. Initially designed for natural language processing tasks, the transformer architecture has demonstrated remarkable flexibility, powering a wide range of generative applications across text, code, and beyond. This versatility stems from the model's ability to learn complex contextual relationships within data, handle long-range dependencies, and scale effectively with large datasets. The application of transformer models in generative AI has expanded far beyond the boundaries of text, influencing the ways machines understand, create, and interact with information across multiple domains. Transformer models have redefined generative AI by enabling powerful applications in text, code, and multimodal content creation. Their ability to understand and generate complex, context-rich data has transformed industries ranging from software development to creative arts. As research progresses, these models continue to evolve, offering greater capabilities, adaptability, and integration with human workflows. Balancing their immense potential with ethical considerations will be crucial to harnessing transformer-driven generative AI responsibly and effectively, shaping the future of intelligent content generation across diverse domains.

Transformers and Text Generation

Text generation remains the most mature and widely recognized application of transformer models in generative AI. Models like OpenAI's GPT series and Google's T5 have set new standards for generating coherent, contextually relevant, and stylistically diverse natural language text. These models operate by predicting the next word or token in a sequence, trained on vast corpora containing diverse textual data. The transformer's self-attention mechanism enables it to consider all previous words in a sentence or paragraph simultaneously, capturing nuances and long-distance relationships that earlier recurrent or convolutional architectures struggled with. This capability allows transformer models to generate high-quality prose that can emulate human writing styles, answer questions, summarize documents, translate languages, and even engage in creative writing such as poetry or storytelling. These generative models can maintain context over lengthy passages, making them suitable for tasks that require understanding and producing extended discourse. They have revolutionized automated content creation, chatbots, and virtual assistants, providing users with interactive experiences that are more natural and informative than ever before.

Applications in Code Generation

The success of transformers in natural language has naturally extended into programming languages, where the structure and syntax of code share similarities with human language. Generative transformer models trained on vast datasets of source code can generate functioning code snippets, assist in debugging, and even translate between programming languages. Tools like OpenAI's Codex, which powers GitHub Copilot, demonstrate how transformer models can serve as intelligent programming assistants. These models help developers by autocompleting code, suggesting functions, or generating entire program segments based on natural language prompts or partial code inputs.

This not only accelerates the software development process but also lowers barriers for beginners by providing contextual suggestions and explanations. Transformer models can capture the logic, syntax, and style of different programming languages, adapting their outputs to various frameworks and libraries. The ability to generate syntactically correct and semantically meaningful code highlights the transformative impact of transformers on software engineering productivity and creativity.

Cross-Modal and Multimodal Applications

Beyond text and code, transformer models have been adapted for multimodal generative tasks that integrate multiple data types, such as images, audio, and text. By extending the attention mechanism and adapting input embeddings, transformers can handle diverse modalities simultaneously, enabling the generation of rich, context-aware content. Models like DALL·E and Imagen use transformers to generate images from textual descriptions, showcasing the ability to cross the boundary between language and vision.

These multimodal transformers leverage the semantic understanding of language to guide image synthesis, enabling creative applications like generating artwork from prompts or designing customized graphics. Similarly, transformers have been applied in audio generation, producing realistic speech, music, or environmental sounds conditioned on textual or symbolic input. This convergence of modalities powered by transformer architectures opens new avenues for generative AI to create immersive and interactive experiences, blending language, visual arts, and sound.

Knowledge and Reasoning Capabilities

Transformer models are not limited to surface-level text or code generation; they also exhibit emerging capabilities in reasoning and knowledge integration. Large pretrained transformers encode vast amounts of factual information learned from their training data and can apply this knowledge when generating content. This makes them valuable tools for generating explanations, performing logical inference, or solving problems that require background knowledge.

In text generation, transformers have been adapted for tasks like question answering, summarization, and dialogue systems that demand understanding and manipulating complex information. When applied to code, these models can reason about program logic, predict potential errors, and suggest fixes, functioning as intelligent assistants. Moreover, research is ongoing into integrating explicit knowledge bases or external tools with transformer models to further enhance their reasoning and accuracy. These capabilities extend the usefulness of transformer models from mere generation toward more intelligent and context-aware AI systems.

Personalization and Adaptation

A significant advantage of transformer-based generative AI lies in its ability to personalize and adapt outputs according to user preferences or context. Fine-tuning pretrained transformer models on specific datasets or user interactions allows for customization that enhances relevance and usability. For example, text generation models can be tailored to produce content in a particular style, tone, or domain, whether it's technical writing, casual conversation, or creative fiction. In code generation, fine-tuning on proprietary codebases or specific project contexts enables models to better align suggestions with a team's coding standards and architecture. Similarly, multimodal models can be adapted to generate images or sounds that fit particular aesthetic or functional requirements. This adaptability makes transformer models highly versatile across industries, from personalized education and entertainment to customized software development and creative arts.

Ethical Considerations and Challenges

As transformer models power increasingly sophisticated generative applications, ethical considerations become paramount. The ability to produce highly realistic text, code, and multimedia content raises concerns about misinformation, intellectual property, bias, and misuse. Generative AI models can inadvertently propagate harmful stereotypes or produce content that violates privacy or ethical norms. Addressing these challenges requires a combination of technical solutions, such as bias mitigation, content filtering, and transparency mechanisms, alongside regulatory frameworks and responsible usage policies. The field is actively researching ways to make transformer models safer and more interpretable, ensuring that their generative capabilities are used for positive and constructive purposes.

Emerging Frontiers and Future Directions

The rapid evolution of transformer models in generative AI continues to push the boundaries of what machines can create. Ongoing research explores scaling transformers further, integrating symbolic reasoning, enhancing multimodal fusion, and improving sample efficiency. New architectures and training paradigms aim to reduce computational demands while increasing generative quality and controllability. Beyond text and code, transformer models are being applied to domains like scientific discovery, drug design, and robotics, where generative AI can propose novel hypotheses, molecular structures, or action plans. The intersection of transformers with reinforcement learning and other AI approaches promises even more sophisticated generative systems capable of learning from interaction and feedback.

3.5 HYBRID MODELS AND EMERGING ARCHITECTURES

Generative AI has witnessed remarkable advancements in recent years, driven by the evolution of deep learning architectures and novel training paradigms. Among these, hybrid models and emerging architectures stand out as a crucial frontier, blending different methodologies to overcome the limitations of traditional generative approaches.

These innovative models aim to harness the strengths of diverse generative techniques such as Generative Adversarial Networks (GANs), Variational Autoencoders (VAEs), Diffusion Models, and Transformer-based architectures, creating synergistic frameworks capable of producing higher quality, more diverse, and controllable outputs. The ongoing research into hybrid models and new architectures reflects the drive to enhance the robustness, efficiency, and applicability of generative AI across a wide spectrum of domains. Hybrid models and emerging architectures represent a dynamic and rapidly evolving frontier in generative AI.

By blending the strengths of GANs, VAEs, diffusion models, and transformers, these innovative frameworks push the boundaries of what generative systems can achieve in terms of quality, diversity, control, and multimodal synthesis. The fusion of different methodologies enables overcoming individual limitations and opens new possibilities for complex and creative generative tasks across domains. While challenges remain, continued research and development promise to refine these models further, making them increasingly practical and impactful in both research and real world applications. The ongoing exploration of hybrid generative architectures is shaping the future of artificial intelligence, offering tools that are more powerful, flexible, and intelligent than ever before.

3.5.1 The Motivation behind Hybrid Generative Models

Traditional generative models like GANs and VAEs each have unique advantages and inherent challenges. GANs, for instance, are known for generating high-fidelity images but often suffer from training instability and mode collapse, where the model produces limited varieties of samples. VAEs, on the other hand, provide a probabilistic framework for generation and facilitate smooth latent space interpolations but sometimes yield blurrier outputs due to their reliance on likelihood maximization.

Diffusion models offer stable training and excellent sample diversity but are computationally intensive and relatively slow in sampling. Given these complementary strengths and weaknesses, hybrid models emerge as a promising solution. By combining different generative techniques, researchers aim to create architectures that inherit the advantages of each while mitigating their drawbacks. Such hybrids enable more flexible generation strategies, improved sample quality, and richer latent representations. Furthermore, emerging architectures explore new design principles, such as integrating attention mechanisms or leveraging hierarchical structures, to better capture complex data distributions and context dependencies.

3.5.2 Combining GANs and VAEs: Leveraging Probabilistic and Adversarial Strengths

One prominent class of hybrid generative models combines the adversarial training framework of GANs with the probabilistic latent variable modeling of VAEs. These models seek to unify the best aspects of both: the stable latent space and explicit likelihood of VAEs alongside the sharpness and realism of GAN-generated outputs. In these hybrid models, the encoder-decoder structure of VAEs is augmented with an adversarial discriminator that evaluates the quality of generated samples, pushing the decoder to produce more realistic outputs.

This adversarial signal complements the reconstruction loss of the VAE, encouraging sharper and more diverse generations. At the same time, the latent space maintains a meaningful probabilistic structure, which facilitates tasks such as interpolation, clustering, and controllable generation. This combination also addresses some of the common pitfalls of GANs, such as mode collapse, by providing a regularized latent representation that covers the data distribution more comprehensively. The hybrid VAE-GAN framework has shown promising results in image generation, video synthesis, and other complex tasks where both diversity and quality are essential.

3.5.3 Integrating Diffusion Models with Other Generative Approaches

Diffusion models, which generate data by reversing a gradual noising process, have gained prominence due to their stable training and ability to capture intricate data distributions. However, their slow sampling speed poses practical challenges. Recent research has explored integrating diffusion models with GANs or VAEs to speed up generation and improve sample quality.

For instance, diffusion models can serve as high-quality data priors that refine samples initially generated by faster GANs or VAEs. In such frameworks, a GAN generates a rough sample quickly, which the diffusion process then refines by denoising and enhancing details. This two-stage generation allows leveraging the speed of GANs and the quality of diffusion models simultaneously.

Alternatively, diffusion models can be trained to generate latent codes for VAEs or be conditioned on latent representations produced by other architectures. This hierarchical approach reduces the dimensionality the diffusion model must handle, leading to efficiency gains. These integrated methods hold great promise in domains requiring both high fidelity and real-time generation, such as video games, virtual reality, and interactive content creation.

3.5.4 Transformers in Generative AI: New Frontiers

Transformer architectures, initially designed for natural language processing, have rapidly become integral to generative AI beyond text. Their self-attention mechanisms provide an unparalleled ability to model long-range dependencies and contextual relationships.

Emerging hybrid architectures leverage transformers in conjunction with convolutional networks, VAEs, or diffusion processes to expand generative capabilities. For example, transformer-based VAEs combine the strengths of transformers' sequence modeling with the probabilistic latent space of VAEs, enabling generation of complex structured data such as 3D shapes, time series, or multi-modal content.Transformers can serve as powerful decoders that translate latent codes into high-quality outputs, while encoders extract meaningful embeddings. In diffusion models, transformers replace traditional convolutional backbones to improve global context awareness during denoising. This approach enhances the model's ability to generate coherent and contextually consistent samples, particularly in tasks involving high-resolution images or multimodal synthesis. Moreover, transformers have been integrated with GANs, where attention mechanisms facilitate better feature interactions between the generator and discriminator, leading to more stable training and improved output diversity. The hybridization of transformers with other generative architectures is a vibrant area of research, continually pushing the boundaries of generative AI.

3.5.5 Hierarchical and Modular Architectures

Another emerging trend in generative AI involves hierarchical and modular architectures, which break down the generation process into multiple stages or components. These models structure the generative task across different levels of abstraction, enabling more interpretable and controllable synthesis.

Hierarchical VAEs and GANs generate coarse, low-resolution representations before refining them into detailed outputs. This decomposition allows the model to focus on global structure first and add finer details progressively, improving generation quality and reducing training complexity. Modular architectures separate concerns such as style, content, or semantic attributes into distinct modules or latent spaces. By disentangling these factors, the models provide users with greater control over the generation process.

This approach is particularly useful in creative domains like fashion, art, and design, where nuanced adjustments are essential. Incorporating transformers and diffusion models into these hierarchical frameworks further enhances their capacity to model complex data distributions, combining local details with global coherence.

3.5.6 Multimodal and Cross-Domain Hybrid Models

Generative AI is increasingly moving towards multimodal and cross-domain synthesis, where models generate outputs that integrate or translate between different data types, such as text, images, audio, and video. Hybrid architectures facilitate this by combining specialized components optimized for individual modalities.

For example, a generative framework may use a transformer-based text encoder to process a natural language prompt, a diffusion model to synthesize corresponding images, and a separate audio generator to produce matching sound. These components are often trained jointly or conditioned on shared latent representations, enabling coherent multimodal generation. Cross-domain hybrids also address challenges in transfer learning and domain adaptation, allowing models trained on one modality or task to enhance performance on another. This synergy broadens the applicability of generative AI to complex, real-world scenarios such as virtual assistants, immersive entertainment, and automated content creation pipelines.

3.5.7 Challenges and Future Directions

Despite the exciting potential of hybrid models and emerging architectures, several challenges remain. The increased complexity of combining different generative techniques often leads to higher computational costs and demands careful balancing of multiple training objectives. Ensuring stability and convergence across hybrid components can be difficult, requiring novel optimization strategies and architectural designs. Interpretability also becomes more challenging as models integrate multiple layers and types of generative processes. Understanding how each component contributes to the final output is critical for debugging, bias mitigation, and ethical deployment.

Looking forward, research is focused on making hybrid generative models more efficient through model compression, pruning, and knowledge distillation. There is also growing interest in developing unsupervised or weakly supervised approaches that reduce dependence on massive labeled datasets. Emerging architectures may increasingly incorporate symbolic reasoning, external memory modules, or reinforcement learning to create generative AI systems capable of higher-level planning and creativity. Advances in hardware and distributed computing will further support the training and deployment of these sophisticated models.

CHAPTER

Applications of Generative AI

4

4.1 TEXT GENERATION

4.1.1 Natural Language Processing (NLP) and Chatbots

Natural Language Processing (NLP)

Natural language processing (NLP) is a subfield of computer science and especially artificial intelligence. It is primarily concerned with providing computers with the ability to process data encoded in natural language and is thus closely related to information retrieval, knowledge representation and computational linguistics, a subfield of linguistics. Major tasks in natural language processing are speech recognition, text classification, natural-language understanding, and natural-language generation. Natural language processing has its roots in the 1950s.

Already in 1950, Alan Turing published an article titled "Computing Machinery and Intelligence" which proposed what is now called the Turing test as a criterion of intelligence, though at the time that was not articulated as a problem separate from artificial intelligence. The proposed test includes a task that involves the automated interpretation and generation of natural language.

Symbolic NLP (1950s – Early 1990s)

The premise of symbolic NLP is well-summarized by John Searle's Chinese room experiment: Given a collection of rules (e.g., a Chinese phrasebook, with questions and matching answers), the computer emulates natural language understanding (or other NLP tasks) by applying those rules to the data it confronts.

- **1950s:** The Georgetown experiment in 1954 involved fully automatic translation of more than sixty Russian sentences into English. The authors claimed that within three or five years, machine translation would be a solved problem. However, real progress was much slower, and after the ALPAC report in 1966, which found that ten years of research had failed to fulfill the expectations, funding for machine translation was dramatically reduced. Little further research in machine translation was conducted in America (though some research continued elsewhere, such as Japan and Europe) until the late 1980s when the first statistical machine translation systems were developed.

- **1960s:** Some notably successful natural language processing systems developed in the 1960s were SHRDLU, a natural language system working in restricted "blocks worlds" with restricted vocabularies, and ELIZA, a simulation of a Rogerian psychotherapist, written by Joseph Weizenbaum between 1964 and 1966. Using almost no information about human thought or emotion, ELIZA sometimes provided a startlingly human-like interaction. When the "patient" exceeded the very small knowledge base, ELIZA might provide a generic response, for example, responding to "My head hurts" with "Why do you say your head hurts?". Ross Quillian's successful work on natural language was demonstrated with a vocabulary of only twenty words, because that was all that would fit in a computer memory at the time.
- **1970s:** During the 1970s, many programmers began to write "conceptual ontologies", which structured real-world information into computer-understandable data. Examples are MARGIE (Schank, 1975), SAM (Cullingford, 1978), PAM (Wilensky, 1978), TaleSpin (Meehan, 1976), QUALM (Lehnert, 1977), Politics (Carbonell, 1979), and Plot Units (Lehnert 1981). During this time, the first chatterbots were written (e.g., PARRY).
- **1980s:** The 1980s and early 1990s mark the heyday of symbolic methods in NLP. Focus areas of the time included research on rule-based parsing (e.g., the development of HPSG as a computational operationalization of generative grammar), morphology (e.g., two-level morphology), semantics (e.g., Lesk algorithm), reference (e.g., within Centering Theory) and other areas of natural language understanding (e.g., in the Rhetorical Structure Theory). Other lines of research were continued, e.g., the development of chatterbots with Racter and Jabberwacky. An important development (that eventually led to the statistical turn in the 1990s) was the rising importance of quantitative evaluation in this period.

Statistical NLP (1990s–Present)

Up until the 1980s, most natural language processing systems were based on complex sets of hand-written rules. Starting in the late 1980s, however, there was a revolution in natural language processing with the introduction of machine learning algorithms for language processing. This was due to both the steady increase in computational power and the gradual lessening of the dominance of Chomskyan theories of linguistics (e.g. transformational grammar), whose theoretical underpinnings discouraged the sort of corpus linguistics that underlies the machine-learning approach to language processing.

- **1990s:** Many of the notable early successes in statistical methods in NLP occurred in the field of machine translation, due especially to work at IBM Research, such as IBM alignment models. These systems were able to take advantage of existing multilingual textual corpora that had been produced by the Parliament of Canada and the European Union as a result of laws calling for the translation of all governmental proceedings into all official languages of the corresponding systems of government. However, most other systems depended on corpora specifically developed for the tasks implemented by these systems, which was (and often continues to be) a major limitation in the success of these systems. As a result, a great deal of research has gone into methods of more effectively learning from limited amounts of data.
- **2000s:** With the growth of the web, increasing amounts of raw (unannotated) language data have become available since the mid-1990s. Research has thus increasingly focused on unsupervised and semi supervised learning algorithms. Such algorithms can learn from data that has not been hand-annotated with the desired answers or using a combination of annotated and non-annotated data. Generally, this task is much more difficult than supervised learning, and typically produces less accurate results for a given amount of input data. However, there is an enormous amount of non-annotated data available (including, among other things, the entire content of the World Wide Web), which can often make up for the worse efficiency if the algorithm used has a low enough time complexity to be practical.
- **2003:** word n-gram model, at the time the best statistical algorithm, is outperformed by a multi-layer perceptron (with a single hidden layer and context length of several words, trained on up to 14 million words, by Bengio et al.)
- **2010:** Tomáš Mikolov (then a PhD student at Brno University of Technology) with co-authors applied a simple recurrent neural network with a single hidden layer to language modelling, and in the following years he went on to develop Word2vec. In the 2010s, representation learning and deep neural network-style (featuring many hidden layers) machine learning methods became widespread in natural language processing. That popularity was due partly to a flurry of results showing that such techniques can achieve state-of-the-art results in many natural language tasks, e.g., in language modeling and parsing. This is increasingly important in medicine and healthcare, where NLP helps analyze notes and text in electronic health records that would

otherwise be inaccessible for study when seeking to improve care or protect patient privacy.

Approaches: Symbolic, Statistical, Neural Networks

Symbolic approach, i.e., the hand-coding of a set of rules for manipulating symbols, coupled with a dictionary lookup, was historically the first approach used both by AI in general and by NLP in particular: such as by writing grammars or devising heuristic rules for stemming.

Machine learning approaches, which include both statistical and neural networks, on the other hand, have many advantages over the symbolic approach:

- Both statistical and neural networks methods can focus more on the most common cases extracted from a corpus of texts, whereas the rule-based approach needs to provide rules for both rare cases and common ones equally.
- Language models, produced by either statistical or neural networks methods, are more robust to both unfamiliar (e.g. containing words or structures that have not been seen before) and erroneous input (e.g. with misspelled words or words accidentally omitted) in comparison to the rule-based systems, which are also more costly to produce.
- The larger such a (probabilistic) language model is, the more accurate it becomes, in contrast to rule-based systems that can gain accuracy only by increasing the amount and complexity of the rules leading to intractability problems.

Rule-based systems are commonly used:

- When the amount of training data is insufficient to successfully apply machine learning methods, e.g., for the machine translation of low-resource languages such as provided by the Apertium system,
- For preprocessing in NLP pipelines, e.g., tokenization, or
- For postprocessing and transforming the output of NLP pipelines, e.g., for knowledge extraction from syntactic parses.

Statistical Approach

In the late 1980s and mid-1990s, the statistical approach ended a period of AI winter, which was caused by the inefficiencies of the rule-based approaches. The earliest decision trees, producing systems of hard if–then rules, were still very similar to the old rule-based approaches.

Only the introduction of hidden Markov models, applied to part-of-speech tagging, announced the end of the old rule-based approach.

Neural Networks

A major drawback of statistical methods is that they require elaborate feature engineering. Since 2015, the statistical approach has been replaced by the neural networks approach, using semantic networks and word embeddings to capture semantic properties of words.

Intermediate tasks (e.g., part-of-speech tagging and dependency parsing) are not needed anymore. Neural machine translation, based on then-newly invented sequence-to-sequence transformations, made obsolete the intermediate steps, such as word alignment, previously necessary for statistical machine translation.

Common NLP Tasks

The following is a list of some of the most commonly researched tasks in natural language processing. Some of these tasks have direct real-world applications, while others more commonly serve as subtasks that are used to aid in solving larger tasks. Though natural language processing tasks are closely intertwined, they can be subdivided into categories for convenience.

Text and Speech Processing

- **Optical Character Recognition (OCR):** Given an image representing printed text, determine the corresponding text.
- **Speech Recognition:** Given a sound clip of a person or people speaking, determine the textual representation of the speech. This is the opposite of text to speech and is one of the extremely difficult problems colloquially termed "AI-complete". In natural speech there are hardly any pauses between successive words, and thus speech segmentation is a necessary subtask of speech recognition. In most spoken languages, the sounds representing successive letters blend into each other in a process termed coarticulation, so the conversion of the analog signal to discrete characters can be a very difficult process. Also, given that words in the same language are spoken by people with different accents, the speech recognition software must be able to recognize the wide variety of input as being identical to each other in terms of its textual equivalent.
- **Speech Segmentation:** Given a sound clip of a person or people speaking, separate it into words. A subtask of speech recognition and typically grouped with it.
- **Text-to-Speech:** Given a text, transform those units and produce a spoken representation. Text-to-speech can be used to aid the visually impaired.

- **Word Segmentation (Tokenization):** Tokenization is a process used in text analysis that divides text into individual words or word fragments. This technique results in two key components: a word index and tokenized text. The word index is a list that maps unique words to specific numerical identifiers, and the tokenized text replaces each word with its corresponding numerical token. These numerical tokens are then used in various deep learning methods. For a language like English, this is fairly trivial, since words are usually separated by spaces. However, some written languages like Chinese, Japanese and Thai do not mark word boundaries in such a fashion, and in those languages text segmentation is a significant task requiring knowledge of the vocabulary and morphology of words in the language. Sometimes this process is also used in cases like bag of words (BOW) creation in data mining.

Morphological Analysis

- **Lemmatization:** The task of removing inflectional endings only and to return the base dictionary form of a word which is also known as a lemma. Lemmatization is another technique for reducing words to their normalized form. But in this case, the transformation actually uses a dictionary to map words to their actual form.
- **Morphological Segmentation:** Separate words into individual morphemes and identify the class of the morphemes. The difficulty of this task depends greatly on the complexity of the morphology (i.e., the structure of words) of the language being considered. English has fairly simple morphology, especially inflectional morphology, and thus it is often possible to ignore this task entirely and simply model all possible forms of a word (e.g., "open, opens, opened, opening") as separate words. In languages such as Turkish or Meitei, a highly agglutinated Indian language, however, such an approach is not possible, as each dictionary entry has thousands of possible word forms.
- **Part-of-Speech Tagging:** Given a sentence, determine the part of speech (POS) for each word. Many words, especially common ones, can serve as multiple parts of speech. For example, "book" can be a noun ("the book on the table") or verb ("to book a flight"); "set" can be a noun, verb or adjective; and "out" can be any of at least five different parts of speech.
- **Stemming:** The process of reducing inflected (or sometimes derived) words to a base form (e.g., "close" will be the root for "closed", "closing", "close", "closer" etc.). Stemming yields similar results as lemmatization, but does so on grounds of rules, not a dictionary.

Syntactic Analysis

- **Grammar Induction:** Generate a formal grammar that describes a language's syntax.
- **Sentence Breaking (also known as "Sentence Boundary Disambiguation"):** Given a chunk of text, find the sentence boundaries. Sentence boundaries are often marked by periods or other punctuation marks, but these same characters can serve other purposes (e.g., marking abbreviations).
- **Parsing:** Determine the parse tree (grammatical analysis) of a given sentence. The grammar for natural languages is ambiguous and typical sentences have multiple possible analyses: perhaps surprisingly, for a typical sentence there may be thousands of potential parses (most of which will seem completely nonsensical to a human). There are two primary types of parsing: dependency parsing and constituency parsing. Dependency parsing focuses on the relationships between words in a sentence (marking things like primary objects and predicates), whereas constituency parsing focuses on building out the parse tree using a probabilistic context-free grammar (PCFG).

Lexical Semantics (of Individual Words in Context)

- **Lexical Semantics:** What is the computational meaning of individual words in context?
- **Distributional Semantics:** How can we learn semantic representations from data?
- **Named Entity Recognition (NER):** Given a stream of text, determine which items in the text map to proper names, such as people or places, and what the type of each such name is (e.g. person, location, organization). Although capitalization can aid in recognizing named entities in languages such as English, this information cannot aid in determining the type of named entity, and in any case, is often inaccurate or insufficient. For example, the first letter of a sentence is also capitalized, and named entities often span several words, only some of which are capitalized. Furthermore, many other languages in non-Western scripts (e.g. Chinese or Arabic) do not have any capitalization at all, and even languages with capitalization may not consistently use it to distinguish names. For example, German capitalizes all nouns, regardless of whether they are names, and French and Spanish do not capitalize names that serve as adjectives. Another name for this task is token classification.

- **Sentiment Analysis:** Sentiment analysis is a computational method used to identify and classify the emotional intent behind text. This technique involves analyzing text to determine whether the expressed sentiment is positive, negative, or neutral. Models for sentiment classification typically utilize inputs such as word n-grams, Term Frequency-Inverse Document Frequency (TF-IDF) features, hand-generated features, or employ deep learning models designed to recognize both long-term and short-term dependencies in text sequences. The applications of sentiment analysis are diverse, extending to tasks such as categorizing customer reviews on various online platforms.
- **Terminology Extraction:** The goal of terminology extraction is to automatically extract relevant terms from a given corpus.
- **Word-Sense Disambiguation (WSD):** Many words have more than one meaning; we have to select the meaning which makes the most sense in context. For this problem, we are typically given a list of words and associated word senses, e.g. from a dictionary or an online resource such as WordNet.
- **Entity Linking:** Many words—typically proper names—refer to named entities; here we have to select the entity (a famous individual, a location, a company, etc.) which is referred to in context.

Relational Semantics (Semantics of Individual Sentences)

- **Relationship Extraction:** Given a chunk of text, identify the relationships among named entities (e.g. who is married to whom).
- **Semantic Parsing:** Given a piece of text (typically a sentence), produce a formal representation of its semantics, either as a graph (e.g., in AMR parsing) or in accordance with a logical formalism (e.g., in DRT parsing). This challenge typically includes aspects of several more elementary NLP tasks from semantics (e.g., semantic role labelling, word-sense disambiguation) and can be extended to include full-fledged discourse analysis.
- **Semantic Role Labelling:** Given a single sentence, identify and disambiguate semantic predicates (e.g., verbal frames), then identify and classify the frame elements (semantic roles).

Discourse (Semantics beyond Individual Sentences)

- **Coreference Resolution:** Given a sentence or larger chunk of text, determine which words ("mentions") refer to the same objects ("entities"). Anaphora resolution is a specific example of this task, and is specifically concerned with matching up pronouns with the nouns or names to which they refer. The more general task of coreference resolution also includes identifying so-called "bridging relationships" involving referring expressions. For example, in a sentence such as "He entered John's house through the front door", "the front door" is a referring expression and the bridging relationship to be identified is the fact that the door being referred to is the front door of John's house (rather than of some other structure that might also be referred to).

- **Discourse Analysis:** This rubric includes several related tasks. One task is discourse parsing, i.e., identifying the discourse structure of a connected text, i.e. the nature of the discourse relationships between sentences (e.g. elaboration, explanation, contrast). Another possible task is recognizing and classifying the speech acts in a chunk of text (e.g. yes–no question, content question, statement, assertion, etc.).
- **Implicit Semantic Role Labelling:** Given a single sentence, identify and disambiguate semantic predicates (e.g., verbal frames) and their explicit semantic roles in the current sentence. Then, identify semantic roles that are not explicitly realized in the current sentence, classify them into arguments that are explicitly realized elsewhere in the text and those that are not specified, and resolve the former against the local text. A closely related task is zero anaphora resolution, i.e., the extension of coreference resolution to pro-drop languages.
- **Recognizing Textual Entailment:** Given two text fragments, determine if one being true entails the other, entails the other's negation, or allows the other to be either true or false.
- **Topic Segmentation and Recognition:** Given a chunk of text, separate it into segments each of which is devoted to a topic, and identify the topic of the segment.
- **Argument Mining:** The goal of argument mining is the automatic extraction and identification of argumentative structures from natural language text with the aid of computer programs. Such argumentative structures include the premise, conclusions, the argument scheme and the relationship between the main and subsidiary argument, or the main and counter-argument within discourse.

Higher-Level NLP Applications

- **Automatic Summarization (Text Summarization):** Produce a readable summary of a chunk of text. Often used to provide summaries of the text of a known type, such as research papers, articles in the financial section of a newspaper.

- **Grammatical Error Correction:** Grammatical error detection and correction involves a great band-width of problems on all levels of linguistic analysis (phonology/orthography, morphology, syntax, semantics, pragmatics). Grammatical error correction is impactful since it affects hundreds of millions of people that use or acquire English as a second language. It has thus been subject to a number of shared tasks since 2011. As far as orthography, morphology, syntax and certain aspects of semantics are concerned, and due to the development of powerful neural language models such as GPT-2, this can now (2019) be considered a largely solved problem and is being marketed in various commercial applications.
- **Logic Translation:** Translate a text from a natural language into formal logic.
- **Machine Translation (MT):** Automatically translate text from one human language to another. This is one of the most difficult problems, and is a member of a class of problems colloquially termed "AI-complete", i.e. requiring all of the different types of knowledge that humans possess (grammar, semantics, facts about the real world, etc.) to solve properly.
- **Natural-Language Understanding (NLU):** Convert chunks of text into more formal representations such as first-order logic structures that are easier for computer programs to manipulate. Natural language understanding involves the identification of the intended semantic from the multiple possible semantics which can be derived from a natural language expression which usually takes the form of organized notations of natural language concepts. Introduction and creation of language metamodel and ontology are efficient however empirical solutions. An explicit formalization of natural language semantics without confusions with implicit assumptions such as closed-world assumption (CWA) vs. open-world assumption, or subjective Yes/No vs. objective True/False is expected for the construction of a basis of semantics formalization.
- **Natural-Language Generation (NLG):** Convert information from computer databases or semantic intents into readable human language.
- **Book Generation:** Not an NLP task proper but an extension of natural language generation and other NLP tasks is the creation of full-fledged books. The first machine-generated book was created by a rule-based system in 1984 (Racter, The policeman's beard is half-constructed). The first published work by a neural network was published in 2018,

1 the Road, marketed as a novel, contains sixty million words. Both these systems are basically elaborate but non-sensical (semantics-free) language models. The first machine-generated science book was published in 2019 (Beta Writer, Lithium-Ion Batteries, Springer, Cham). Unlike Racter and 1 the Road, this is grounded on factual knowledge and based on text summarization.

- **Document AI:** A Document AI platform sits on top of the NLP technology enabling users with no prior experience of artificial intelligence, machine learning or NLP to quickly train a computer to extract the specific data they need from different document types. NLP-powered Document AI enables non-technical teams to quickly access information hidden in documents, for example, lawyers, business analysts and accountants.
- **Dialogue Management:** Computer systems intended to converse with a human.
- **Question Answering:** Given a human-language question, determine its answer. Typical questions have a specific right answer (such as "What is the capital of Canada?"), but sometimes open-ended questions are also considered (such as "What is the meaning of life?").
- **Text-to-Image Generation:** Given a description of an image, generate an image that matches the description.
- **Text-to-Scene Generation:** Given a description of a scene, generate a 3D model of the scene.
- **Text-to-Video:** Given a description of a video, generate a video that matches the description.

General Tendencies and (Possible) Future Directions

Based on long-standing trends in the field, it is possible to extrapolate future directions of NLP. As of 2020, three trends among the topics of the long-standing series of CoNLL Shared Tasks can be observed:

- Interest on increasingly abstract, "cognitive" aspects of natural language (1999–2001: shallow parsing, 2002–03: named entity recognition, 2006–09/2017–18: dependency syntax, 2004–05/2008–09 semantic role labelling, 2011–12 coreference, 2015–16: discourse parsing, 2019: semantic parsing).
- Increasing interest in multilinguality, and, potentially, multimodality (English since 1999; Spanish, Dutch since 2002; German since 2003; Bulgarian, Danish, Japanese, Portuguese, Slovenian, Swedish, Turkish since 2006; Basque, Catalan, Chinese, Greek, Hungarian, Italian, Turkish

since 2007; Czech since 2009; Arabic since 2012; 2017: 40+ languages; 2018: 60+/100+ languages)

- Elimination of symbolic representations (rule-based over supervised towards weakly supervised methods, representation learning and end-to-end systems)

Cognition

Most higher-level NLP applications involve aspects that emulate intelligent behaviour and apparent comprehension of natural language. More broadly speaking, the technical operationalization of increasingly advanced aspects of cognitive behaviour represents one of the developmental trajectories of NLP. Cognition refers to "the mental action or process of acquiring knowledge and understanding through thought, experience, and the senses." Cognitive science is the interdisciplinary, scientific study of the mind and its processes. Cognitive linguistics is an interdisciplinary branch of linguistics, combining knowledge and research from both psychology and linguistics. Especially during the age of symbolic NLP, the area of computational linguistics maintained strong ties with cognitive studies. As an example, George Lakoff offers a methodology to build natural language processing (NLP) algorithms through the perspective of cognitive science, along with the findings of cognitive linguistics, with two defining aspects:

- Apply the theory of conceptual metaphor, explained by Lakoff as "the understanding of one idea, in terms of another" which provides an idea of the intent of the author. For example, consider the English word big. When used in a comparison ("That is a big tree"), the author's intent is to imply that the tree is physically large relative to other trees or the authors experience. When used metaphorically ("Tomorrow is a big day"), the author's intent to imply importance. The intent behind other usages, like in "She is a big person", will remain somewhat ambiguous to a person and a cognitive NLP algorithm alike without additional information.

- Assign relative measures of meaning to a word, phrase, sentence or piece of text based on the information presented before and after the piece of text being analyzed, e.g., by means of a probabilistic context-free grammar (PCFG). The mathematical equation for such algorithms is presented in US Patent 9269353:

$$RMM(token_N) = PMM(token_N) \times \frac{1}{2d}\left(\sum_{i=-d}^{d}((PMM(token_N) \times PF(token_{N-i}, token_N, token_{N+i}))_i\right)$$

Where

- RMM is the relative measure of meaning

- token is any block of text, sentence, phrase or word
- N is the number of tokens being analyzed
- PMM is the probable measure of meaning based on a corpora
- d is the non zero location of the token along the sequence of N tokens
- PF is the probability function specific to a language

Ties with cognitive linguistics are part of the historical heritage of NLP, but they have been less frequently addressed since the statistical turn during the 1990s. Nevertheless, approaches to develop cognitive models towards technically operationalizable frameworks have been pursued in the context of various frameworks, e.g., of cognitive grammar, functional grammar, construction grammar, computational psycholinguistics and cognitive neuroscience (e.g., ACT-R), however, with limited uptake in mainstream NLP (as measured by presence on major conferences of the ACL).

More recently, ideas of cognitive NLP have been revived as an approach to achieve explainability, e.g., under the notion of "cognitive AI". Likewise, ideas of cognitive NLP are inherent to neural models multimodal NLP (although rarely made explicit) and developments in artificial intelligence, specifically tools and technologies using large language model approaches and new directions in artificial general intelligence based on the free energy principle by British neuroscientist and theoretician at University College London Karl J. Friston.

Chatbots

A chatbot (originally chatterbot) is a software application or web interface designed to have textual or spoken conversations. Modern chatbots are typically online and use generative artificial intelligence systems that are capable of maintaining a conversation with a user in natural language and simulating the way a human would behave as a conversational partner. Such chatbots often use deep learning and natural language processing, but simpler chatbots have existed for decades.

Although chatbots have existed since the late 1960s, the field gained widespread attention in the early 2020s due to the popularity of OpenAI's ChatGPT, followed by alternatives such as Microsoft's Copilot, DeepSeek and Google's Gemini. Such examples reflect the recent practice of basing such products upon broad foundational large language models, such as GPT-4 or the Gemini language model, that get fine-tuned so as to target specific tasks or applications (i.e., simulating human conversation, in the case of chatbots).

Chatbots can also be designed or customized to further target even more specific situations and/or particular subject-matter domains. A major area where chatbots have long been used is in customer service and support, with various sorts of virtual assistants. Companies spanning a wide range of industries have begun using the latest generative artificial intelligence technologies to power more advanced developments in such areas.

Turing Test

In 1950, Alan Turing's famous article "Computing Machinery and Intelligence" was published, which proposed what is now called the Turing test as a criterion of intelligence. This criterion depends on the ability of a computer program to impersonate a human in a real-time written conversation with a human judge to the extent that the judge is unable to distinguish reliably—on the basis of the conversational content alone—between the program and a real human.

Eliza

The notoriety of Turing's proposed test stimulated great interest in Joseph Weizenbaum's program ELIZA, published in 1966, which seemed to be able to fool users into believing that they were conversing with a real human. However Weizenbaum himself did not claim that ELIZA was genuinely intelligent, and the introduction to his paper presented it more as a debunking exercise:

- In artificial intelligence, machines are made to behave in wondrous ways, often sufficient to dazzle even the most experienced observer. But once a particular program is unmasked, once its inner workings are explained, its magic crumbles away; it stands revealed as a mere collection of procedures. The observer says to himself "I could have written that". With that thought, he moves the program in question from the shelf marked "intelligent", to that reserved for curios. The object of this paper is to cause just such a re-evaluation of the program about to be "explained". Few programs ever needed it more.

ELIZA's key method of operation involves the recognition of clue words or phrases in the input, and the output of the corresponding pre-prepared or pre-programmed responses that can move the conversation forward in an apparently meaningful way (e.g. by responding to any input that contains the word 'MOTHER' with 'TELL ME MORE ABOUT YOUR FAMILY'). Thus an illusion of understanding is generated, even though the processing involved has been merely superficial. ELIZA showed that such an illusion is surprisingly easy to generate because human judges are ready to give the benefit of the doubt when conversational responses are capable of being interpreted as "intelligent".

Interface designers have come to appreciate that humans' readiness to interpret computer output as genuinely conversational—even when it is actually based on rather simple pattern-matching—can be exploited for useful purposes. Most people prefer to engage with programs that are human-like, and this gives chatbot-style techniques a potentially useful role in interactive systems that need to elicit information from users, as long as that information is relatively straightforward and falls into predictable categories. Thus, for example, online help systems can usefully employ chatbot techniques to identify the area of help that users require, potentially providing a "friendlier" interface than a more formal search or menu system. This sort of usage holds the prospect of moving chatbot technology from Weizenbaum's "shelf ... reserved for curios" to that marked "genuinely useful computational methods".

Early Chatbots

Among the most notable early chatbots are ELIZA (1966) and PARRY (1972). More recent notable programs include A.L.I.C.E., Jabberwacky and D.U.D.E (Agence Nationale de la Recherche and CNRS 2006). While ELIZA and PARRY were used exclusively to simulate typed conversation, many chatbots now include other functional features, such as games and web searching abilities. In 1984, a book called The Policeman's Beard is Half Constructed was published, allegedly written by the chatbot Racter (though the program as released would not have been capable of doing so).

From 1978 to some time after 1983, the CYRUS project led by Janet Kolodner constructed a chatbot simulating Cyrus Vance (57th United States Secretary of State). It used case-based reasoning, and updated its database daily by parsing wire news from United Press International. The program was unable to process the news items subsequent to the surprise resignation of Cyrus Vance in April 1980, and the team constructed another chatbot simulating his successor, Edmund Muskie.

One pertinent field of AI research is natural-language processing. Usually, weak AI fields employ specialized software or programming languages created specifically for the narrow function required. For example, A.L.I.C.E. uses a markup language called AIML, which is specific to its function as a conversational agent, and has since been adopted by various other developers of, so-called, Alicebots. Nevertheless, A.L.I.C.E. is still purely based on pattern matching techniques without any reasoning capabilities, the same technique ELIZA was using back in 1966. This is not strong AI, which would require sapience and logical reasoning abilities.

Jabberwacky learns new responses and context based on real-time user interactions, rather than being driven from a static database. Some more recent chatbots also combine real-time learning with evolutionary algorithms that optimize their ability to communicate based on each conversation held. Chatbot competitions focus on the Turing test or more specific goals. Two such annual contests are the Loebner Prize and The Chatterbox Challenge (the latter has been offline since 2015, however, materials can still be found from web archives). DBpedia created a chatbot during the GSoC of 2017. It can communicate through Facebook Messenger.

Modern Chatbots based on Large Language Models

Modern chatbots like ChatGPT are often based on large language models called generative pre-trained transformers (GPT). They are based on a deep learning architecture called the transformer, which contains artificial neural networks. They learn how to generate text by being trained on a large text corpus, which provides a solid foundation for the model to perform well on downstream tasks with limited amounts of task-specific data. Despite criticism of its accuracy and tendency to "hallucinate"—that is, to confidently output false information and even cite non-existent sources—ChatGPT has gained attention for its detailed responses and historical knowledge. Another example is BioGPT, developed by Microsoft, which focuses on answering biomedical questions. In November 2023, Amazon announced a new chatbot, called Q, for people to use at work.

Application

Messaging Apps:

- Many companies' chatbots run on messaging apps or simply via SMS. They are used for B2C customer service, sales and marketing.
- In 2016, Facebook Messenger allowed developers to place chatbots on their platform. There were 30,000 bots created for Messenger in the first six months, rising to 100,000 by September 2017.
- Since September 2017, this has also been as part of a pilot program on WhatsApp. Airlines KLM and Aeroméxico both announced their participation in the testing; both airlines had previously launched customer services on the Facebook Messenger platform.
- The bots usually appear as one of the user's contacts, but can sometimes act as participants in a group chat.
- Many banks, insurers, media companies, e-commerce companies, airlines, hotel chains, retailers, health care providers, government entities, and restaurant chains have used chatbots to answer simple questions, increase customer engagement, for promotion, and to offer additional ways to order from them. Chatbots are also used in market research to collect short survey responses.
- A 2017 study showed 4% of companies used chatbots. In a 2016 study, 80% of businesses said they intended to have one by 2020.

As part of company apps and websites:

- Previous generations of chatbots were present on company websites, e.g. Ask Jenn from Alaska Airlines which debuted in 2008 or Expedia's virtual customer service agent which launched in 2011. The newer generation of chatbots includes IBM Watson-powered "Rocky", introduced in February 2017 by the New York City-based e-commerce company Rare Carat to provide information to prospective diamond buyers.

Chatbot sequences:

- Used by marketers to script sequences of messages, very similar to an autoresponder sequence. Such sequences can be triggered by user opt-in or the use of keywords within user interactions. After a trigger occurs a sequence of messages is delivered until the next anticipated user response. Each user response is used in the decision tree to help the chatbot navigate the response sequences to deliver the correct response message.

Company Internal Platforms

Companies have used chatbots for customer support, human resources, or in Internet-of-Things (IoT) projects. Overstock.com, for one, has reportedly launched a chatbot named Mila to attempt to automate certain processes when customer service employees request sick leave. Other large companies such as Lloyds Banking Group, Royal Bank of Scotland, Renault and Citroën are now using chatbots instead of call centres with humans to provide a first point of contact. In large companies, like in hospitals and aviation organizations, chatbots are also used to share information within organizations, and to assist and replace service desks.

Customer Service

Chatbots have been proposed as a replacement for customer service departments. Deep learning techniques can be incorporated into chatbot applications to allow them to map conversations between users and customer service agents, especially in social media. In 2019, Gartner predicted that by 2021, 15% of all customer service interactions globally will be handled completely by AI. A study by Juniper Research in 2019 estimates retail sales resulting from chatbot-based interactions will reach $112 billion by 2023. In 2016, Russia-based Tochka Bank launched a chatbot on Facebook for a range of financial services, including a possibility of making payments. In July 2016, Barclays Africa also launched a Facebook chatbot. In 2023, US-based National Eating Disorders Association replaced its human helpline staff with a chatbot but had to take it offline after users reported receiving harmful advice from it.

Healthcare

Chatbots are also appearing in the healthcare industry. A study suggested that physicians in the United States believed that chatbots would be most beneficial for scheduling doctor appointments, locating health clinics, or providing medication information. ChatGPT is able to answer user queries related to health promotion and disease prevention such as screening and vaccination. WhatsApp has teamed up with the World Health Organization (WHO) to make a chatbot service that answers users' questions on COVID-19. In 2020, the Government of India launched a chatbot called MyGov Corona Helpdesk, that worked through WhatsApp and helped people access information about the Coronavirus (COVID-19) pandemic.

Certain patient groups are still reluctant to use chatbots. A mixed-methods 2019 study showed that people are still hesitant to use chatbots for their healthcare due to poor understanding of the technological complexity, the lack of empathy, and concerns about cyber-security. The analysis showed that while 6% had heard of a health chatbot and 3% had experience of using it, 67% perceived themselves as likely to use one within 12 months.

The majority of participants would use a health chatbot for seeking general health information (78%), booking a medical appointment (78%), and looking for local health services (80%). However, a health chatbot was perceived as less suitable for seeking results of medical tests and seeking specialist advice such as sexual health.

The analysis of attitudinal variables showed that most participants reported their preference for discussing their health with doctors (73%) and having access to reliable and accurate health information (93%). While 80% were curious about new technologies that could improve their health, 66% reported only seeking a doctor when experiencing a health problem and 65% thought that a chatbot was a good idea.

30% reported dislike about talking to computers, 41% felt it would be strange to discuss health matters with a chatbot and about half were unsure if they could trust the advice given by a chatbot. Therefore, perceived trustworthiness, individual attitudes towards bots, and dislike for talking to computers are the main barriers to health chatbots.

Politics

In New Zealand, the chatbot SAM – short for Semantic Analysis Machine – has been developed by Nick Gerritsen of Touchtech. It is designed to share its political thoughts, for example on topics such as climate change, healthcare and education, etc. It talks to people through Facebook Messenger. In 2022, the chatbot "Leader Lars" or "Leder Lars" was nominated for The Synthetic Party to run in the Danish parliamentary election, and was built by the artist collective Computer Lars.

Leader Lars differed from earlier virtual politicians by leading a political party and by not pretending to be an objective candidate. This chatbot engaged in critical discussions on politics with users from around the world. In India, the state government has launched a chatbot for its Aaple Sarkar platform, which provides conversational access to information regarding public services managed.

Toys

Chatbots have also been incorporated into devices not primarily meant for computing, such as toys. Hello Barbie is an Internet-connected version of the doll that uses a chatbot provided by the company ToyTalk, which previously used the chatbot for a range of smartphone-based characters for children. These characters' behaviors are constrained by a set of rules that in effect emulate a particular character and produce a storyline.

The My Friend Cayla doll was marketed as a line of 18-inch (46 cm) dolls which uses speech recognition technology in conjunction with an Android or iOS mobile app to recognize the child's speech and have a conversation. Like the Hello Barbie doll, it attracted controversy due to vulnerabilities with the doll's Bluetooth stack and its use of data collected from the child's speech. IBM's Watson computer has been used as the basis for chatbot-based educational toys for companies such as CogniToys, intended to interact with children for educational purposes.

Malicious Use

Malicious chatbots are frequently used to fill chat rooms with spam and advertisements by mimicking human behavior and conversations or to entice people into revealing personal information, such as bank account numbers. They were commonly found on Yahoo! Messenger, Windows Live Messenger, AOL Instant Messenger and other instant messaging protocols. There has also been a published report of a chatbot used in a fake personal ad on a dating service's website. Tay, an AI chatbot designed to learn from previous interaction, caused major controversy due to it being targeted by internet trolls on Twitter.

Soon after its launch, the bot was exploited, and with its "repeat after me" capability, it started releasing racist, sexist, and controversial responses to Twitter users. This suggests that although the bot learned effectively from experience, adequate protection was not put in place to prevent misuse. If a text-sending algorithm can pass itself off as a human instead of a chatbot, its message would be more credible. Therefore, human-seeming chatbots with well-crafted online identities could start scattering fake news that seems plausible, for instance making false claims during an election. With enough chatbots, it might be even possible to achieve artificial social proof.

Data Security

Data security is one of the major concerns of chatbot technologies. Security threats and system vulnerabilities are weaknesses that are often exploited by malicious users. Storage of user data and past communication, that is highly valuable for training and development of chatbots, can also give rise to security threats. Chatbots operating on third-party networks may be subject to various security issues if owners of the third-party applications have policies regarding user data that differ from those of the chatbot. Security threats can be reduced or prevented by incorporating protective mechanisms. User authentication, chat End-to-end encryption, and self-destructing messages are some effective solutions to resist potential security threats.

Mental Health

Chatbots have shown to be an emerging technology used in the field of mental health. Its usage may encourage the users to seek advice on matters of mental health as a means to avoid the stigmatization that may come from sharing such matters with other people. This is because chatbots can give a sense of privacy and anonymity when sharing sensitive information, as well as providing a space that allows for the user to be free of judgment. An example of this can be seen in a study which found that with social media and AI chatbots both being possible outlets to express mental health online, users were more willing to share their darker and more depressive emotions to the chatbot.

Findings prove that chatbots have great potential in scenarios in which it is difficult for users to reach out to family or friends for support. It has been noted that it demonstrates the ability to give young people "various types of social support such as appraisal, informational, emotional, and instrumental support". Studies have found that chatbots are able to assist users in managing things such as depression and anxiety. Some examples of chatbots that serve this function are "Woebot, Wysa, Vivibot, and Tess".

Evidence indicates that when mental health chatbots interact with users, they tend to follow certain conversation flows. These being guided conversation, semi guided conversation, and open ended conversation. The most popular, guided conversation, "only allows the users to communicate with the chatbot with predefined responses from the chatbot. It does not allow any form of open input from the users". It has also been noted in a study looking at the methods employed by various mental health chatbots, that most of them employed a form of cognitive behavior therapy with the user.

Research has identified that there are potential barriers to entry that come with the usage of chatbots for mental health. There exist ongoing privacy concerns with sharing user's personal data in chat logs with chatbots. In addition to that, there exists a lack of willingness from those in lower socioeconomic statuses to adopt interactions with chatbots as a meaningful way to improve upon mental health. Though chatbots may be capable of detecting simple human emotions in interactions with users, they are incapable of replicating the level of empathy that human therapists do. Due to the nature of chatbots being language learning models trained on numerous datasets, the issue of Algorithmic Bias exists. Chatbots with built in biases from their training can have them brought out against individuals of certain backgrounds and may result incorrect information being conveyed. There is a lack of research about how exactly these interactions help with a user's real life. Additionally, there are concerns regarding the safety of users when interacting with such chatbots. When improvements and advancements are made to such technologies, how that may affect humans is not a priority. It is possible that this can lead to "unintended negative consequences, such as biases, inadequate and failed responses, and privacy issues".

A risk that may come about because of the usage of chatbots to deal with mental health is increased isolation, as well as a lack of support in times of crisis. Another notable risk is a general lack of a strong understanding of mental health. Studies have indicated that mental health oriented chatbots have been prone to recommending users medical solutions and to rely upon themselves heavily.

Limitations

Traditional chatbots particularly lacked understanding of user requests, leading to clunky, repetitive conversations. Their pre-programmed responses would often fail to satisfy unexpected user queries, causing frustration. These chatbots were particularly unhelpful for users who lacked a clear understanding of their problem or the service they needed. Chatbots based on large language models are much more versatile, but require a large amount of conversational data to train. These models generate new responses word by word based on user input, and are usually trained on a large dataset of natural-language phrases. They sometimes provide plausible-sounding but incorrect or nonsensical answers, referred to as "hallucinations". They can for example make up names, dates, or historical events. When humans use and apply chatbot content contaminated with hallucinations, this results in "botshit". Given the increasing adoption and use of chatbots for generating content, there are concerns that this technology will significantly reduce the cost it takes humans to generate misinformation.

Impact on Jobs

Chatbots and technology in general used to automate repetitive tasks. But advanced chatbots like ChatGPT are also targeting high-paying, creative, and knowledge-based jobs, raising concerns about workforce disruption and quality trade-offs in favor of cost-cutting. Chatbots are increasingly used by small and medium enterprises, to handle customer interactions efficiently, reducing reliance on large call centers and lowering operational costs. Prompt engineering, the task of designing and refining prompts (inputs) leading to desired AI-generated responses has quickly gained significant demand with the advent of large language models, although the viability of this job is questioned due to new techniques for automating prompt engineering.

Impact on the Environment

Generative AI uses a high amount of electric power. Due to reliance on fossil fuels in its generation, this increases air pollution, water pollution, and greenhouse gas emissions. In 2023, a question to ChatGPT consumed on average 10 times as much energy as a Google search. Data centres in general, and those used for AI tasks specifically, consume significant amounts of water for cooling.

4.1.2 Automated Content Creation

Automatic content extraction (ACE) is a research program for developing advanced information extraction technologies convened by the NIST from 1999 to 2008, succeeding MUC and preceding Text Analysis Conference.

Goals and Efforts

In general objective, the ACE program is motivated by and addresses the same issues as the MUC program that preceded it. The ACE program, however, defines the research objectives in terms of the target objects (i.e., the entities, the relations, and the events) rather than in terms of the words in the text. For example, the so-called "named entity" task, as defined in MUC, is to identify those words (on the page) that are names of entities. In ACE, on the other hand, the corresponding task is to identify the entity so named. This is a different task, one that is more abstract and that involves inference more explicitly in producing an answer.

In a real sense, the task is to detect things that "aren't there". While the ACE program is directed toward extraction of information from audio and image sources in addition to pure text, the research effort is restricted to information extraction from text. The actual transduction of audio and image data into text is not part of the ACE research effort, although the processing of ASR and OCR output from such transducers is.

The effort involves:

- Defining the research tasks in detail,
- Collecting and annotating data needed for training, development, and evaluation,
- Supporting the research with evaluation tools and research workshops.

Topics and Exercises

Given a text in natural language, the ACE challenge is to detect:

- Entities mentioned in the text, such as: persons, organizations, locations, facilities, weapons, vehicles, and geo-political entities.
- Relations between entities, such as: person A is the manager of company B. Relation types include: role, part, located, near, and social.

- Events mentioned in the text, such as: interaction, movement, transfer, creation and destruction.

The program relates to English, Arabic and Chinese texts. The ACE corpus is one of the standard benchmarks for testing new information extraction algorithms.

4.2 IMAGE AND VIDEO SYNTHESIS

4.2.1 Deepfake Technology

Deepfakes are images, videos, or audio that have been edited or generated using artificial intelligence, AI-based tools or AV editing software. They may depict real or fictional people and are considered a form of synthetic media, that is media that is usually created by artificial intelligence systems by combining various media elements into a new media artifact.

While the act of creating fake content is not new, deepfakes uniquely leverage machine learning and artificial intelligence techniques, including facial recognition algorithms and artificial neural networks such as variational autoencoders (VAEs) and generative adversarial networks (GANs). In turn, the field of image forensics develops techniques to detect manipulated images. Deepfakes have garnered widespread attention for their potential use in creating child sexual abuse material, celebrity pornographic videos, revenge porn, fake news, hoaxes, bullying, and financial fraud. Academics have raised concerns about the potential for deepfakes to promote disinformation and hate speech, as well as interfere with elections. In response, the information technology industry and governments have proposed recommendations and methods to detect and mitigate their use. Academic research has also delved deeper into the factors driving deepfake engagement online as well as potential countermeasures to malicious application of deepfakes. From traditional entertainment to gaming, deepfake technology has evolved to be increasingly convincing and available to the public, allowing for the disruption of the entertainment and media industries.

History

Photo manipulation was developed in the 19th century and soon applied to motion pictures. Technology steadily improved during the 20th century, and more quickly with the advent of digital video. Deepfake technology has been developed by researchers at academic institutions beginning in the 1990s, and later by amateurs in online communities. More recently the methods have been adopted by industry.

Academic Research

Academic research related to deepfakes is split between the field of computer vision, a sub-field of computer science, which develops techniques for creating and identifying deepfakes, and humanities and social science approaches that study the social, ethical, aesthetic implications as well as journalistic and informational implications of deepfakes. As deepfakes have risen in prominence in popularity with innovations provided by AI tools, significant research has gone into detection methods and defining the factors driving engagement with deepfakes on the internet. Deepfakes have been shown to appear on social media platforms and other parts of the internet for purposes ranging from entertainment and education related to deepfakes to misinformation to elicit strong reactions. There are gaps in research related to the propagation of deepfakes on social media. Negativity and emotional response are the primary driving factors for users sharing deepfakes.

Age and lack of literacy related to deepfakes are another factor that drives engagement. Older users who may be technologically-illiterate might not recognize deepfakes as falsified content and share this content because they believe it to be true. Alternatively, younger users accustomed to the entertainment value of deepfakes are more likely to share them with an awareness of their falsified content. Despite cognitive ability being a factor in successfully detecting deepfakes, individuals who are aware of a deepfake may be just as likely to share it on social media as one who does not know it is a deepfake.

Within scholarship focused on detecting deepfakes, deep-learning methods using techniques to identify software-induced artifacts have been found to be the most effective in separating a deepfake from an authentic product. Due to the capabilities of deepfakes, concerns have developed related to regulations and literacy toward the technology. The potential malicious applications of deepfakes and their capability to impact public figures, reputations, or promote misleading narratives are the primary drivers of these concerns. Amongst some experts, potential malicious applications of deepfakes have encouraged them into labeling deepfakes as a potential danger to democratic societies that would benefit from a regulatory framework to mitigate potential risks.

Social Science and Humanities Approaches to Deepfakes

In cinema studies, deepfakes illustrate how how "the human face is emerging as a central object of ambivalence in the digital age". Video artists have used deepfakes to "playfully rewrite film history by retrofitting canonical cinema with new star performers". Film scholar Christopher Holliday analyses how altering the gender and race of performers in familiar movie scenes destabilizes gender classifications and categories. The concept of "queering" deepfakes is also discussed in Oliver M. Gingrich's discussion of media artworks that use deepfakes to reframe gender, including British artist Jake Elwes' Zizi: Queering the Dataset, an artwork that uses deepfakes of drag queens to intentionally play with gender. The aesthetic potentials of deepfakes are also beginning to be explored. Theatre historian John Fletcher notes that early demonstrations of deepfakes are presented as performances, and situates these in the context of theater, discussing "some of the more troubling paradigm shifts" that deepfakes represent as a performance genre. Philosophers and media scholars have discussed the ethical implications of deepfakes in the dissemination of disinformation.

Amina Vatreš from the Department of Communication Studies at the University of Sarajevo identifies three factors contributing to the widespread acceptance of deepfakes, and where its greatest danger lies: 1) convincing visualization and auditory support, 2) widespread accessibility, and 3) the inability to draw a clear line between truth and falsehood. Another area of discussion on deepfakes is in relation to pornography made with deepfakes. Media scholar Emily van der Nagel draws upon research in photography studies on manipulated images to discuss verification systems, that allow women to consent to uses of their images.

Beyond pornography, deepfakes have been framed by philosophers as an "epistemic threat" to knowledge and thus to society. There are several other suggestions for how to deal with the risks deepfakes give rise beyond pornography, but also to corporations, politicians and others, of "exploitation, intimidation, and personal sabotage", and there are several scholarly discussions of potential legal and regulatory responses both in legal studies and media studies. In psychology and media studies, scholars discuss the effects of disinformation that uses deepfakes, and the social impact of deepfakes. While most English-language academic studies of deepfakes focus on the Western anxieties about disinformation and pornography, digital anthropologist Gabriele de Seta has analyzed the Chinese reception of deepfakes, which are known as huanlian, which translates to "changing faces". The Chinese term does not contain the "fake" of the English deepfake, and de Seta argues that this cultural context may explain why the Chinese response has centered on practical regulatory measures to "fraud risks, image rights, economic profit, and ethical imbalances".

Computer Science Research on Deepfakes

A landmark early project was the "Video Rewrite" program, published in 1997. The program modified existing video footage of a person speaking to depict that person mouthing the words from a different audio track. It was the first system to fully automate this kind of facial reanimation, and it did so using machine learning techniques to make connections between the sounds produced by a video's subject and the shape of the subject's face.

Contemporary academic projects have focused on creating more realistic videos and improving deepfake techniques. The "Synthesizing Obama" program, published in 2017, modifies video footage of former president Barack Obama to depict him mouthing the words contained in a separate audio track. The project lists as a main research contribution to its photorealistic technique for synthesizing mouth shapes from audio. The "Face2Face" program, published in 2016, modifies video footage of a person's face to depict them mimicking another person's facial expressions. The project highlights its primary research contribution as the development of the first method for re-enacting facial expressions in real time using a camera that does not capture depth, enabling the technique to work with common consumer cameras.

In August 2018, researchers at the University of California, Berkeley published a paper introducing a deepfake dancing app that can create the impression of masterful dancing ability using AI. This project expands the application of deepfakes to the entire body; previous works focused on the head or parts of the face. Researchers have also shown that deepfakes are expanding into other domains such as medical imagery.

In this work, it was shown how an attacker can automatically inject or remove lung cancer in a patient's 3D CT scan. The result was so convincing that it fooled three radiologists and a state-of-the-art lung cancer detection AI. To demonstrate the threat, the authors successfully performed the attack on a hospital in a White hat penetration test.

A survey of deepfakes, published in May 2020, provides a timeline of how the creation and detection deepfakes have advanced over the last few years. The survey identifies that researchers have been focusing on resolving the following challenges of deepfake creation:

- **Generalization:** High-quality deepfakes are often achieved by training on hours of footage of the target. This challenge is to minimize the amount of training data and the time to train the model required to produce quality images and to enable the execution of trained models on new identities (unseen during training).
- **Paired Training:** Training a supervised model can produce high-quality results, but requires data pairing. This is the process of finding examples of inputs and their desired outputs for the model to learn from. Data pairing is laborious and impractical when training on multiple identities and facial behaviors. Some solutions include self-supervised training (using frames from the same video), the use of unpaired networks such as Cycle-GAN, or the manipulation of network embeddings.
- **Identity Leakage:** This is where the identity of the driver (i.e., the actor controlling the face in a reenactment) is partially transferred to the generated face. Some solutions proposed include attention mechanisms, few-shot learning, disentanglement, boundary conversions, and skip connections.

- **Occlusions:** When part of the face is obstructed with a hand, hair, glasses, or any other item then artifacts can occur. A common occlusion is a closed mouth which hides the inside of the mouth and the teeth. Some solutions include image segmentation during training and in-painting.
- **Temporal Coherence:** In videos containing deepfakes, artifacts such as flickering and jitter can occur because the network has no context of the preceding frames. Some researchers provide this context or use novel temporal coherence losses to help improve realism. As the technology improves, the interference is diminishing.

Amateur Development

The term deepfake originated in late 2017 from a Reddit user named "deepfakes". He, along with other members of Reddit's "r/deepfakes", shared deepfakes they created; many videos involved celebrities' faces swapped onto the bodies of actors in pornographic videos, while non-pornographic content included many videos with actor Nicolas Cage's face swapped into various movies. Other online communities remain, including Reddit communities that do not share pornography, such as "r/SFWdeepfakes" (short for "safe for work deepfakes"), in which community members share deepfakes depicting celebrities, politicians, and others in non-pornographic scenarios. Other online communities continue to share pornography on platforms that have not banned deepfake pornography.

Commercial Development

In January 2018, a proprietary desktop application called "FakeApp" was launched. This app allows users to easily create and share videos with their faces swapped with each other. As of 2019, "FakeApp" had been largely replaced by open-source alternatives such as "Faceswap", command line-based "DeepFaceLab", and web-based apps such as DeepfakesWeb.com Larger companies started to use deepfakes. Corporate training videos can be created using deepfaked avatars and their voices, for example Synthesia, which uses deepfake technology with avatars to create personalized videos. The mobile app Momo created the application Zao which allows users to superimpose their face on television and movie clips with a single picture. As of 2019 the Japanese AI company DataGrid made a full body deepfake that could create a person from scratch. As of 2020 audio deepfakes, and AI software capable of detecting deepfakes and cloning human voices after 5 seconds of listening time also exist. A mobile deepfake app, Impressions, was launched in March 2020. It was the first app for the creation of celebrity deepfake videos from mobile phones.

Resurrection

Deepfake technology's ability to fabricate messages and actions of others can include deceased individuals. On 29 October 2020, Kim Kardashian posted a video featuring a hologram of her late father Robert Kardashian created by the company Kaleida, which used a combination of performance, motion tracking, SFX, VFX and DeepFake technologies to create the illusion. In 2020, a deepfake video of Joaquin Oliver, a victim of the Parkland shooting was created as part of a gun safety campaign.

Oliver's parents partnered with nonprofit Change the Ref and McCann Health to produce a video in which Oliver to encourage people to support gun safety legislation and politicians who back do so as well. In 2022, a deepfake video of Elvis Presley was used on the program America's Got Talent 17. A TV commercial used a deepfake video of Beatles member John Lennon, who was murdered in 1980.

Techniques

Deepfakes rely on a type of neural network called an autoencoder. These consist of an encoder, which reduces an image to a lower dimensional latent space, and a decoder, which reconstructs the image from the latent representation. Deepfakes utilize this architecture by having a universal encoder which encodes a person in to the latent space. The latent representation contains key features about their facial features and body posture. This can then be decoded with a model trained specifically for the target. This means the target's detailed information will be superimposed on the underlying facial and body features of the original video, represented in the latent space.

A popular upgrade to this architecture attaches a generative adversarial network to the decoder. A GAN trains a generator, in this case the decoder, and a discriminator in an adversarial relationship. The generator creates new images from the latent representation of the source material, while the discriminator attempts to determine whether or not the image is generated. This causes the generator to create images that mimic reality extremely well as any defects would be caught by the discriminator. Both algorithms improve constantly in a zero sum game. This makes deepfakes difficult to combat as they are constantly evolving; any time a defect is determined, it can be corrected.

Applications

Acting

Digital clones of professional actors have appeared in films before, and progress in deepfake technology is expected to further the accessibility and effectiveness of such clones. The use of AI technology was a major issue in the 2023 SAG-AFTRA strike, as new techniques enabled the capability of generating and storing a digital likeness to use in place of actors. Disney has improved their visual effects using high-resolution deepfake face swapping technology. Disney improved their technology through progressive training programmed to identify facial expressions, implementing a face-swapping feature, and iterating in order to stabilize and refine the output. This high-resolution deepfake technology saves significant operational and production costs. Disney's deepfake generation model can produce AI-generated media at a 1024 x 1024 resolution, as opposed to common models that produce media at a 256 x 256 resolution. The technology allows Disney to de-age characters or revive deceased actors. Similar technology was initially used by fans to unofficially insert faces into existing media, such as overlaying Harrison Ford's young face onto Han Solo's face in Solo: A Star Wars Story. Disney used deepfakes for the characters of Princess Leia and Grand Moff Tarkin in Rogue One.

The 2020 documentary Welcome to Chechnya used deepfake technology to obscure the identity of the people interviewed, so as to protect them from retaliation. Creative Artists Agency has developed a facility to capture the likeness of an actor "in a single day", to develop a digital clone of the actor, which would be controlled by the actor or their estate alongside other personality rights. Companies which have used digital clones of professional actors in advertisements include Puma, Nike and Procter & Gamble. Deepfakes allowed for the use of David Beckham in a campaign using nearly nine languages to raise awareness the fight against Malaria. In the 2024 Indian Tamil science fiction action thriller The Greatest of All Time, the teenage version of Vijay's character Jeevan is portrayed by Ayaz Khan. Vijay's teenage face was then attained by AI deepfake.

Art

Deepfakes are also being used in education and media to create realistic videos and interactive content, which offer new ways to engage audiences. However, they also bring risks, especially for spreading false information, which has led to calls for responsible use and clear rules. In March 2018 the multidisciplinary artist Joseph Ayerle published the video artwork Un'emozione per sempre 2.0 (English title: The Italian Game). The artist worked with Deepfake technology to create an AI actor, a synthetic version of 80s movie star Ornella Muti, traveling in time from 1978 to 2018.

The Massachusetts Institute of Technology referred this artwork in the study "Collective Wisdom". The artist used Ornella Muti's time travel to explore generational reflections, while also investigating questions about the role of provocation in the world of art. For the technical realization Ayerle used scenes of photo model Kendall Jenner. The program replaced Jenner's face by an AI calculated face of Ornella Muti. As a result, the AI actor has the face of the Italian actor Ornella Muti and the body of Kendall Jenner. Deepfakes have been widely used in satire or to parody celebrities and politicians. The 2020 webseries Sassy Justice, created by

Trey Parker and Matt Stone, heavily features the use of deepfaked public figures to satirize current events and raise awareness of deepfake technology.

Blackmail

Deepfakes can be used to generate blackmail materials that falsely incriminate a victim. A report by the American Congressional Research Service warned that deepfakes could be used to blackmail elected officials or those with access to classified information for espionage or influence purposes. Alternatively, since the fakes cannot reliably be distinguished from genuine materials, victims of actual blackmail can now claim that the true artifacts are fakes, granting them plausible deniability. The effect is to void credibility of existing blackmail materials, which erases loyalty to blackmailers and destroys the blackmailer's control. This phenomenon can be termed "blackmail inflation", since it "devalues" real blackmail, rendering it worthless. It is possible to utilize commodity GPU hardware with a small software program to generate this blackmail content for any number of subjects in huge quantities, driving up the supply of fake blackmail content limitlessly and in highly scalable fashion.

Entertainment

- On June 8, 2022, Daniel Emmet, a former AGT contestant, teamed up with the AI startup Metaphysic AI, to create a hyperrealistic deepfake to make it appear as Simon Cowell. Cowell, notoriously known for severely critiquing contestants, was on stage interpreting "You're The Inspiration" by Chicago. Emmet sang on stage as an image of Simon Cowell emerged on the screen behind him in flawless synchronicity.
- On August 30, 2022, Metaphysic AI had 'deep-fake' Simon Cowell, Howie Mandel and Terry Crews singing opera on stage.
- On September 13, 2022, Metaphysic AI performed with a synthetic version of Elvis Presley for the finals of America's Got Talent.
- The MIT artificial intelligence project 15.ai has been used for content creation for multiple Internet fandoms, particularly on social media.
- In 2023 the bands ABBA and KISS partnered with Industrial Light & Magic and Pophouse Entertainment to develop deepfake avatars capable of performing virtual concerts.

Fraud and Scams

Fraudsters and scammers make use of deepfakes to trick people into fake investment schemes, financial fraud, cryptocurrencies, sending money, and following endorsements. The likenesses of celebrities and politicians have been used for large-scale scams, as well as those of private individuals, which are used in spearphishing attacks. According to the Better Business Bureau, deepfake scams are becoming more prevalent. These scams are responsible for an estimated $12 billion in fraud losses globally. According to a recent report these numbers are expected to reach $40 Billion over the next three years.

Fake endorsements have misused the identities of celebrities like Taylor Swift, Tom Hanks, Oprah Winfrey, and Elon Musk; news anchors like Gayle King and Sally Bundock; and politicians like Lee Hsien Loong and Jim Chalmers. Videos of them have appeared in online advertisements on YouTube, Facebook, and TikTok, who have policies against synthetic and manipulated media.

Ads running these videos are seen by millions of people. A single Medicare fraud campaign had been viewed more than 195 million times across thousands of videos. Deepfakes have been used for: a fake giveaway of Le Creuset cookware for a "shipping fee" without receiving the products, except for hidden monthly charges; weight-loss gummies that charge significantly more than what was said; a fake iPhone giveaway; and fraudulent get-rich-quick, investment, and cryptocurrency schemes.

Many ads pair AI voice cloning with "decontextualized video of the celebrity" to mimic authenticity. Others use a whole clip from a celebrity before moving to a different actor or voice. Some scams may involve real-time deepfakes. Celebrities have been warning people of these fake endorsements, and to be more vigilant against them. Celebrities are unlikely to file lawsuits against every person operating deepfake scams, as "finding and suing anonymous social media users is resource intensive," though cease and desist letters to social media companies work in getting videos and ads taken down. Audio deepfakes have been used as part of social engineering scams, fooling people into thinking they are receiving instructions from a trusted individual. In 2019, a U.K.-based energy firm's CEO was scammed over the phone when he was ordered to transfer €220,000 into a Hungarian bank account by an individual who reportedly used audio deepfake technology to impersonate the voice of the firm's parent company's chief executive. As of 2023, the combination advances in deepfake technology, which could clone an individual's voice from a recording of a few seconds to a minute, and new text generation tools, enabled automated impersonation scams, targeting victims using a convincing digital clone of a friend or relative.

Identity Masking

Audio deepfakes can be used to mask a user's real identity. In online gaming, for example, a player may want to choose a voice that sounds like their in-game character when speaking to other players. Those who are subject to harassment, such as women, children, and transgender people, can use these "voice skins" to hide their gender or age.

Memes

In 2020, an internet meme emerged utilizing deepfakes to generate videos of people singing the chorus of "Baka Mitai", a song from the game Yakuza 0 in the video game series Like a Dragon. In the series, the melancholic song is sung by the player in a karaoke minigame. Most iterations of this meme use a 2017 video uploaded by user Dobbsyrules, who lip syncs the song, as a template.

Politics

- In February 2018, in separate videos, the face of the Argentine President Mauricio Macri had been replaced by the face of Adolf Hitler, and Angela Merkel's face has been replaced with Donald Trump's.
- In April 2018, Jordan Peele collaborated with Buzzfeed to create a deepfake of Barack Obama with Peele's voice; it served as a public service announcement to increase awareness of deepfakes.
- In January 2019, Fox affiliate KCPQ aired a deepfake of Trump during his Oval Office address, mocking his appearance and skin colour. The employee found responsible for the video was subsequently fired.
- In June 2019, the United States House Intelligence Committee held hearings on the potential malicious use of deepfakes to sway elections.
- In April 2020, the Belgian branch of Extinction Rebellion published a deepfake video of Belgian Prime Minister Sophie Wilmès on Facebook. The video promoted a possible link between deforestation and COVID-19. It had more than 100,000 views within 24 hours and received many comments. On the Facebook page where the video appeared, many users interpreted the deepfake video as genuine.
- During the 2020 US presidential campaign, many deepfakes surfaced purporting Joe Biden in cognitive decline—falling asleep during an interview, getting lost, and misspeaking—all bolstering rumors of his decline.
- During the 2020 Delhi Legislative Assembly election campaign, the Delhi Bharatiya Janata Party used similar technology to distribute a version of an English-language campaign advertisement by its leader, Manoj Tiwari, translated into Haryanvi to target Haryana voters. A voiceover was provided by an actor, and AI trained using video of Tiwari speeches was used to lip-sync the video to the new voiceover. A party staff member described it as a "positive" use of deepfake technology, which allowed them to "convincingly approach the target audience even if the candidate didn't speak the language of the voter."

- In 2020, Bruno Sartori produced deepfakes parodying politicians like Jair Bolsonaro and Donald Trump.
- In April 2021, politicians in a number of European countries were approached by pranksters Vovan and Lexus, who are accused by critics of working for the Russian state. They impersonated Leonid Volkov, a Russian opposition politician and chief of staff of the Russian opposition leader Alexei Navalny's campaign, allegedly through deepfake technology. However, the pair told The Verge that they did not use deepfakes, and just used a look-alike.
- In May 2023, a deepfake video of Vice President Kamala Harris supposedly slurring her words and speaking nonsensically about today, tomorrow and yesterday went viral on social media.
- In June 2023, in the United States, Ron DeSantis's presidential campaign used a deepfake to misrepresent Donald Trump.
- In March 2024, during India's state assembly elections, deepfake technology was widely employed by political candidates to reach out to voters. Many politicians used AI-generated deepfakes created by startup The Indian Deepfaker, founded by Divyendra Singh Jadoun, to translate their speeches into multiple regional languages, allowing them to engage with diverse linguistic communities across the country. This surge in the use of deepfakes for political campaigns marked a significant shift in electioneering tactics in India.

Social Media

Deepfakes have begun to see use in popular social media platforms, notably through Zao, a Chinese deepfake app that allows users to substitute their own faces onto those of characters in scenes from films and television shows such as Romeo + Juliet and Game of Thrones. The app originally faced scrutiny over its invasive user data and privacy policy, after which the company put out a statement claiming it would revise the policy.

In January 2020 Facebook announced that it was introducing new measures to counter this on its platforms. The Congressional Research Service cited unspecified evidence as showing that foreign intelligence operatives used deepfakes to create social media accounts with the purposes of recruiting individuals with access to classified information.

In 2021, realistic deepfake videos of actor Tom Cruise were released on TikTok, which went viral and garnered more than tens of millions of views. The deepfake videos featured an "artificial intelligence-generated doppelganger" of Cruise doing various activities such as teeing off at the golf course, showing off a coin trick, and biting into a lollipop. The creator of the clips, Belgian VFX Artist Chris Umé, said he first got interested in deepfakes in 2018 and saw the "creative potential" of them.

Sockpuppets

Deepfake photographs can be used to create sockpuppets, non-existent people, who are active both online and in traditional media. A deepfake photograph appears to have been generated together with a legend for an apparently non-existent person named Oliver Taylor, whose identity was described as a university student in the United Kingdom. The Oliver Taylor persona submitted opinion pieces in several newspapers and was active in online media attacking a British legal academic and his wife, as "terrorist sympathizers."

The academic had drawn international attention in 2018 when he commenced a lawsuit in Israel against NSO, a surveillance company, on behalf of people in Mexico who alleged they were victims of NSO's phone hacking technology. Reuters could find only scant records for Oliver Taylor and "his" university had no records for him. Many experts agreed that the profile photo is a deepfake. Several newspapers have not retracted articles attributed to him or removed them from their websites. It is feared that such techniques are a new battleground in disinformation.

Collections of deepfake photographs of non-existent people on social networks have also been deployed as part of Israeli partisan propaganda. The Facebook page "Zionist Spring" featured photos of non-existent persons along with their "testimonies" purporting to explain why they have abandoned their left-leaning politics to embrace right-wing politics, and the page also contained large numbers of posts from Prime Minister of Israel Benjamin Netanyahu and his son and from other Israeli right wing sources.

The photographs appear to have been generated by "human image synthesis" technology, computer software that takes data from photos of real people to produce a realistic composite image of a non-existent person. In much of the "testimonies," the reason given for embracing the political right was the shock of learning of alleged incitement to violence against the prime minister. Right wing Israeli television broadcasters then broadcast the "testimonies" of these non-existent people based on the fact that they were being "shared" online. The broadcasters aired these "testimonies" despite being unable to find such people, explaining "Why does the origin matter?" Other Facebook fake profiles—profiles of fictitious individuals—contained material that allegedly contained such incitement against the right wing prime minister, in response to which the prime minister complained that there was a plot to murder him.

Concerns and Counter Measures

Though fake photos have long been plentiful, faking motion pictures has been more difficult, and the presence of deepfakes increases the difficulty of classifying videos as genuine or not. AI researcher Alex Champandard has said people should know how fast things can be corrupted with deepfake technology, and that the problem is not a technical one, but rather one to be solved by trust in information and journalism.

Computer science associate professor Hao Li of the University of Southern California states that deepfakes created for malicious use, such as fake news, will be even more harmful if nothing is done to spread awareness of deepfake technology. Li predicted that genuine videos and deepfakes would become indistinguishable in as soon as half a year, as of October 2019, due to rapid advancement in artificial intelligence and computer graphics. Former Google fraud czar Shuman Ghosemajumder has called deepfakes an area of "societal concern" and said that they will inevitably evolve to a point at which they can be generated automatically, and an individual could use that technology to produce millions of deepfake videos.

Credibility of Information

A primary pitfall is that humanity could fall into an age in which it can no longer be determined whether a medium's content corresponds to the truth. Deepfakes are one of a number of tools for disinformation attack, creating doubt, and undermining trust. They have a potential to interfere with democratic functions in societies, such as identifying collective agendas, debating issues, informing decisions, and solving problems though the exercise of political will. People may also start to dismiss real events as fake.

Defamation

Deepfakes possess the ability to damage individual entities tremendously. This is because deepfakes are often targeted at one individual, and/or their relations to others in hopes to create a narrative powerful enough to influence public opinion or beliefs. This can be done through deepfake voice phishing, which manipulates audio to create fake phone calls or conversations.

Another method of deepfake use is fabricated private remarks, which manipulate media to convey individuals voicing damaging comments. The quality of a negative video or audio does not need to be that high. As long as someone's likeness and actions are recognizable, a deepfake can hurt their reputation. In September 2020 Microsoft made public that they are developing a Deepfake detection software tool.

Beyond publicfigure defamation, deepfakes are increasingly used in K–12 and highereducation settings to target peers with false portrayals that extend well beyond static images or text messages. Students have reported encountering synthetic videos depicting classmates in nonconsensual intimate acts and experiencing academic or social disruptions as a result. Schools and universities frequently find themselves illequipped to address these incidents, as most antibullying policies predate AIgenerated media and focus narrowly on oncampus behavior or studentowned devices. When deepfake harassment originates offcampus—via private social networks, encrypted messaging, or servers hosted overseas—administrators struggle to determine jurisdiction, balance freespeech concerns, and coordinate with law enforcement. To close these gaps, legal scholars recommend updating both state and federal antibullying statutes to explicitly include "nonconsensual synthetic imagery" alongside traditional definitions of harassment. Concurrently, integrating AIliteracy curricula—covering deepfake detection techniques, ethical considerations, and responsible digital citizenship—can empower students to recognize, report, and resist deepfake bullying before it escalates.

Cyberbullying

With the rise of accessible deepfake tools—ranging from opensource platforms like DeepFaceLab and Faceswap to userfriendly mobile apps such as Zao and Impressions—malicious actors have begun weaponizing synthetic media as a novel form of cyberbullying. Termed "deepfake bullying," these attacks can take many forms: perpetrators may superimpose a student's face onto videos of underage drinking or drug use, create fabricated nude images without consent, or manufacture scenes of criminal behavior to falsely implicate victims.Because modern generative adversarial networks can produce hyperrealistic results, targets often cannot distinguish real from fake, causing intense embarrassment and panic when content first appears. Once released, deepfake content tends to circulate rapidly across messaging apps, social feeds, and even private chat groups, where it can be downloaded, reedited, and recirculated—subjecting victims to repeated retraumatization and a persistent fear of new exposures. Psychological assessments of affected students report elevated levels of anxiety, depression, and social withdrawal; some victims have withdrawn from school activities or changed schools entirely to escape ongoing harassment.In response, educators, school counselors, and childpsychology experts are calling for explicit policies that define deepfake bullying as a disciplinary offense, mandate immediate content takedowns, and require traumainformed support structures—such as specialized counseling services, peersupport hotlines, and restorativejustice circles—to help victims regain a sense of safety and agency.

Audio Detection

Detecting fake audio is a highly complex task that requires careful attention to the audio signal in order to achieve good performance. Using deep learning, preprocessing of feature design and masking augmentation have been proven effective in improving performance.

Video Detection

Most of the academic research surrounding deepfakes focuses on the detection of deepfake videos. One approach to deepfake detection is to use algorithms to recognize patterns and pick up subtle inconsistencies that arise in deepfake videos. For example, researchers have developed automatic systems that examine videos for errors such as irregular blinking patterns of lighting. This approach has been criticized because deepfake detection is characterized by a "moving goal post" where the production of deepfakes continues to change and improve as algorithms to detect deepfakes improve. In order to assess the most effective algorithms for detecting deepfakes, a coalition of leading technology companies hosted the Deepfake Detection Challenge to accelerate the technology for identifying manipulated content. The winning model of the Deepfake Detection Challenge was 65% accurate on the holdout set of 4,000 videos. A team at Massachusetts Institute of Technology published a paper in December 2021 demonstrating that ordinary humans are 69–72% accurate at identifying a random sample of 50 of these videos.

A team at the University of Buffalo published a paper in October 2020 outlining their technique of using reflections of light in the eyes of those depicted to spot deepfakes with a high rate of success, even without the use of an AI detection tool, at least for the time being. In the case of well-documented individuals such as political leaders, algorithms have been developed to distinguish identity-based features such as patterns of facial, gestural, and vocal mannerisms and detect deep-fake impersonators.

Another team led by Wael AbdAlmageed with Visual Intelligence and Multimedia Analytics Laboratory (VIMAL) of the Information Sciences Institute at the University Of Southern California developed two generations of deepfake detectors based on convolutional neural networks. The first generation used recurrent neural networks to spot spatio-temporal inconsistencies to identify visual artifacts left by the deepfake generation process. The algorithm achieved 96% accuracy on FaceForensics++, the only large-scale deepfake benchmark available at that time. The second generation used end-to-end deep networks to differentiate between artifacts and high-level semantic facial information using two-branch networks.

The first branch propagates colour information while the other branch suppresses facial content and amplifies low-level frequencies using Laplacian of Gaussian (LoG). Further, they included a new loss function that learns a compact representation of bona fide faces, while dispersing the representations (i.e. features) of deepfakes. VIMAL's approach showed state-of-the-art performance on FaceForensics++ and Celeb-DF benchmarks, and on March 16, 2022 (the same day of the release), was used to identify the deepfake of Volodymyr Zelensky out-of-the-box without any retraining or knowledge of the algorithm with which the deepfake was created.

Other techniques suggest that blockchain could be used to verify the source of the media. For instance, a video might have to be verified through the ledger before it is shown on social media platforms. With this technology, only videos from trusted sources would be approved, decreasing the spread of possibly harmful deepfake media. Digitally signing of all video and imagery by cameras and video cameras, including smartphone cameras, was suggested to fight deepfakes. That allows tracing every photograph or video back to its original owner that can be used to pursue dissidents. One easy way to uncover deepfake video calls consists in asking the caller to turn sideways.

Prevention

Henry Ajder who works for Deeptrace, a company that detects deepfakes, says there are several ways to protect against deepfakes in the workplace. Semantic passwords or secret questions can be used when holding important conversations. Voice authentication and other biometric security features should be up to date. Educate employees about deepfakes.

Media Literacy and deepfakes

Due to the capability of deepfakes to fool viewers and believably mimic a person, research has indicated that the concept of truth through observation cannot be fully relied on. Additionally, literacy of the technology among populations could be called into question due to the relatively new success of convincing deepfakes.

When combined with increasing ease of access to the technology, this has led to the concern amongst some experts that some societies are not prepared to interact with deepfakes organically without potential consequences from sharing misinformation and disinformation. Media literacy has been considered as a potential counter to "prime" a viewer to identify a deepfake when they encounter one organically by engendering critical thinking. While media literacy education can have conflicting results in the overall success in detecting deepfakes, research has indicated that critical thinking and a skeptical outlook toward a presented piece of media are effective at assisting an individual in determining a deepfake. Media literacy frameworks promote critical analysis of media and the motivations behind the presentation of the associated content. Media literacy shows promise as a potential cognitive countermeasure when interacting with malicious deepfakes.

Controversies

In March 2024, a video clip was shown from the Buckingham Palace, where Kate Middleton had cancer and she was undergoing chemotherapy. However, the clip fuelled rumours that the woman in that clip was an AI deepfake. UCLA's race director Johnathan Perkins doubted she had cancer, and further speculated that she could be in critical condition or dead.

Politics

Recently, the use of deepfakes has inspired research on deepfake's capability and effects when used in disinformation campaigns. This capability has raised concerns, partly due to the potential of deepfakes to circumvent a person's skepticism and influence their views on an issue. Due to the continued advancement in technology that improves deceptive capabilities of deepfakes, some scholars believe that deepfakes could pose a significant threat to democratic societies. Studies have investigated the effects of political deepfakes. In two separate studies focusing on Dutch participants, it was found that deepfakes have varying effects on an audience.

As a tool of disinformation, deepfakes did not necessarily produce stronger reactions or shifts in viewpoints than traditional textual disinformation. However, deepfakes did produce a reassuring effect on individuals who held preconceived notions that aligned with the viewpoint promoted by the deepfake disinformation in the study. Additionally, deepfakes are effective when designed to target a specific demographic segment related to a particular issue. "Microtargeting" involves understanding nuanced political issues of a specific demographic to create a targeted deepfake. The targeted deepfake is then used to connect with and influence the viewpoint of that demographic. Targeted deepfakes were found to be notably effective by the researchers. Research has also found that the political effects of deepfakes are not necessarily as straightforward or assured. Researchers in the United Kingdom uncovered that deepfake political disinformation does not have a guaranteed effect on populations beyond indications that it may sow distrust or uncertainty in a source that provides the deepfake. The implications of distrust in sources led researchers to conclude that deepfakes may have outsized effect in a "low-trust" information environment where public institutions are not trusted by the public. Across the world, there are key instances where deepfakes have been used to misrepresent well-known politicians and other public figures.

Example Events

- **Barack Obama:** On April 17, 2018, American actor Jordan Peele, BuzzFeed, and Monkeypaw Productions posted a deepfake of Barack Obama to YouTube, which depicted Barack Obama cursing and calling Donald Trump names. In this deepfake, Peele's voice and face were transformed and manipulated into those of Obama. The intent of this video was to portray the dangerous consequences and power of deepfakes, and how deepfakes can make anyone say anything.
- **Donald Trump:** On May 5, 2019, Derpfakes posted a deepfake of Donald Trump to YouTube, based on a skit Jimmy Fallon performed on The Tonight Show. In the original skit (aired May 4, 2016), Jimmy Fallon dressed as Donald Trump and pretended to participate in a phone call

with Barack Obama, conversing in a manner that presented him to be bragging about his primary win in Indiana. In the deepfake, Jimmy Fallon's face was transformed into Donald Trump's face, with the audio remaining the same. This deepfake video was produced by Derpfakes with a comedic intent. In March 2023, a series of images appeared to show New York Police Department officers restraining Trump. The images, created using Midjourney, were initially posted on Twitter by Eliot Higgins but were later re-shared without context, leading some viewers to believe they were real photographs.

- **Nancy Pelosi:** In 2019, a clip from Nancy Pelosi's speech at the Center for American Progress (given on May 22, 2019) in which the video was slowed down, in addition to the pitch of the audio being altered, to make it seem as if she were drunk, was widely distributed on social media. Critics argue that this was not a deepfake, but a shallowfake—a less sophisticated form of video manipulation.
- **Mark Zuckerberg:** In May 2019, two artists collaborating with the company CannyAI created a deepfake video of Facebook founder Mark Zuckerberg talking about harvesting and controlling data from billions of people. The video was part of an exhibit to educate the public about the dangers of artificial intelligence.
- **Kim Jong-un and Vladimir Putin:** On September 29, 2020, deepfakes of North Korean leader Kim Jong-un and Russian President Vladimir Putin were uploaded to YouTube, created by a nonpartisan advocacy group RepresentUs. The deepfakes of Kim and Putin were meant to air publicly as commercials to relay the notion that interference by these leaders in US elections would be detrimental to the United States' democracy. The commercials also aimed to shock Americans to realize how fragile democracy is, and how media and news can significantly influence the country's path regardless of credibility. However, while the commercials included an ending comment detailing that the footage was not real, they ultimately did not air due to fears and sensitivity regarding how Americans may react. On June 5, 2023, an unknown source broadcast a reported deepfake of Vladimir Putin on multiple radio and television networks. In the clip, Putin appears to deliver a speech announcing the invasion of Russia and calling for a general mobilization of the army.
- **Volodymyr Zelenskyy:** On March 16, 2022, a one-minute long deepfake video depicting Ukraine's president Volodymyr Zelenskyy seemingly telling his soldiers to lay down their arms and surrender during the 2022 Russian invasion of Ukraine was circulated on social media.

Russian social media boosted it, but after it was debunked, Facebook and YouTube removed it. Twitter allowed the video in tweets where it was exposed as a fake, but said it would be taken down if posted to deceive people. Hackers inserted the disinformation into a live scrolling-text news crawl on TV station Ukraine 24, and the video appeared briefly on the station's website in addition to false claims that Zelenskyy had fled his country's capital, Kyiv. It was not immediately clear who created the deepfake, to which Zelenskyy responded with his own video, saying, "We don't plan to lay down any arms. Until our victory."

- **Wolf News:** In late 2022, pro-China propagandists started spreading deepfake videos purporting to be from "Wolf News" that used synthetic actors. The technology was developed by a London company called Synthesia, which markets it as a cheap alternative to live actors for training and HR videos.
- **Pope Francis:** In March 2023, an anonymous construction worker from Chicago used Midjourney to create a fake image of Pope Francis in a white Balenciaga puffer jacket. The image went viral, receiving over twenty million views. Writer Ryan Broderick dubbed it "the first real mass-level AI misinformation case". Experts consulted by Slate characterized the image as unsophisticated: "you could have made it on Photoshop five years ago".
- **Keir Starmer:** In October 2023, a deepfake audio clip of the UK Labour Party leader Keir Starmer abusing staffers was released on the first day of a Labour Party conference. The clip purported to be an audio tape of Starmer abusing his staffers.
- **Rashmika Mandanna:** In early November 2023, a famous South Indian actor, Rashmika Mandanna fell prey to DeepFake when a morphed video of a famous British-Indian influencer, Zara Patel, with Rashmika's face started to float on social media. Zara Patel claims to not be involved in its creation.
- **Bongbong Marcos:** In April 2024, a deepfake video misrepresenting Philippine President Bongbong Marcos was released. It is a slideshow accompanied by a deepfake audio of Marcos purportedly ordering the Armed Forces of the Philippines and special task force to act "however appropriate" should China attack the Philippines. The video was released amidst tensions related to the South China Sea dispute. The Presidential Communications Office has said that there is no such directive from the president and said a foreign actor might be behind the fabricated media. Criminal charges has been filed by the Kapisanan

ng mga Brodkaster ng Pilipinas in relation to the deepfake media. On July 22, 2024, a video of Marcos purportedly snorting illegal drugs was released by Claire Contreras, a former supporter of Marcos. Dubbed as the polvoron video, the media noted its consistency with the insinuation of Marcos' predecessor—Rodrigo Duterte—that Marcos is a drug addict; the video was also shown at a Hakbang ng Maisug rally organized by people aligned with Duterte. Two days later, the Philippine National Police and the National Bureau of Investigation, based on their own findings, concluded that the video was created using AI; they further pointed out inconsistencies with the person on the video with Marcos, such as details on the two people's ears.

- **Joe Biden:** Prior to the 2024 United States presidential election, phone calls imitating the voice of the incumbent Joe Biden were made to dissuade people from voting for him. The person responsible for the calls was charged with voter suppression and impersonating a candidate. The FCC proposed to fine him US$6 million and Lingo Telecom, the company that allegedly relayed the calls, $2 million.
- **Arup Group:** The firm Arup Group lost $25 million in 2024 from a deepfake scam.

Responses

Social Media Platforms

Twitter (later X) is taking active measures to handle synthetic and manipulated media on their platform. In order to prevent disinformation from spreading, Twitter is placing a notice on tweets that contain manipulated media and/or deepfakes that signal to viewers that the media is manipulated. There will also be a warning that appears to users who plan on retweeting, liking, or engaging with the tweet.

Twitter will also work to provide users a link next to the tweet containing manipulated or synthetic media that links to a Twitter Moment or credible news article on the related topic—as a debunking action. Twitter also has the ability to remove any tweets containing deepfakes or manipulated media that may pose a harm to users' safety. In order to better improve Twitter's detection of deepfakes and manipulated media, Twitter asked users who are interested in partnering with them to work on deepfake detection solutions to fill out a form.

"In August 2024, the secretaries of state of Minnesota, Pennsylvania, Washington, Michigan and New Mexico penned an open letter to X owner Elon Musk urging modifications to its AI chatbot Grok's new text-to-video generator, added in August 2024, stating that it had disseminated election misinformation. Facebook has taken efforts towards encouraging the creation of deepfakes in order to develop state of the art deepfake detection software. Facebook was the prominent partner in hosting the Deepfake Detection Challenge (DFDC), held December 2019, to 2114 participants who generated more than 35,000 models. The top performing models with the highest detection accuracy were analyzed for similarities and differences; these findings are areas of interest in further research to improve and refine deepfake detection models. Facebook has also detailed that the platform will be taking down media generated with artificial intelligence used to alter an individual's speech. However, media that has been edited to alter the order or context of words in one's message would remain on the site but be labeled as false, since it was not generated by artificial intelligence.

On 31 January 2018, Gfycat began removing all deepfakes from its site. On Reddit, the r/deepfakes subreddit was banned on 7 February 2018, due to the policy violation of "involuntary pornography". In the same month, representatives from Twitter stated that they would suspend accounts suspected of posting non-consensual deepfake content. Chat site Discord has taken action against deepfakes in the past, and has taken a general stance against deepfakes. In September 2018, Google added "involuntary synthetic pornographic imagery" to its ban list, allowing anyone to request the block of results showing their fake nudes. In February 2018, Pornhub said that it would ban deepfake videos on its website because it is considered "non consensual content" which violates their terms of service. They also stated previously to Mashable that they will take down content flagged as deepfakes. Writers from Motherboard reported that searching "deepfakes" on Pornhub still returned multiple recent deepfake videos.

Facebook has previously stated that they would not remove deepfakes from their platforms. The videos will instead be flagged as fake by third-parties and then have a lessened priority in user's feeds. This response was prompted in June 2019 after a deepfake featuring a 2016 video of Mark Zuckerberg circulated on Facebook and Instagram. In May 2022, Google officially changed the terms of service for their Jupyter Notebook colabs, banning the use of their colab service for the purpose of creating deepfakes. This came a few days after a VICE article had been published, claiming that "most deepfakes are non-consensual porn" and that the main use of popular deepfake software DeepFaceLab (DFL), "the most important technology powering the vast majority of this generation of deepfakes" which often was used in combination with Google colabs, would be to create non-consensual pornography, by pointing to the fact that among many other well-known examples of third-party DFL implementations such as deepfakes commissioned by The Walt Disney Company, official music videos, and web series Sassy Justice by the creators of South Park, DFL's GitHub page also links to deepfake porn website Mr.Deepfakes and participants of the DFL Discord server also participate on Mr.Deepfakes.

Legislation

In the United States, there have been some responses to the problems posed by deepfakes. In 2018, the Malicious Deep Fake Prohibition Act was introduced to the US Senate; in 2019, the Deepfakes Accountability Act was introduced in the 116th United States Congress by U.S. representative for New York's 9th congressional district Yvette Clarke. Several states have also introduced legislation regarding deepfakes, including Virginia, Texas, California, and New York; charges as varied as identity theft, cyberstalking, and revenge porn have been pursued, while more comprehensive statutes are urged.

Among U.S. legislative efforts, on 3 October 2019, California governor Gavin Newsom signed into law Assembly Bills No. 602 and No. 730. Assembly Bill No. 602 provides individuals targeted by sexually explicit deepfake content made without their consent with a cause of action against the content's creator. Assembly Bill No. 730 prohibits the distribution of malicious deepfake audio or visual media targeting a candidate running for public office within 60 days of their election. U.S. representative Yvette Clarke introduced H.R. 5586: Deepfakes Accountability Act into the 118th United States Congress on September 20, 2023 in an effort to protect national security from threats posed by deepfake technology. U.S. representative María Salazar introduced H.R. 6943: No AI Fraud Act into the 118th United States Congress on January 10, 2024, to establish specific property rights of individual physicality, including voice.

In November 2019, China announced that deepfakes and other synthetically faked footage should bear a clear notice about their fakeness starting in 2020. Failure to comply could be considered a crime the Cyberspace Administration of China stated on its website. The Chinese government seems to be reserving the right to prosecute both users and online video platforms failing to abide by the rules. The Cyberspace Administration of China, the Ministry of Industry and Information Technology, and the Ministry of Public Security jointly issued the Provision on the Administration of Deep Synthesis Internet Information Service in November 2022. China's updated Deep Synthesis Provisions (Administrative Provisions on Deep Synthesis in Internet-Based Information Services) went into effect in January 2023.

In the United Kingdom, producers of deepfake material could be prosecuted for harassment, but deepfake production was not a specific crime until 2023, when the Online Safety Act was passed, which made deepfakes illegal; the UK plans to expand the Act's scope to criminalize deepfakes created with "intention to cause distress" in 2024.

In Canada, in 2019, the Communications Security Establishment released a report which said that deepfakes could be used to interfere in Canadian politics, particularly to discredit politicians and influence voters. As a result, there are multiple ways for citizens in Canada to deal with deepfakes if they are targeted by them. In February 2024, bill C-63 was tabled in the 44th Canadian Parliament in order to enact the Online Harms Act, which would amend Criminal Code, and other Acts. An earlier version of the Bill, C-36, was ended by the dissolution of the 43rd Canadian Parliament in September 2021.

In India, there are no direct laws or regulation on AI or deepfakes, but there are provisions under the Indian Penal Code and Information Technology Act 2000/2008, which can be looked at for legal remedies, and the new proposed Digital India Act will have a chapter on AI and deepfakes in particular, as per the MoS Rajeev Chandrasekhar.

In Europe, the European Union's 2024 Artificial Intelligence Act (AI Act) takes a risk-based approach to regulating AI systems, including deepfakes. It establishes categories of "unacceptable risk," "high risk," "specific/limited or transparency risk", and "minimal risk" to determine the level of regulatory obligations for AI providers and users. However, the lack of clear definitions for these risk categories in the context of deepfakes creates potential challenges for effective implementation. Legal scholars have raised concerns about the classification of deepfakes intended for political misinformation or the creation of non-consensual intimate imagery. Debate exists over whether such uses should always be considered "high-risk" AI systems, which would lead to stricter regulatory requirements.

In August 2024, the Irish Data Protection Commission (DPC) launched court proceedings against X for its unlawful use of the personal data of over 60 million EU/EEA users, in order to train its AI technologies, such as its chatbot Grok.

Response from DARPA

In 2016, the Defense Advanced Research Projects Agency (DARPA) launched the Media Forensics (MediFor) program which was funded through 2020. MediFor aimed at automatically spotting digital manipulation in images and videos, including Deepfakes. In the summer of 2018, MediFor held an event where individuals competed to create AI-generated videos, audio, and images as well as automated tools to detect these deepfakes. According to the MediFor program, it established a framework of three tiers of information—digital integrity, physical integrity and semantic integrity—to generate one integrity score in an effort to enable accurate detection of manipulated media. In 2019, DARPA hosted a "proposers day" for the Semantic Forensics (SemaFor) program where researchers were driven to prevent viral spread of AI-manipulated media. DARPA and the Semantic Forensics Program were also working together to detect AI-manipulated media through efforts in training computers to utilize common sense, logical reasoning. Built on the MediFor's technologies, SemaFor's attribution algorithms infer if digital media originates from a particular organization or individual, while characterization algorithms determine whether media was generated or manipulated for malicious purposes. In March 2024, SemaFor published an analytic catalog that offers the public access to open-source resources developed under SemaFor.

4.2.2 Artistic Style Transfer and Creative Applications

Artistic style transfer represents one of the most fascinating and visually compelling applications of generative artificial intelligence. By blending the content of one image with the stylistic elements of another, AI systems can generate artworks that reinterpret photographs in the aesthetic manner of famous painters or unique artistic styles. This technology has bridged the gap between computation and creativity, enabling artists, designers, and even casual users to explore new visual possibilities that were once limited to manual techniques.

As AI-driven tools become increasingly sophisticated, the creative potential of style transfer is expanding across various domains such as visual arts, fashion, entertainment, and user-generated content. Artistic style transfer exemplifies how generative AI can transform the creative process across a multitude of disciplines. By merging computational power with artistic intuition, it enables new forms of expression, personalization, and collaboration.

From digital art and fashion design to media production and everyday creativity, style transfer has broadened the scope of what is possible in visual aesthetics. As the technology continues to evolve, it holds the potential to reshape the creative industries and democratize access to artistic innovation, making the act of creation more inclusive, experimental, and dynamic than ever before.

Understanding Artistic Style Transfer

At its core, artistic style transfer is a process in which an algorithm extracts the structural or semantic content from a source image and recombines it with the texture, color, and brushwork style of a target artwork. This capability was made possible by advancements in convolutional neural networks (CNNs), particularly through the pioneering work of researchers who demonstrated that deep neural networks trained for image recognition could also capture stylistic information. A neural network processes an image through a series of layers, each of which captures different levels of abstraction.

Lower layers tend to identify edges and simple textures, while higher layers grasp complex features such as shapes and arrangements. Style transfer algorithms exploit this hierarchical structure by computing a content representation from higher layers and a style representation from lower layers. By optimizing a new image that simultaneously aligns with the content features of the input photo and the style features of the artwork, the algorithm generates a novel image that visually merges the two.

Evolution of Style Transfer Techniques

The original implementations of style transfer were computationally intensive, relying on iterative optimization techniques that required minutes or even hours to produce a single image. These methods, though powerful, were impractical for real-time applications. To address this limitation, researchers developed feed-forward networks that could learn to apply a particular style in one pass, significantly reducing generation time.

Further developments introduced models capable of multi-style and arbitrary style transfer, enabling a single network to apply many different styles or any new style without retraining. These advances often rely on conditional instance normalization, attention mechanisms, or adaptive feature modulation, which allow the model to flexibly adapt to varying stylistic inputs. Another branch of research has explored generative adversarial networks (GANs) and transformers for style transfer. These models have brought greater realism, diversity, and controllability to generated outputs, making AI-generated art more expressive and aligned with human expectations. The progress in these architectures has also facilitated better handling of complex textures, spatial coherence, and semantic awareness, allowing for more convincing and aesthetically pleasing results.

Applications in Visual Arts

In the visual arts, style transfer offers a new medium for artistic experimentation and expression. Digital artists use these tools to reimagine photographs or original artworks in the styles of van Gogh, Picasso, Monet, and many other historical figures, or to create entirely novel aesthetic blends. This capability democratizes access to artistic tools, allowing individuals without formal training to produce visually compelling pieces. Museums and galleries have also embraced style transfer to engage audiences in interactive exhibits, where visitors can transform their portraits into classical art styles or remix iconic paintings.

These experiences blend cultural heritage with modern technology, fostering greater appreciation and interaction with art. Additionally, style transfer has inspired new forms of digital art that challenge traditional boundaries. Artists can now generate entire series or animations by applying consistent styles across multiple frames, leading to hybrid forms of visual storytelling that merge fine art with digital media. The blending of different visual vocabularies, made possible by AI, reflects the evolving nature of creativity in the digital age.

Creative Applications in Design and Fashion

Beyond traditional art, style transfer has found a strong foothold in design and fashion. Designers use AI-generated textures and patterns to create innovative fabrics, prints, and product designs that are both unique and visually impactful.

By applying various artistic styles to base designs, creators can rapidly explore a vast design space, generating ideas that might not have emerged through manual sketching or rendering alone. In fashion, AI tools support the customization and personalization of apparel. Consumers can input their preferred styles or reference artworks, and the system can generate clothing items that reflect those preferences. This approach aligns with the growing trend of personalized fashion, where individuals seek unique expressions of identity through customized garments. Interior design is another field where style transfer is making an impact. Architects and designers can visualize spaces with different artistic aesthetics, helping clients explore themes ranging from classical elegance to contemporary minimalism. Style transfer allows for rapid prototyping and ideation, shortening the design cycle and enhancing creative freedom.

Integration in Media and Entertainment

Media and entertainment industries are leveraging style transfer to enhance visual storytelling, video production, and interactive experiences. In filmmaking and animation, directors can apply consistent visual styles to entire scenes or sequences, achieving cohesive aesthetics that would otherwise require intensive manual work. Style transfer also supports the creation of stylized cinematography, where scenes are rendered in the visual language of graphic novels, impressionist paintings, or abstract art. Video games benefit from this technology by offering customizable visual modes that transform the appearance of game environments. Players can experience the same game world through different artistic lenses, increasing replay value and engagement. Some games incorporate AI-generated art as part of their narrative or world-building, blending procedural content generation with creative direction. In music videos and promotional content, style transfer adds artistic flair and uniqueness. Visual artists can animate lyrics or imagery in styles that resonate with the themes and emotions of the content, deepening the connection between visuals and audio.

Social Media and User-Generated Content

The accessibility of style transfer tools through mobile apps and online platforms has made them popular among social media users. Applications like Prisma, DeepArt, and many others enable users to apply art styles to their photos with just a few taps. This ease of use has contributed to the viral spread of stylized images and a growing culture of AI-enhanced self-expression. User-generated content platforms encourage creativity by offering tools that let users remix their photos, videos, and even live streams in real-time using style transfer filters. These features not only entertain but also empower users to craft distinct digital identities. Influencers, content creators, and brands use stylized visuals to stand out in crowded digital spaces, enhancing their storytelling and branding.

Challenges and Future Directions

Despite its impressive progress, artistic style transfer still faces several challenges. Maintaining semantic coherence while applying complex styles remains a technical hurdle, especially in scenes with multiple objects, varied lighting, or high-resolution textures. Some algorithms struggle with preserving facial features or important details, leading to distortions or artifacts. Another issue involves style generalization. While models trained on known artworks perform well, transferring styles from arbitrary inputs, such as user sketches or unknown art forms, can be less reliable. Improving models' adaptability and interpretability is essential for broader adoption.

Ethical concerns have also emerged, particularly regarding copyright and originality. As style transfer becomes more advanced, distinguishing between human and machine-generated art may become increasingly difficult. This raises questions about artistic credit, authorship, and the potential commodification of creative expression. Looking forward, research is focused on making style transfer more robust, controllable, and interpretable. Interactive systems that allow users to guide the transfer process more intuitively, such as selecting regions of interest or adjusting style intensity, are gaining popularity. Multi-modal style transfer, which combines text, audio, or motion cues with visual styles, is also an exciting area of development, promising richer and more immersive creative tools.

4.3 MUSIC AND AUDIO GENERATION

4.3.1 AI Composers

Artificial intelligence has become a transformative force across numerous creative domains, and in the world of music, AI composers are emerging as one of the most intriguing developments. AI composers are systems that generate music autonomously or semi-autonomously using advanced algorithms, neural networks, and machine learning techniques. These systems are capable of analyzing massive amounts of musical data, learning stylistic patterns, and composing original works that imitate or extend human creativity.

As the technology matures, AI is not only becoming a tool for assisting musicians but is also starting to redefine the very process of musical creation. AI composers represent a revolutionary advancement at the intersection of music and technology. By learning from vast musical datasets and generating original compositions, these systems challenge traditional notions of creativity, authorship, and artistic process. Whether used as collaborative tools, educational aids, or independent creators, AI composers are reshaping the landscape of music in profound ways. As the technology continues to evolve, it promises to open new avenues for artistic expression, cultural preservation, and musical discovery, heralding an era where human imagination and machine intelligence compose in harmony.

The Foundations of AI-Generated Music

The idea of machines generating music dates back to the early experiments with algorithmic composition in the mid-20th century. Composers like Iannis Xenakis and Lejaren Hiller explored mathematical models and probabilistic rules to create music, laying the groundwork for future developments. These early approaches lacked the complexity and nuance of human composition, but they introduced a fundamental concept: that music could be broken down into logical patterns and generated algorithmically. With the advent of machine learning and deep learning, AI composers have moved far beyond rule-based systems.

Neural networks, especially recurrent neural networks (RNNs) and long short-term memory (LSTM) networks, have enabled machines to learn from sequences of musical data, capturing time-dependent structures such as melody, harmony, and rhythm. These models learn patterns from massive musical corpora and generate new pieces by predicting the next note or chord in a sequence. More recently, transformer models and variational autoencoders have further advanced AI composition by enabling longer memory spans, stylistic consistency, and structural complexity in generated music.

How AI Composers Work

AI composers generally rely on large datasets of existing music to learn the structure and syntax of musical languages. These datasets can include classical symphonies, jazz improvisations, pop songs, and even non-Western musical traditions. The training process involves feeding these datasets into neural networks, which then learn to model relationships between notes, chords, motifs, and other musical elements. Once trained, an AI composer can generate music by sampling from the learned probability distributions. Some models require a seed input or prompt, such as a melody fragment or chord progression, while others can compose music from scratch.

More advanced systems incorporate user input or constraints, such as tempo, mood, or instrumentation, allowing composers and producers to direct the creative process while still leveraging AI's generative power. AI composition is not limited to symbolic music, such as MIDI data. Some models also generate raw audio using techniques like WaveNet, GANs, or diffusion models. These approaches allow for the synthesis of music with realistic instrument sounds, timbral textures, and production quality, expanding the scope of what AI can achieve in music generation.

Applications in the Music Industry

AI composers are finding applications across the music industry, from composing background scores to assisting human musicians in songwriting. In the realm of film, television, and video games, AI-generated music is increasingly used to produce mood-specific background tracks at scale. These applications benefit from AI's ability to quickly generate long, consistent pieces in various styles, saving time and costs for content creators. In commercial music production, AI tools assist songwriters by suggesting chord progressions, melodies, or harmonies. These systems act as creative collaborators, offering musical ideas that might inspire new directions or overcome creative blocks.

For example, platforms like AIVA, Amper Music, and OpenAI's MuseNet allow users to generate entire compositions or enhance existing ideas with stylistic variations. Live performance is another area where AI composers are making an impact. Musicians have begun collaborating with AI in real-time, using machine-generated outputs as inputs for improvisation or interactive installations. These performances blur the line between human and machine creativity, offering audiences unique experiences that evolve with each interaction.

AI Composers and Music Education

AI tools are also revolutionizing music education by serving as personalized tutors and compositional aids. Students can analyze AI-generated compositions to understand musical forms, styles, and harmonic relationships. AI systems can offer feedback on student compositions or provide suggestions for improvements, creating a more interactive and responsive learning environment. Furthermore, AI can help democratize music creation for individuals without formal training.

By lowering the barrier to entry, AI composers empower more people to experiment with music and express themselves creatively. This democratization aligns with broader trends in digital media, where user-generated content and participatory culture are reshaping artistic production.

The Debate on Creativity and Originality

The rise of AI composers has sparked significant debate regarding the nature of creativity and the role of the human artist. Critics argue that AI-generated music lacks genuine emotional depth, intentionality, or cultural context. They contend that while AI can mimic styles and generate novel combinations, it does so without experiencing or understanding music in the way humans do. Proponents, however, view AI as a new medium of expression that expands human creativity rather than replacing it.

They point out that many great artists have historically used technological tools—from the piano to the synthesizer—to explore new sounds and ideas. In this view, AI is simply another step in the evolution of musical tools, providing novel possibilities for composition and experimentation. The question of authorship also arises when AI contributes significantly to a musical work. Who owns the rights to an AI-composed song? Should credit go to the programmer, the user, or the AI itself? Legal and ethical frameworks are still catching up with these developments, and how society resolves these issues will shape the future of AI in music.

Expanding Cultural Horizons

One of the most promising aspects of AI composers is their potential to explore and preserve diverse musical traditions. By training models on non-Western music, folk styles, or historical archives, AI systems can help rediscover forgotten forms and generate new compositions inspired by global musical cultures. This capability fosters cross-cultural understanding and artistic innovation, promoting inclusivity in music creation. Moreover, AI can assist in musicological research by analyzing large-scale musical corpora, identifying stylistic trends, and generating hypothetical compositions that reflect historical or theoretical models. This intersection of AI and musicology offers new tools for scholars and educators to study the evolution and diversity of music.

Future Directions and Challenges

The future of AI composers is full of potential but also fraught with challenges. As models become more sophisticated, there is a growing need for transparency and interpretability. Understanding how an AI system generates music—what patterns it learns, how it makes decisions—can help users trust and control the creative process. Another challenge is ensuring diversity and fairness in training data. If AI composers are trained predominantly on Western, male-dominated repertoires, they may reinforce existing biases in music production and marginalize other voices. Curating diverse and representative datasets is crucial for building inclusive AI systems. Human-AI collaboration is likely to become a central theme in future developments. Rather than aiming for fully autonomous AI composers, many researchers and musicians envision hybrid systems that support co-creation. These systems will combine the computational power of AI with human intuition, emotion, and cultural insight, leading to richer and more meaningful musical experiences.

4.3.2 Speech Synthesis

Speech synthesis is the artificial production of human speech. A computer system used for this purpose is called a speech synthesizer, and can be implemented in software or hardware products. A text-to-speech (TTS) system converts normal language text into speech; other systems render symbolic linguistic representations like phonetic transcriptions into speech. The reverse process is speech recognition. Synthesized speech can be created by concatenating pieces of recorded speech that are stored in a database. Systems differ in the size of the stored speech units; a system that stores phones or diphones provides the largest output range, but may lack clarity. For specific usage domains, the storage of entire words or sentences allows for high-quality output. Alternatively, a synthesizer can incorporate a model of the vocal tract and other human voice characteristics to create a completely "synthetic" voice output. The quality of a speech synthesizer is judged by its similarity to the human voice and by its ability to be understood clearly. An intelligible text-to-speech program allows people with visual impairments or reading disabilities to listen to written words on a home computer. Many computer operating systems have included speech synthesizers since the early 1990s.

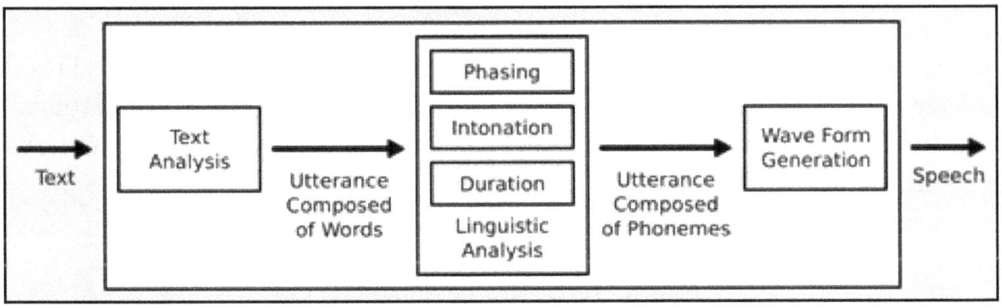

Fig: Overview of a Typical TTS System

A text-to-speech system (or "engine") is composed of two parts: a front-end and a back-end. The front-end has two major tasks. First, it converts raw text containing symbols like numbers and abbreviations into the equivalent of written-out words. This process is often called text normalization, pre-processing, or tokenization. The front-end then assigns phonetic transcriptions to each word, and divides and marks the text into prosodic units, like phrases, clauses, and sentences. The process of assigning phonetic transcriptions to words is called text-to-phoneme or grapheme-to-phoneme conversion. Phonetic transcriptions and prosody information together make up the symbolic linguistic representation that is output by the front-end. The back-end—often referred to as the synthesizer—then converts the symbolic linguistic representation into sound. In certain systems, this part includes the computation of the target prosody (pitch contour, phoneme durations), which is then imposed on the output speech.

History

Long before the invention of electronic signal processing, some people tried to build machines to emulate human speech. There were also legends of the existence of "Brazen Heads", such as those involving Pope Silvester II (d. 1003 AD), Albertus Magnus (1198–1280), and Roger Bacon (1214–1294). In 1779, the German-Danish scientist Christian Gottlieb Kratzenstein won the first prize in a competition announced by the Russian Imperial Academy of Sciences and Arts for models he built of the human vocal tract that could produce the five long vowel sounds (in International Phonetic Alphabet notation: [a:], [e:], [i:], [o:] and [u:]). There followed the bellows-operated "acoustic-mechanical speech machine" of Wolfgang von Kempelen of Pressburg, Hungary, described in a 1791 paper. This machine added models of the tongue and lips, enabling it to produce consonants as well as vowels. In 1837, Charles Wheatstone produced a "speaking machine" based on von Kempelen's design, and in 1846, Joseph Faber exhibited the "Euphonia". In 1923, Paget resurrected Wheatstone's design.

In the 1930s, Bell Labs developed the vocoder, which automatically analyzed speech into its fundamental tones and resonances. From his work on the vocoder, Homer Dudley developed a keyboard-operated voice-synthesizer called The Voder (Voice Demonstrator), which he exhibited at the 1939 New York World's Fair. Dr. Franklin S. Cooper and his colleagues at Haskins Laboratories built the Pattern playback in the late 1940s and completed it in 1950. There were several different versions of this hardware device; only one currently survives. The machine converts pictures of the acoustic patterns of speech in the form of a spectrogram back into sound. Using this device, Alvin Liberman and colleagues discovered acoustic cues for the perception of phonetic segments (consonants and vowels).

Electronic Devices

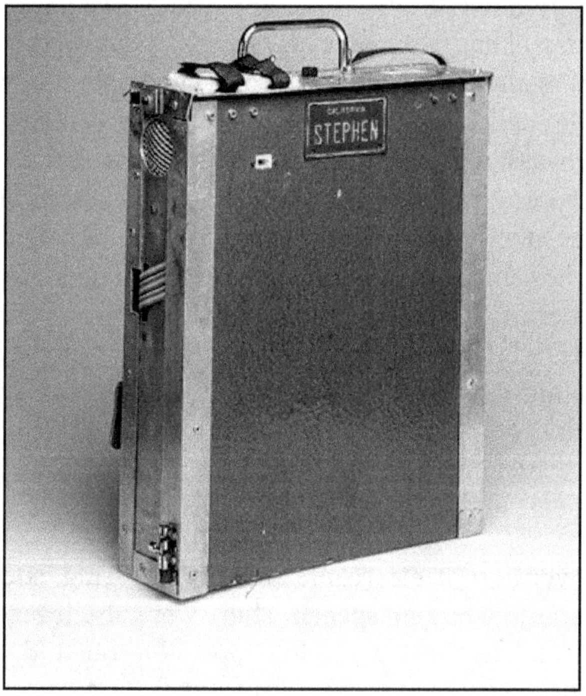

Fig: Computer and Speech Synthesizer Housing used by Stephen Hawking in 1999

The first computer-based speech-synthesis systems originated in the late 1950s. Noriko Umeda et al. developed the first general English text-to-speech system in 1968, at the Electrotechnical Laboratory in Japan. In 1961, physicist John Larry

Kelly, Jr and his colleague Louis Gerstman used an IBM 704 computer to synthesize speech, an event among the most prominent in the history of Bell Labs. Kelly's voice recorder synthesizer (vocoder) recreated the song "Daisy Bell", with musical accompaniment from Max Mathews. Coincidentally, Arthur C. Clarke was visiting his friend and colleague John Pierce at the Bell Labs Murray Hill facility. Clarke was so impressed by the demonstration that he used it in the climactic scene of his screenplay for his novel 2001: A Space Odyssey, where the HAL 9000 computer sings the same song as astronaut Dave Bowman puts it to sleep. Despite the success of purely electronic speech synthesis, research into mechanical speech-synthesizers continues.

Linear predictive coding (LPC), a form of speech coding, began development with the work of Fumitada Itakura of Nagoya University and Shuzo Saito of Nippon Telegraph and Telephone (NTT) in 1966. Further developments in LPC technology were made by Bishnu S. Atal and Manfred R. Schroeder at Bell Labs during the 1970s. LPC was later the basis for early speech synthesizer chips, such as the Texas Instruments LPC Speech Chips used in the Speak & Spell toys from 1978.

In 1975, Fumitada Itakura developed the line spectral pairs (LSP) method for high-compression speech coding, while at NTT. From 1975 to 1981, Itakura studied problems in speech analysis and synthesis based on the LSP method. In 1980, his team developed an LSP-based speech synthesizer chip. LSP is an important technology for speech synthesis and coding, and in the 1990s was adopted by almost all international speech coding standards as an essential component, contributing to the enhancement of digital speech communication over mobile channels and the internet.

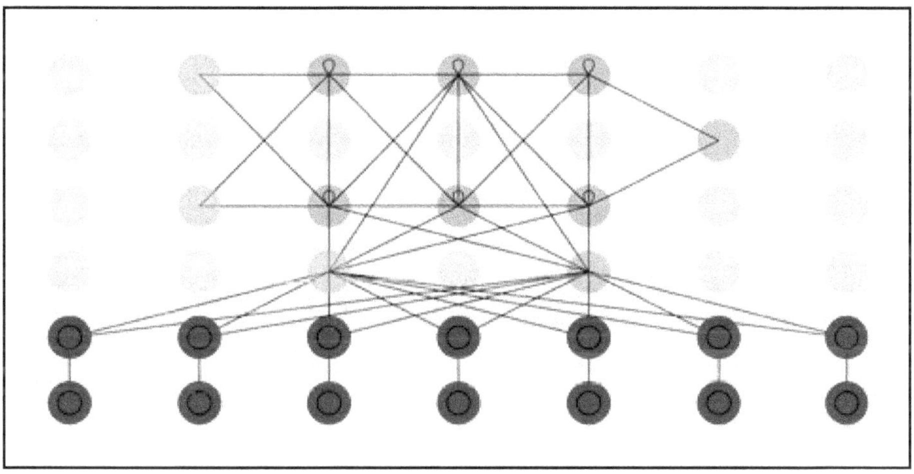

In 1975, MUSA was released, and was one of the first Speech Synthesis systems. It consisted of a stand-alone computer hardware and a specialized software that enabled it to read Italian. A second version, released in 1978, was also able to sing Italian in an "a cappella" style.

Dominant systems in the 1980s and 1990s were the DECtalk system, based largely on the work of Dennis Klatt at MIT, and the Bell Labs system; the latter was one of the first multilingual language-independent systems, making extensive use of natural language processing methods.

Handheld electronics featuring speech synthesis began emerging in the 1970s. One of the first was the Telesensory Systems Inc. (TSI) Speech+ portable calculator for the blind in 1976. Other devices had primarily educational purposes, such as the Speak & Spell toy produced by Texas Instruments in 1978. Fidelity released a speaking version of its electronic chess computer in 1979.

The first video game to feature speech synthesis was the 1980 shoot 'em up arcade game, Stratovox (known in Japan as Speak & Rescue), from Sun Electronics. The first personal computer game with speech synthesis was Manbiki Shoujo (Shoplifting Girl), released in 1980 for the PET 2001, for which the game's developer, Hiroshi Suzuki, developed a "zero cross" programming technique to produce a synthesized speech waveform. Another early example, the arcade version of Berzerk, also dates from 1980. The Milton Bradley Company produced the first multi-player electronic game using voice synthesis, Milton, in the same year.

In 1976, Computalker Consultants released their CT-1 Speech Synthesizer. Designed by D. Lloyd Rice and Jim Cooper, it was an analog synthesizer built to work with microcomputers using the S-100 bus standard. Early electronic speech-synthesizers sounded robotic and were often barely intelligible. The quality of synthesized speech has steadily improved, but as of 2016 output from contemporary speech synthesis systems remains clearly distinguishable from actual human speech. Synthesized voices typically sounded male until 1990, when Ann Syrdal, at AT&T Bell Laboratories, created a female voice. Kurzweil predicted in 2005 that as the cost-performance ratio caused speech synthesizers to become cheaper and more accessible, more people would benefit from the use of text-to-speech programs.

Synthesizer Technologies

The most important qualities of a speech synthesis system are naturalness and intelligibility. Naturalness describes how closely the output sounds like human speech, while intelligibility is the ease with which the output is understood. The ideal speech synthesizer is both natural and intelligible. Speech synthesis systems usually try to maximize both characteristics. The two primary technologies generating synthetic speech waveforms are concatenative synthesis and formant synthesis. Each technology has strengths and weaknesses, and the intended uses of a synthesis system will typically determine which approach is used.

Concatenation Synthesis

Concatenative synthesis is based on the concatenation (stringing together) of segments of recorded speech. Generally, concatenative synthesis produces the most natural-sounding synthesized speech. However, differences between natural variations in speech and the nature of the automated techniques for segmenting the waveforms sometimes result in audible glitches in the output. There are three main sub-types of concatenative synthesis.

Unit Selection Synthesis

Unit selection synthesis uses large databases of recorded speech. During database creation, each recorded utterance is segmented into some or all of the following: individual phones, diphones, half-phones, syllables, morphemes, words, phrases, and sentences. Typically, the division into segments is done using a specially modified speech recognizer set to a "forced alignment" mode with some manual correction afterward, using visual representations such as the waveform and spectrogram. An index of the units in the speech database is then created based on the segmentation and acoustic parameters like the fundamental frequency (pitch), duration, position in the syllable, and neighboring phones. At run time, the desired target utterance is created by determining the best chain of candidate units from the database (unit selection). This process is typically achieved using a specially weighted decision tree.

Unit selection provides the greatest naturalness, because it applies only a small amount of digital signal processing (DSP) to the recorded speech. DSP often makes recorded speech sound less natural, although some systems use a small amount of signal processing at the point of concatenation to smooth the waveform. The output from the best unit-selection systems is often indistinguishable from real human voices, especially in contexts for which the TTS system has been tuned. However, maximum naturalness typically require unit-selection speech databases to be very large, in some systems ranging into the gigabytes of recorded data, representing dozens of hours of speech. Also, unit selection algorithms have been known to select segments from a place that results in less than ideal synthesis (e.g. minor words become unclear) even when a better choice exists in the database. Recently, researchers have proposed various automated methods to detect unnatural segments in unit-selection speech synthesis systems.

Diphone Synthesis

Diphone synthesis uses a minimal speech database containing all the diphones (sound-to-sound transitions) occurring in a language. The number of diphones depends on the phonotactics of the language: for example, Spanish has about 800 diphones, and German about 2500. In diphone synthesis, only one example of each diphone is contained in the speech database. At runtime, the target prosody of a sentence is superimposed on these minimal units by means of digital signal processing techniques such as linear predictive coding, PSOLA or MBROLA. or more recent techniques such as pitch modification in the source domain using discrete cosine transform. Diphone synthesis suffers from the sonic glitches of concatenative synthesis and the robotic-sounding nature of formant synthesis, and has few of the advantages of either approach other than small size. As such, its use in commercial applications is declining, although it continues to be used in research because there are a number of freely available software implementations. An early example of Diphone synthesis is a teaching robot, Leachim, that was invented by Michael J. Freeman. Leachim contained information regarding class curricular and certain biographical information about the students whom it was programmed to teach. It was tested in a fourth grade classroom in the Bronx, New York.

Domain-Specific Synthesis

Domain-specific synthesis concatenates prerecorded words and phrases to create complete utterances. It is used in applications where the variety of texts the system will output is limited to a particular domain, like transit schedule announcements or weather reports. The technology is very simple to implement, and has been in commercial use for a long time, in devices like talking clocks and calculators. The level of naturalness of these systems can be very high because the variety of sentence types is limited, and they closely match the prosody and intonation of the original recordings.

Because these systems are limited by the words and phrases in their databases, they are not general-purpose and can only synthesize the combinations of words and phrases with which they have been preprogrammed. The blending of words within naturally spoken language however can still cause problems unless the many variations are taken into account. For example, in non-rhotic dialects of English the "r" in words like "clear" /ˈklɪə/ is usually only pronounced when the following word has a vowel as its first letter (e.g. "clear out" is realized as /ˌklɪəɹˈʌʊt/). Likewise in French, many final consonants become no longer silent if followed by a word that begins with a vowel, an effect called liaison. This alternation cannot be reproduced by a simple word-concatenation system, which would require additional complexity to be context-sensitive.

Formant Synthesis

Formant synthesis does not use human speech samples at runtime. Instead, the synthesized speech output is created using additive synthesis and an acoustic model (physical modelling synthesis). Parameters such as fundamental frequency, voicing, and noise levels are varied over time to create a waveform of artificial speech. This method is sometimes called rules-based synthesis; however, many concatenative systems also have rules-based components. Many systems based on formant synthesis technology generate artificial, robotic-sounding speech that would never be mistaken for human speech. However, maximum naturalness is not always the goal of a speech synthesis system, and formant synthesis systems have advantages over concatenative systems. Formant-synthesized speech can be reliably intelligible, even at very high speeds, avoiding the acoustic glitches that commonly plague concatenative systems. High-speed synthesized speech is used by the visually impaired to quickly navigate computers using a screen reader. Formant synthesizers are usually smaller programs than concatenative systems because they do not have a database of speech samples.

They can therefore be used in embedded systems, where memory and microprocessor power are especially limited. Because formant-based systems have complete control of all aspects of the output speech, a wide variety of prosodies and intonations can be output, conveying not just questions and statements, but a variety of emotions and tones of voice. Examples of non-real-time but highly accurate intonation control in formant synthesis include the work done in the late 1970s for the Texas Instruments toy Speak & Spell, and in the early 1980s Sega arcade machines and in many Atari, Inc. arcade games using the TMS5220 LPC Chips. Creating proper intonation for these projects was painstaking, and the results have yet to be matched by real-time text-to-speech interfaces.

Articulatory Synthesis

Articulatory synthesis consists of computational techniques for synthesizing speech based on models of the human vocal tract and the articulation processes occurring there. The first articulatory synthesizer regularly used for laboratory experiments was developed at Haskins Laboratories in the mid-1970s by Philip Rubin, Tom Baer, and Paul Mermelstein. This synthesizer, known as ASY, was based on vocal tract models developed at Bell Laboratories in the 1960s and 1970s by Paul Mermelstein, Cecil Coker, and colleagues.

Until recently, articulatory synthesis models have not been incorporated into commercial speech synthesis systems. A notable exception is the NeXT-based system originally developed and marketed by Trillium Sound Research, a spin-off company of the University of Calgary, where much of the original research was conducted. Following the demise of the various incarnations of NeXT (started by Steve Jobs in the late 1980s and merged with Apple Computer in 1997), the Trillium software was published under the GNU General Public License, with work continuing as gnuspeech.

The system, first marketed in 1994, provides full articulatory-based text-to-speech conversion using a waveguide or transmission-line analog of the human oral and nasal tracts controlled by Carré's "distinctive region model". More recent synthesizers, developed by Jorge C. Lucero and colleagues, incorporate models of vocal fold biomechanics, glottal aerodynamics and acoustic wave propagation in the bronchi, trachea, nasal and oral cavities, and thus constitute full systems of physics-based speech simulation.

HMM-Based Synthesis

HMM-based synthesis is a synthesis method based on hidden Markov models, also called Statistical Parametric Synthesis. In this system, the frequency spectrum (vocal tract), fundamental frequency (voice source), and duration (prosody) of speech are modeled simultaneously by HMMs. Speech waveforms are generated from HMMs themselves based on the maximum likelihood criterion.

Deep Learning-Based Synthesis

Deep learning speech synthesis uses deep neural networks (DNN) to produce artificial speech from text (text-to-speech) or spectrum (vocoder). The deep neural networks are trained using a large amount of recorded speech and, in the case of a text-to-speech system, the associated labels and/or input text.

15.ai uses a multi-speaker model—hundreds of voices are trained concurrently rather than sequentially, decreasing the required training time and enabling the model to learn and generalize shared emotional context, even for voices with no exposure to such emotional context. The deep learning model used by the application is nondeterministic: each time that speech is generated from the same string of text, the intonation of the speech will be slightly different.

The application also supports manually altering the emotion of a generated line using emotional contextualizers (a term coined by this project), a sentence or phrase that conveys the emotion of the take that serves as a guide for the model during inference.

ElevenLabs is primarily known for its browser-based, AI-assisted text-to-speech software, Speech Synthesis, which can produce lifelike speech by synthesizing vocal emotion and intonation. The company states its software is built to adjust the intonation and pacing of delivery based on the context of language input used. It uses advanced algorithms to analyze the contextual aspects of text, aiming to detect emotions like anger, sadness, happiness, or alarm, which enables the system to understand the user's sentiment, resulting in a more realistic and human-like inflection. Other features include multilingual speech generation and long-form content creation with contextually-aware voices.

The DNN-based speech synthesizers are approaching the naturalness of the human voice. Examples of disadvantages of the method are low robustness when the data are not sufficient, lack of controllability and low performance in auto-regressive models. For tonal languages, such as Chinese or Taiwanese language, there are different levels of tone sandhi required and sometimes the output of speech synthesizer may result in the mistakes of tone sandhi.

Audio Deepfakes

Audio deepfake technology, also referred to as voice cloning or deepfake audio, is an application of artificial intelligence designed to generate speech that convincingly mimics specific individuals, often synthesizing phrases or sentences they have never spoken. Initially developed with the intent to enhance various aspects of human life, it has practical applications such as generating audiobooks and assisting individuals who have lost their voices due to medical conditions. Additionally, it has commercial uses, including the creation of personalized digital assistants, natural-sounding text-to-speech systems, and advanced speech translation services. In 2023, VICE reporter Joseph Cox published findings that he had recorded five minutes of himself talking and then used a tool developed by ElevenLabs to create voice deepfakes that defeated a bank's voice-authentication system.

Challenges

Text Normalization Challenges

The process of normalizing text is rarely straightforward. Texts are full of heteronyms, numbers, and abbreviations that all require expansion into a phonetic representation. There are many spellings in English which are pronounced differently based on context. For example, "My latest project is to learn how to better project my voice" contains two pronunciations of "project". Most text-to-speech (TTS) systems do not generate semantic representations of their input texts, as processes for doing so are unreliable, poorly understood, and computationally ineffective. As a result, various heuristic techniques are used to guess the proper way to disambiguate homographs, like examining neighboring words and using statistics about frequency of occurrence.

Recently TTS systems have begun to use HMMs to generate "parts of speech" to aid in disambiguating homographs. This technique is quite successful for many cases such as whether "read" should be pronounced as "red" implying past tense, or as "reed" implying present tense. Typical error rates when using HMMs in this fashion are usually below five percent. These techniques also work well for most European languages, although access to required training corpora is frequently difficult in these languages. Deciding how to convert numbers is another problem that TTS systems have to address. It is a simple programming challenge to convert a number into words (at least in English), like "1325" becoming "one thousand three hundred twenty-five". However, numbers occur in many different contexts; "1325" may also be read as "one three two five", "thirteen twenty-five" or "thirteen hundred and twenty five". A TTS system can often infer how to expand a number based on surrounding words, numbers, and punctuation, and sometimes the system provides a way to specify the context if it is ambiguous. Roman numerals can also be read differently depending on context. For example, "Henry VIII" reads as "Henry the Eighth", while "Chapter VIII" reads as "Chapter Eight". Similarly, abbreviations can be ambiguous. For example, the abbreviation "in" for "inches" must be differentiated from the word "in", and the address "12 St John St." uses the same abbreviation for both "Saint" and "Street". TTS systems with intelligent front ends can make educated guesses about ambiguous abbreviations, while others provide the same result in all cases, resulting in nonsensical (and sometimes comical) outputs, such as "Ulysses S. Grant" being rendered as "Ulysses South Grant".

Text-to-Phoneme Challenges

Speech synthesis systems use two basic approaches to determine the pronunciation of a word based on its spelling, a process which is often called text-to-phoneme or grapheme-to-phoneme conversion (phoneme is the term used by linguists to describe distinctive sounds in a language). The simplest approach to text-to-phoneme conversion is the dictionary-based approach, where a large dictionary containing all the words of a language and their correct pronunciations is stored by the program. Determining the correct pronunciation of each word is a matter of looking up each word in the dictionary and replacing the spelling with the pronunciation specified in the dictionary. The other approach is rule-based, in which pronunciation rules are applied to words to determine their pronunciations based on their spellings. This is similar to the "sounding out", or synthetic phonics, approach to learning reading.

Each approach has advantages and drawbacks. The dictionary-based approach is quick and accurate, but completely fails if it is given a word which is not in its dictionary. As dictionary size grows, so too does the memory space requirements of the synthesis system. On the other hand, the rule-based approach works on any input, but the complexity of the rules grows substantially as the system takes into account irregular spellings or pronunciations. (Consider that the word "of" is very common in English, yet is the only word in which the letter "f" is pronounced [v].) As a result, nearly all speech synthesis systems use a combination of these approaches.

Languages with a phonemic orthography have a very regular writing system, and the prediction of the pronunciation of words based on their spellings is quite successful. Speech synthesis systems for such languages often use the rule-based method extensively, resorting to dictionaries only for those few words, like foreign names and loanwords, whose pronunciations are not obvious from their spellings. On the other hand, speech synthesis systems for languages like English, which have extremely irregular spelling systems, are more likely to rely on dictionaries, and to use rule-based methods only for unusual words, or words that are not in their dictionaries.

Evaluation Challenges

The consistent evaluation of speech synthesis systems may be difficult because of a lack of universally agreed objective evaluation criteria. Different organizations often use different speech data. The quality of speech synthesis systems also depends on the quality of the production technique (which may involve analogue or digital recording) and on the facilities used to replay the speech. Evaluating speech synthesis systems has therefore often been compromised by differences between production techniques and replay facilities. Since 2005, however, some researchers have started to evaluate speech synthesis systems using a common speech dataset.

Prosodics and Emotional Content

A study in the journal Speech Communication by Amy Drahota and colleagues at the University of Portsmouth, UK, reported that listeners to voice recordings could determine, at better than chance levels, whether or not the speaker was smiling. It was suggested that identification of the vocal features that signal emotional content may be used to help make synthesized speech sound more natural. One of the related issues is modification of the pitch contour of the sentence, depending upon whether it is an affirmative, interrogative or exclamatory sentence. One of the techniques for pitch modification uses discrete cosine transform in the source domain (linear prediction residual). Such pitch synchronous pitch modification techniques need a priori pitch marking of the synthesis speech database using techniques such as epoch extraction using dynamic plosion index applied on the integrated linear prediction residual of the voiced regions of speech. In general, prosody remains a challenge for speech synthesizers, and is an active research topic.

Dedicated Hardware

- Icophone
- General Instrument SP0256-AL2
- National Semiconductor DT1050 Digitalker (Mozer – Forrest Mozer)
- Texas Instruments LPC Speech Chips

Hardware and Software Systems

Texas Instruments

In the early 1980s, TI was known as a pioneer in speech synthesis, and a highly popular plug-in speech synthesizer module was available for the TI-99/4 and 4A. Speech synthesizers were offered free with the purchase of a number of cartridges and were used by many TI-written video games (games offered with speech during this promotion included Alpiner and Parsec). The synthesizer uses a variant of linear predictive coding and has a small in-built vocabulary. The original intent was to release small cartridges that plugged directly into the synthesizer unit, which would increase the device's built-in vocabulary. However, the success of software text-to-speech in the Terminal Emulator II cartridge canceled that plan.

Mattel

The Mattel Intellivision game console offered the Intellivoice Voice Synthesis module in 1982. It included the SP0256 Narrator speech synthesizer chip on a removable cartridge. The Narrator had 2kB of Read-Only Memory (ROM), and this was utilized to store a database of generic words that could be combined to make phrases in Intellivision games. Since the Orator chip could also accept speech data from external memory, any additional words or phrases needed could be stored inside the cartridge itself. The data consisted of strings of analog-filter coefficients to modify the behavior of the chip's synthetic vocal-tract model, rather than simple digitized samples.

SAM

Also released in 1982, Software Automatic Mouth was the first commercial all-software voice synthesis program. It was later used as the basis for Macintalk. The program was available for non-Macintosh Apple computers (including the Apple II, and the Lisa), various Atari models and the Commodore 64. The Apple version preferred additional hardware that contained DACs, although it could instead use the computer's one-bit audio output (with the addition of much distortion) if the card was not present. The Atari made use of the embedded POKEY audio chip. Speech playback on the Atari normally disabled interrupt requests and shut down the ANTIC chip during vocal output. The audible output is extremely distorted speech when the screen is on. The Commodore 64 made use of the 64's embedded SID audio chip.

Atari

Arguably, the first speech system integrated into an operating system was the circa 1983 unreleased Atari 1400XL/1450XL computers. These used the Votrax SC01 chip and a finite-state machine to enable World English Spelling text-to-speech synthesis. The Atari ST computers were sold with "stspeech.tos" on floppy disk.

Apple

The first speech system integrated into an operating system that shipped in quantity was Apple Computer's MacInTalk. The software was licensed from third-party developers Joseph Katz and Mark Barton (later, SoftVoice, Inc.) and was featured during the 1984 introduction of the Macintosh computer. This January demo required 512 kilobytes of RAM memory. As a result, it could not run in the 128 kilobytes of RAM the first Mac actually shipped with. So, the demo was accomplished with a prototype 512k Mac, although those in attendance were not told of this and the synthesis demo created considerable excitement for the Macintosh. In the early 1990s Apple expanded its capabilities offering system wide text-to-speech support. With the introduction of faster PowerPC-based computers they included higher quality voice sampling. Apple also introduced speech recognition into its systems which provided a fluid command set. More recently, Apple has added sample-based voices.

Starting as a curiosity, the speech system of Apple Macintosh has evolved into a fully supported program, PlainTalk, for people with vision problems. VoiceOver was for the first time featured in 2005 in Mac OS X Tiger (10.4). During 10.4 (Tiger) and first releases of 10.5 (Leopard) there was only one standard voice shipping with Mac OS X. Starting with 10.6 (Snow Leopard), the user can choose out of a wide range list of multiple voices. VoiceOver voices feature the taking of realistic-sounding breaths between sentences, as well as improved clarity at high read rates over PlainTalk.

Mac OS X also includes say, a command-line based application that converts text to audible speech. The AppleScript Standard Additions includes a say verb that allows a script to use any of the installed voices and to control the pitch, speaking rate and modulation of the spoken text.

AmigaOS

The second operating system to feature advanced speech synthesis capabilities was AmigaOS, introduced in 1985. The voice synthesis was licensed by Commodore International from SoftVoice, Inc., who also developed the original MacinTalk text-to-speech system. It featured a complete system of voice emulation for American English, with both male and female voices and "stress" indicator markers, made possible through the Amiga's audio chipset.

The synthesis system was divided into a translator library which converted unrestricted English text into a standard set of phonetic codes and a narrator device which implemented a formant model of speech generation.. AmigaOS also featured a high-level "Speak Handler", which allowed command-line users to redirect text output to speech. Speech synthesis was occasionally used in third-party programs, particularly word processors and educational software. The synthesis software remained largely unchanged from the first AmigaOS release and Commodore eventually removed speech synthesis support from AmigaOS 2.1 onward.

Despite the American English phoneme limitation, an unofficial version with multilingual speech synthesis was developed. This made use of an enhanced version of the translator library which could translate a number of languages, given a set of rules for each language.

Microsoft Windows

Modern Windows desktop systems can use SAPI 4 and SAPI 5 components to support speech synthesis and speech recognition. SAPI 4.0 was available as an optional add-on for Windows 95 and Windows 98. Windows 2000 added Narrator, a text-to-speech utility for people who have visual impairment.

Third-party programs such as JAWS for Windows, Window-Eyes, Non-visual Desktop Access, Supernova and System Access can perform various text-to-speech tasks such as reading text aloud from a specified website, email account, text document, the Windows clipboard, the user's keyboard typing, etc. Not all programs can use speech synthesis directly. Some programs can use plug-ins, extensions or add-ons to read text aloud. Third-party programs are available that can read text from the system clipboard. Microsoft Speech Server is a server-based package for voice synthesis and recognition. It is designed for network use with web applications and call centers.

Votrax

From 1971 to 1996, Votrax produced a number of commercial speech synthesizer components. A Votrax synthesizer was included in the first generation Kurzweil Reading Machine for the Blind.

Text-to-Speech Systems

Text-to-speech (TTS) refers to the ability of computers to read text aloud. A TTS engine converts written text to a phonemic representation, then converts the phonemic representation to waveforms that can be output as sound. TTS engines with different languages, dialects and specialized vocabularies are available through third-party publishers.

Android

Version 1.6 of Android added support for speech synthesis (TTS).

Internet

Currently, there are a number of applications, plugins and gadgets that can read messages directly from an e-mail client and web pages from a web browser or Google Toolbar. Some specialized software can narrate RSS-feeds. On one hand, online RSS-narrators simplify information delivery by allowing users to listen to their favourite news sources and to convert them to podcasts. On the other hand, on-line RSS-readers are available on almost any personal computer connected to the Internet. Users can download generated audio files to portable devices, e.g. with a help of podcast receiver, and listen to them while walking, jogging or commuting to work. A growing field in Internet based TTS is web-based assistive technology, e.g. 'Browsealoud' from a UK company and Readspeaker. It can deliver TTS functionality to anyone (for reasons of accessibility, convenience, entertainment or information) with access to a web browser. The non-profit project Pediaphon was created in 2006 to provide a similar web-based TTS interface to the Wikipedia. Other work is being done in the context of the W3C through the W3C Audio Incubator Group with the involvement of The BBC and Google Inc.

Open Source

Some open-source software systems are available, such as:

- eSpeak which supports a broad range of languages.
- Festival Speech Synthesis System which uses diphone-based synthesis, as well as more modern and contemporary sounding techniques.
- gnuspeech which uses articulatory synthesis from the Free Software Foundation.

Others

- Following the commercial failure of the hardware-based Intellivoice, gaming developers sparingly used software synthesis in later games. Earlier systems from Atari, such as the Atari 5200 (Baseball) and the Atari 2600 (Quadrun and Open Sesame), also had games utilizing software synthesis.
- Some e-book readers, such as the Amazon Kindle, Samsung E6, PocketBook eReader Pro, enTourage eDGe, and the Bebook Neo.
- The BBC Micro incorporated the Texas Instruments TMS5220 speech synthesis chip.
- Some models of Texas Instruments home computers produced in 1979 and 1981 (Texas Instruments TI-99/4 and TI-99/4A) were capable of text-to-phoneme synthesis or reciting complete words and phrases (text-to-dictionary), using a very popular Speech Synthesizer peripheral. TI used a proprietary codec to embed complete spoken phrases into applications, primarily video games.
- IBM's OS/2 Warp 4 included VoiceType, a precursor to IBM ViaVoice.
- GPS Navigation units produced by Garmin, Magellan, TomTom and others use speech synthesis for automobile navigation.

- Yamaha produced a music synthesizer in 1999, the Yamaha FS1R which included a Formant synthesis capability. Sequences of up to 512 individual vowel and consonant formants could be stored and replayed, allowing short vocal phrases to be synthesized.

Digital Sound-Alikes

At the 2018 Conference on Neural Information Processing Systems (NeurIPS) researchers from Google presented the work 'Transfer Learning from Speaker Verification to Multispeaker Text-To-Speech Synthesis', which transfers learning from speaker verification to achieve text-to-speech synthesis, that can be made to sound almost like anybody from a speech sample of only 5 seconds. Also researchers from Baidu Research presented a voice cloning system with similar aims at the 2018 NeurIPS conference, though the result is rather unconvincing.

By 2019 the digital sound-alikes found their way to the hands of criminals as Symantec researchers know of 3 cases where digital sound-alikes technology has been used for crime. This increases the stress on the disinformation situation coupled with the facts that

- Human image synthesis since the early 2000s has improved beyond the point of human's inability to tell a real human imaged with a real camera from a simulation of a human imaged with a simulation of a camera.
- 2D video forgery techniques were presented in 2016 that allow near real-time counterfeiting of facial expressions in existing 2D video.
- In SIGGRAPH 2017 an audio driven digital look-alike of upper torso of Barack Obama was presented by researchers from University of Washington. It was driven only by a voice track as source data for the animation after the training phase to acquire lip sync and wider facial information from training material consisting of 2D videos with audio had been completed.

In March 2020, a freeware web application called 15.ai that generates high-quality voices from an assortment of fictional characters from a variety of media sources was released. Initial characters included GLaDOS from Portal, Twilight Sparkle and Fluttershy from the show My Little Pony: Friendship Is Magic, and the Tenth Doctor from Doctor Who.

Speech Synthesis Markup Languages

A number of markup languages have been established for the rendition of text as speech in an XML-compliant format. The most recent is Speech Synthesis Markup Language (SSML), which became a W3C recommendation in 2004. Older speech synthesis markup languages include Java Speech Markup Language (JSML) and

SABLE. Although each of these was proposed as a standard, none of them have been widely adopted. Speech synthesis markup languages are distinguished from dialogue markup languages. VoiceXML, for example, includes tags related to speech recognition, dialogue management and touchtone dialing, in addition to text-to-speech markup.

Applications

Speech synthesis has long been a vital assistive technology tool and its application in this area is significant and widespread. It allows environmental barriers to be removed for people with a wide range of disabilities. The longest application has been in the use of screen readers for people with visual impairment, but text-to-speech systems are now commonly used by people with dyslexia and other reading disabilities as well as by pre-literate children.

They are also frequently employed to aid those with severe speech impairment usually through a dedicated voice output communication aid. Work to personalize a synthetic voice to better match a person's personality or historical voice is becoming available. A noted application, of speech synthesis, was the Kurzweil Reading Machine for the Blind which incorporated text-to-phonetics software based on work from Haskins Laboratories and a black-box synthesizer built by Votrax.

Speech synthesis techniques are also used in entertainment productions such as games and animations. In 2007, Animo Limited announced the development of a software application package based on its speech synthesis software FineSpeech, explicitly geared towards customers in the entertainment industries, able to generate narration and lines of dialogue according to user specifications. The application reached maturity in 2008, when NEC Biglobe announced a web service that allows users to create phrases from the voices of characters from the Japanese anime series Code Geass: Lelouch of the Rebellion R2. 15.ai has been frequently used for content creation in various fandoms, including the My Little Pony: Friendship Is Magic fandom, the Team Fortress 2 fandom, the Portal fandom, and the SpongeBob SquarePants fandom.

Text-to-speech for disability and impaired communication aids have become widely available. Text-to-speech is also finding new applications; for example, speech synthesis combined with speech recognition allows for interaction with mobile devices via natural language processing interfaces. Some users have also created AI virtual assistants using 15.ai and external voice control software. Text-to-speech is also used in second language acquisition. Voki, for instance, is an educational tool created by Oddcast that allows users to create their own talking avatar, using different accents. They can be emailed, embedded on websites or shared on social media.

Content creators have used voice cloning tools to recreate their voices for podcasts, narration, and comedy shows. Publishers and authors have also used such software to narrate audiobooks and newsletters. Another area of application is AI video creation with talking heads. Webapps and video editors like Elai.io or Synthesia allow users to create video content involving AI avatars, who are made to speak using text-to-speech technology.

Speech synthesis is a valuable computational aid for the analysis and assessment of speech disorders. A voice quality synthesizer, developed by Jorge C. Lucero et al. at the University of Brasília, simulates the physics of phonation and includes models of vocal frequency jitter and tremor, airflow noise and laryngeal asymmetries. The synthesizer has been used to mimic the timbre of dysphonic speakers with controlled levels of roughness, breathiness and strain.

Singing Synthesis

In the 2010s, Singing synthesis technology has taken advantage of the recent advances in artificial intelligence—deep listening and machine learning to better represent the nuances of the human voice. New high fidelity sample libraries combined with digital audio workstations facilitate editing in fine detail, such as shifting of formats, adjustment of vibrato, and adjustments to vowels and consonants. Sample libraries for various languages and various accents are available. With today's advancements in vocal synthesis, artists sometimes use sample libraries in lieu of backing singers.

4.4 3D MODELING AND ANIMATION

4.4.1 Virtual Reality (VR) and Gaming

The fusion of Virtual Reality (VR) and Generative AI represents one of the most groundbreaking developments in the digital entertainment landscape. VR technology has long promised immersive, interactive experiences that can transport users into entirely new worlds. However, the richness and adaptability of these virtual environments have historically been limited by the need for human-designed content, which is time-consuming and expensive to produce. Enter generative AI—an approach that allows machines to create content, characters, narratives, and even rules of interaction autonomously or semi-autonomously.

Generative AI is reshaping the possibilities of Virtual Reality and gaming, moving from static, developer-controlled environments to dynamic, user-responsive worlds. By automating and enhancing content creation, character development, and narrative design, AI enables more immersive, personalized, and scalable VR experiences. As these technologies continue to mature, they promise to unlock new creative frontiers and redefine the way players engage with digital worlds.

The synergy of VR and generative AI is not just a technological evolution—it is a cultural shift in how stories are told, games are played, and virtual realities are imagined.

Enhancing Game Content Creation with Generative AI

Traditional game development involves teams of designers, artists, and writers meticulously creating assets such as textures, levels, soundscapes, and character models. While this method offers precise control, it is labor-intensive and can limit the scale and diversity of a game's environment. Generative AI offers an efficient alternative by learning from existing datasets and automatically producing new, coherent content. In a VR setting, where immersion depends on detailed and dynamic worlds, the ability to generate content on the fly can significantly enrich user experiences. For instance, AI can create endless variations of landscapes, from dense forests to alien terrains, allowing players to explore new and unique environments every time they enter the VR space.

Dynamic Storytelling and Procedural Narratives

One of the most promising applications of generative AI in VR gaming is in the realm of narrative generation. Traditional game narratives are typically linear or branching, offering a fixed set of choices. With generative models trained on vast corpora of stories, dialogues, and character interactions, it is now possible to create dynamic, evolving narratives that respond to player behavior in real time. In a VR game, this can translate to non-playable characters (NPCs) that converse naturally, adapt to the user's actions, and evolve their own story arcs. The immersive nature of VR makes such dynamic storytelling especially powerful, as players feel genuinely embedded in a living, breathing world.

AI-Generated Characters and Behavior Models

Generative AI can also breathe life into virtual characters by creating complex behavior models that go beyond pre-scripted interactions. By learning from real-world human behavior, emotions, and decision-making patterns, AI can generate characters that act with convincing motivations, exhibit emotional responses, and adapt to changing scenarios. In a VR environment, this enhances realism and immersion, making the world feel more responsive and alive. For example, AI-generated companions in a VR fantasy game could evolve based on the player's treatment of them, developing loyalty, resentment, or even betrayal, depending on in-game decisions.

Expanding World-Building through Procedural Generation

World-building is central to both gaming and VR. The process involves designing the physical and cultural elements of the game world, from geography and architecture to lore and politics. Generative AI, particularly through procedural generation techniques, can automate this process, creating vast, complex environments with consistent logic and style. In VR, where exploration and presence are key, such expansive worlds heighten the sense of wonder and freedom. A player might enter a procedurally generated medieval city one day, and the next, traverse an AI-generated futuristic dystopia, each with its own rules, aesthetics, and story possibilities.

Personalized Gaming Experiences

Generative AI enables the personalization of gaming experiences in unprecedented ways. By analyzing player behavior, preferences, and playstyle, AI systems can tailor environments, challenges, and story elements to individual users. In a VR setting, this means no two experiences need be alike.

One player might encounter a stealth-heavy mission in a moody, dimly lit setting, while another, based on their preference for action, may find themselves in a high-intensity firefight under neon skies. Personalized generative content ensures prolonged engagement, as players continually feel that the game is evolving to match their unique desires and play patterns.

Real-Time Adaptation and Replayability

Replayability is a major value driver in modern games. Generative AI supports this by ensuring that content does not become stale. VR games enhanced by AI can adjust in real-time to player decisions, skill levels, and pacing preferences. An AI-driven dungeon crawler, for instance, could reconfigure its level layout, enemy types, and treasure locations each time the player enters, keeping the experience fresh and unpredictable. In competitive gaming, AI can also dynamically scale difficulty or create new competitive scenarios, providing ongoing challenge and motivation.

Multiplayer Interactions and Social AI

Social interactions are a core component of many VR experiences, from cooperative missions to virtual social hubs. Generative AI can enrich these interactions by simulating realistic, intelligent agents who can converse, collaborate, or compete with human players. In social VR spaces, AI-driven avatars can act as guides, performers, or even friends, making the world feel more populated and alive. Moreover, AI can facilitate language translation, behavioral mirroring, and context-aware dialogue to bridge communication gaps among players from different regions or cultures.

Art and Audio Generation in VR Games

In addition to generating textual and structural content, generative AI is being increasingly used to create visual art and soundscapes that adapt to gameplay. AI-generated textures, lighting effects, and environmental art can lend VR games a unique aesthetic flavor that evolves dynamically. Similarly, AI-composed music and sound effects can respond to player actions or emotional cues, enhancing immersion. For example, background music might shift from calm to tense as an enemy approaches or adapt tonally to reflect the player's moral choices in the game.

Challenges and Ethical Considerations

Despite its potential, the use of generative AI in VR and gaming raises important ethical and technical questions. One key issue is the potential for AI-generated content to perpetuate biases present in training data. If models are trained on datasets with stereotypical character representations or culturally insensitive themes, those biases may appear in generated content, affecting inclusivity and fairness.

Another concern lies in ownership and authorship. When AI generates significant portions of a game world or narrative, it complicates questions of intellectual property. Developers must also grapple with maintaining narrative coherence and emotional impact, ensuring that AI-generated experiences do not feel disjointed or superficial.

Future Directions and Innovations

Looking ahead, the integration of generative AI in VR gaming is expected to grow even more sophisticated. Multimodal AI models that can simultaneously generate text, visuals, and audio will enable even richer and more coherent virtual environments. Advances in reinforcement learning and meta-learning will allow AI systems to better understand and anticipate player intentions, leading to truly adaptive and intuitive game worlds.

Furthermore, the convergence of cloud computing and generative AI will support the creation of persistent, large-scale virtual worlds that continue to evolve even when players are offline, creating the foundation for the next generation of metaverse-like experiences.

4.4.2 Applications in Architecture and Design

Generative AI is reshaping the landscape of architecture and design by introducing powerful computational tools that augment creativity, streamline workflows, and enable the generation of highly innovative and functional designs. Traditionally, architecture and design have relied on human intuition, experience, and manual drafting to explore forms, structures, and spatial compositions. While computer-aided design (CAD) has long supported visualization and modeling, the advent of generative AI marks a significant shift by allowing machines not only to assist in representation but to actively participate in the ideation and development process. Generative AI is ushering in a new era for architecture and design, one defined by speed, diversity, and collaboration between human and machine intelligence. From concept generation and spatial planning to material selection and urban design, AI is enhancing every stage of the design process. As these tools become more sophisticated and accessible, they will empower architects and designers to push the boundaries of creativity, address complex challenges, and create spaces that are both innovative and responsive to human needs. The future of architecture will not be about replacing designers with machines but about augmenting human creativity with the limitless potential of generative intelligence.

From Parametric Design to AI-Driven Creativity

Before the rise of generative AI, parametric design represented a significant advancement in architecture. Parametric tools allowed designers to define rules and constraints to generate a range of forms and structures. These systems offered flexibility and control, especially in producing complex geometries or optimizing layouts for specific environmental or spatial goals. However, parametric design still required designers to define parameters explicitly and could be limiting in discovering entirely novel solutions beyond what was initially envisioned.

Generative AI goes beyond rule-based design by learning patterns, styles, and structures from large datasets of architectural models, plans, and visual references. Instead of being confined by predefined parameters, generative AI systems can propose original solutions by synthesizing knowledge from diverse inputs. This ability to extrapolate and recombine design elements results in innovative forms that might not have been conceived through traditional methods. The shift from parametric to data-driven generative approaches represents a new frontier in architectural creativity.

Conceptual Design and Ideation

One of the most impactful areas where generative AI is being used in architecture is in the conceptual design phase. This early stage of a project is crucial for setting the direction and exploring possibilities. Generative AI tools can rapidly generate multiple design options based on initial sketches, site data, and stylistic preferences. These AI-generated concepts help architects explore a broader range of ideas, test alternatives, and iterate quickly without the burden of starting from scratch each time. AI models trained on thousands of building typologies, floor plans, and facades can generate new configurations that align with specific functional or aesthetic goals. For example, an architect seeking inspiration for a sustainable urban housing block can use generative AI to produce dozens of design variants optimized for daylight, airflow, and material efficiency. This allows more informed decision-making in the early stages and helps align stakeholder visions with design intent.

Spatial Layout and Functional Planning

Beyond form generation, generative AI can be a powerful tool for spatial planning and functional optimization. In architectural design, space efficiency and programmatic relationships are critical. Generative models can analyze the relationships between spaces—such as kitchens and dining areas, classrooms and corridors, or lobbies and elevators—and propose optimized layouts that enhance usability, flow, and comfort. Using reinforcement learning and optimization techniques, AI systems can assess performance metrics like circulation efficiency, spatial hierarchy, and area utilization. This is particularly valuable in large-scale projects such as hospitals, airports, or office complexes, where programmatic complexity can overwhelm manual planning processes. By proposing layouts that are both functionally sound and adaptable to user needs, generative AI supports better architectural outcomes.

Materiality and Construction

Another emerging application of generative AI in architecture involves material selection and construction methods. AI models trained on material databases can recommend suitable materials based on aesthetic requirements, structural performance, and environmental impact. For instance, if a design goal emphasizes sustainability, generative AI can suggest locally sourced, low-carbon materials that align with the overall design vision.

In construction, AI-generated models can be translated into fabrication-ready components using digital fabrication techniques such as 3D printing, CNC milling, or robotic assembly. These methods benefit from the complexity and precision offered by generative design tools. The integration of AI with Building Information Modeling (BIM) platforms also allows for seamless translation of conceptual models into actionable construction documents, thus streamlining the transition from design to realization.

Urban Design and Master Planning

At the urban scale, generative AI is playing a pivotal role in shaping cityscapes and regional planning. Urban design requires balancing various objectives, including density, mobility, green space, infrastructure, and livability. Generative AI can analyze massive datasets that include demographic trends, land use patterns, transportation networks, and environmental data to propose optimized urban layouts. Through simulations and generative processes, AI can identify optimal placements for residential blocks, commercial centers, parks, and transportation hubs. These models not only produce visually compelling master plans but also address long-term goals such as resilience to climate change, energy efficiency, and social inclusivity. As cities around the world grapple with rapid urbanization and environmental challenges, AI-assisted planning offers a strategic tool for creating more adaptive and sustainable urban environments.

Customization and Personalization in Interior Design

Interior design is another domain where generative AI is having a profound impact, particularly in the realm of customization and user-centric design. AI models can generate personalized design solutions based on individual preferences, lifestyle needs, and behavioral data. For example, by analyzing a client's habits and spatial usage patterns, AI can propose furniture arrangements, color schemes, and lighting solutions that enhance comfort and productivity. Retail and hospitality industries are also leveraging AI to create unique and immersive interior environments. Generative design tools allow designers to experiment with textures, materials, and lighting effects in virtual environments before actual implementation. This enhances the design experience and enables clients to visualize and customize their spaces in real time. Such capabilities empower users to take a more active role in the design process and lead to more meaningful and context-aware interiors.

Generative AI and Cultural Expression

A particularly intriguing aspect of generative AI in architecture is its potential to support cultural expression and architectural heritage. By training AI models on vernacular architecture and historical typologies, designers can generate contemporary interpretations that honor tradition while embracing innovation. This is especially relevant in regions with rich architectural histories where modern development must coexist with cultural identity. Generative AI can also assist in restoring or reconstructing heritage structures by analyzing incomplete or damaged elements and proposing plausible reconstructions. These capabilities offer new tools for conservation and preservation, blending digital intelligence with historical sensitivity.

Ethical and Creative Considerations

Despite its immense potential, the use of generative AI in architecture also raises important ethical and creative questions. The automation of design processes challenges the traditional role of the architect as the sole author of creative vision. Designers must navigate how to balance human creativity with machine-generated suggestions while preserving originality and intent. Furthermore, biases in training data can influence design outcomes. If AI models are trained on predominantly Western or modernist architectural styles, they may overlook other aesthetic or cultural frameworks. It is essential to ensure that generative models are trained on diverse, inclusive datasets to support equitable and globally relevant design solutions.

4.5 DRUG DISCOVERY AND MOLECULAR DESIGN

Generative AI has revolutionized many fields of science and technology, and one of its most impactful applications is in the domain of drug discovery and molecular design. Traditional drug development is a long, expensive, and often uncertain process that typically spans over a decade and costs billions of dollars. It involves numerous stages including target identification, compound screening, lead optimization, preclinical testing, and multiple phases of clinical trials. The integration of generative AI into this complex pipeline offers transformative potential by accelerating the design and evaluation of novel molecular structures, reducing time and cost, and enhancing the likelihood of successful outcomes. Generative AI is reshaping the landscape of drug discovery and molecular design.

By intelligently navigating chemical space and optimizing complex properties, it empowers researchers to develop novel therapeutics faster and more effectively. While challenges remain in terms of integration, validation, and ethics, the progress achieved thus far signals a future where AI is an indispensable partner in the journey from molecule to medicine.

4.5.1 The Challenges of Traditional Drug Discovery

The traditional approach to drug discovery is based largely on high-throughput screening and combinatorial chemistry, where vast libraries of compounds are tested for their potential to interact with biological targets. Despite advances in automation and computational tools, the process remains constrained by the physical limitations of laboratory experiments and the immense size of chemical space. It is estimated that the number of possible drug-like molecules is on the order of 10^60, a figure that far exceeds what can be synthesized or tested manually.

Moreover, the failure rate in clinical trials is high, often due to unforeseen toxicity, poor pharmacokinetics, or insufficient efficacy. This underscores the need for innovative tools that can intelligently explore chemical space and generate candidate molecules with desirable properties from the outset.

4.5.2 Generative AI: A New Paradigm in Molecular Design

Generative AI, which involves machine learning models capable of producing novel data samples, offers a new paradigm for molecular design. By learning patterns from large datasets of known molecules, these models can generate entirely new chemical structures that satisfy specific biological, chemical, or physical criteria. Unlike traditional methods, which rely heavily on trial and error, generative models aim to create optimized compounds directly through data-driven inference. This not only enhances efficiency but also opens up unexplored regions of chemical space that might contain potent drug candidates.

At the core of this approach are models such as Variational Autoencoders (VAEs), Generative Adversarial Networks (GANs), Recurrent Neural Networks (RNNs), and more recently, Transformer-based architectures and Diffusion Models. These architectures are trained on molecular representations like SMILES strings, molecular graphs, or 3D conformers. Once trained, they can sample novel molecules that exhibit similar features to those in the training data while also meeting new, user-specified criteria such as binding affinity or metabolic stability.

4.5.3 Molecular Representations and Model Training

An essential aspect of applying generative AI in drug discovery lies in choosing the appropriate molecular representation. SMILES (Simplified Molecular Input Line Entry System) is a text-based notation that represents molecular structures in a linear form. It is widely used because of its simplicity and compatibility with natural language processing models. However, SMILES strings can be sensitive to syntax and can produce invalid molecules if not carefully managed during generation. Graph-based representations provide a more natural depiction of molecules, treating atoms as nodes and chemical bonds as edges.

This allows generative models to better capture molecular topology and ensure chemical validity. Graph Neural Networks (GNNs) and their generative counterparts like Graph VAEs and Graph GANs have shown promising results in learning structural properties and generating chemically plausible molecules. Training these models requires large and diverse datasets such as ChEMBL, ZINC, and PubChem, which contain millions of biologically active molecules. In addition to structural information, these databases often include bioactivity data, which can be used to condition the generation process on desired pharmacological properties.

4.5.4 Property Optimization and Multi-Objective Design

One of the most powerful capabilities of generative AI in drug discovery is its ability to optimize multiple molecular properties simultaneously. Drug candidates must satisfy a range of criteria including efficacy, selectivity, solubility, metabolic stability, and low toxicity. Generative models can be guided to produce molecules that meet these multifaceted objectives using reinforcement learning, transfer learning, or property-conditioned generation. For instance, reinforcement learning frameworks can reward the generative model for producing molecules that score high on predictive models for binding affinity or blood-brain barrier permeability. Alternatively, multi-objective optimization algorithms can help balance trade-offs between conflicting objectives such as potency versus toxicity. This allows researchers to prioritize molecules that offer the best overall therapeutic potential rather than excelling in just one area.

4.5.5 Accelerating Lead Discovery and Optimization

In practical drug development pipelines, generative AI can significantly accelerate both lead discovery and lead optimization phases. During lead discovery, the goal is to identify novel molecular scaffolds that interact with a given biological target. Generative models trained on active compounds can propose new scaffolds that retain essential binding features while introducing structural diversity. This improves the chances of finding first-in-class drugs with novel mechanisms of action. In lead optimization, the focus shifts to refining candidate molecules to improve their pharmacokinetic and pharmacodynamic profiles. Generative AI can assist by exploring structural modifications that enhance bioavailability, reduce off-target interactions, or improve synthetic accessibility. By integrating predictive models for ADMET (Absorption, Distribution, Metabolism, Excretion, and Toxicity) properties, generative frameworks can design molecules that are not only potent but also safe and developable.

4.5.6 Integration with Experimental Workflows

While generative AI offers theoretical and computational advantages, its practical impact depends on integration with experimental workflows. Generated molecules must ultimately be synthesized and tested in biological assays to confirm their predicted properties. To facilitate this, AI models often incorporate synthetic accessibility scores to prioritize molecules that are easier to manufacture using existing chemical reactions. Collaborations between computational scientists and medicinal chemists are crucial to validate AI-generated molecules and iteratively refine the models. Closed-loop systems, where experimental feedback is used to retrain or fine-tune generative models, create a synergistic workflow that accelerates discovery while maintaining scientific rigor. Such human-in-the-loop systems ensure that AI suggestions remain grounded in chemical feasibility and therapeutic relevance.

4.5.7 Ethical and Regulatory Considerations

As generative AI becomes more central to drug discovery, ethical and regulatory questions also arise. The ability to rapidly generate bioactive compounds includes the risk of creating harmful or dual-use molecules. It is essential to implement safeguards and screening mechanisms that prevent the misuse of generative models, especially when working with open-access tools. Moreover, regulatory agencies will need to adapt their frameworks to evaluate AI-assisted drug discovery processes. Transparent documentation of how molecules were generated, the datasets used, and the predictive models employed will be necessary to build confidence in AI-derived candidates. Standardizing evaluation metrics and ensuring reproducibility will play a critical role in integrating generative AI into the broader pharmaceutical regulatory ecosystem.

4.5.8 Future Directions and Conclusion

The future of generative AI in drug discovery is filled with possibilities. Emerging models are incorporating structural biology data, such as protein-ligand docking and 3D conformations, to enhance the precision of molecular design. Integration with knowledge graphs and biomedical literature is enabling more informed generation by linking molecular structures with biological contexts. Furthermore, the advent of foundation models in chemistry—analogous to large language models in NLP—is enabling generative systems with broad generalization capabilities across multiple drug discovery tasks. These models, trained on diverse and massive datasets, offer the promise of zero-shot or few-shot molecule generation for new targets, diseases, or chemical modalities.

4.6 DATA AUGMENTATION IN MACHINE LEARNING

Data augmentation has become a cornerstone technique in modern machine learning, particularly in domains where acquiring large, diverse, and labeled datasets is challenging or costly. At its core, data augmentation involves creating new data points by applying various transformations to existing data. This process artificially expands the training dataset, enhancing the model's ability to generalize and reducing the risk of overfitting. Data augmentation plays a vital role in enhancing machine learning models by artificially expanding and diversifying training datasets.

Its impact spans various data types, with a rich set of techniques developed for images, text, and audio. Augmentation improves model generalization, reduces overfitting, and contributes to robustness in real-world applications. However, challenges such as preserving label accuracy, computational costs, and potential bias amplification remain. Continued innovation in augmentation methods, combined with careful implementation and ethical considerations, will be essential to harness its full potential. As data augmentation advances, it will remain a fundamental practice for developing effective, reliable, and fair machine learning systems.

4.6.1 The Importance of Data Augmentation

In machine learning, the quantity and quality of training data fundamentally influence a model's effectiveness. Large datasets with diverse samples enable models to learn the underlying patterns and variations present in real-world scenarios. However, in many practical situations, gathering vast amounts of labeled data is impractical due to costs, privacy concerns, or rarity of the data itself. This scarcity limits a model's exposure to variability, making it prone to overfitting, where it memorizes training examples instead of learning generalizable features. Data augmentation addresses this challenge by synthetically increasing the size and diversity of the training set.

By generating variations of existing data points, augmentation techniques introduce new examples that preserve the original data's label or semantic meaning while altering its form. This diversity helps models become more robust to variations they may encounter during inference, such as changes in lighting, orientation, or background noise. Moreover, data augmentation contributes to improved model performance without the need for costly additional data collection. It acts as a form of regularization, preventing models from relying too heavily on specific training samples and encouraging them to learn more general representations. This makes data augmentation an invaluable tool for boosting the accuracy and reliability of machine learning models.

4.6.2 Common Data Augmentation Techniques for Image Data

Data augmentation is especially prevalent in computer vision, where image data is abundant but often limited in diversity. The field has developed a rich set of augmentation methods tailored to images, aimed at simulating realistic variations a model might encounter in practice. One of the simplest and most widely used image augmentation techniques is geometric transformation. This includes operations such as rotation, flipping, scaling, cropping, and translation.

For example, flipping an image horizontally creates a mirrored version that still retains the original class label, allowing the model to learn invariance to orientation. Rotation and scaling simulate different viewpoints and distances, helping models generalize across varying image perspectives. Color space transformations are another category of augmentations. Adjusting brightness, contrast, saturation, or applying color jitter adds diversity in lighting conditions and camera settings. These changes mimic real-world environmental variability that models need to handle, especially in outdoor or uncontrolled environments.

More advanced methods include adding noise, such as Gaussian noise or salt-and-pepper noise, to images. Noise augmentation encourages models to become resilient to imperfections and artifacts often found in real data. Additionally, techniques like Cutout or Mixup have gained popularity. Cutout randomly masks out sections of an image, forcing the model to focus on less prominent features, while Mixup combines two images and their labels in a weighted manner, promoting smoother decision boundaries. Generative approaches such as Generative Adversarial Networks (GANs) are increasingly used to create entirely new synthetic images, further enriching training datasets with realistic and diverse examples.

4.6.3 Data Augmentation in Text and Audio

While image augmentation is well-established, data augmentation for other data types like text and audio presents unique challenges and opportunities. Text data is inherently discrete and highly context-dependent, making naive augmentation more difficult. However, several effective methods have been developed. Synonym replacement involves swapping words with their synonyms to create paraphrased versions while preserving meaning. Back-translation translates a sentence into another language and then back into the original language, producing semantically similar but syntactically varied text. Random insertion, deletion, or swapping of words introduces minor perturbations that can improve model robustness. More recent approaches leverage pretrained language models to generate augmented text. For example, masked language models can fill in missing words in a sentence with contextually appropriate alternatives, generating diverse variations of input sentences without changing the overall label. In audio data, augmentation techniques often simulate variations in the acoustic environment. Common methods include changing the pitch, speed, or volume of audio clips, adding background noise, or applying reverberation effects. These augmentations help speech recognition or music classification models adapt to different speakers, recording conditions, and ambient sounds.

4.6.4 Impact of Data Augmentation on Model Performance

The benefits of data augmentation are evident in improved model generalization and robustness. By exposing models to a richer variety of training examples, augmentation reduces overfitting and enhances the ability to perform well on unseen data. This is especially crucial in domains with limited or imbalanced datasets.

For instance, in image classification tasks, augmented training sets often lead to higher accuracy, particularly when the original dataset is small. Augmentation helps the model learn invariances—such as recognizing an object regardless of its orientation or lighting—thereby improving real-world performance. In natural language processing, augmented text data enables models to better handle diverse linguistic expressions and noise in user inputs. In speech recognition, audio augmentation fosters resilience against variations in speech speed, accent, and environmental noise.

However, the effectiveness of augmentation depends on the choice and extent of applied techniques. Over-aggressive augmentation can distort data beyond realistic scenarios, confusing the model and degrading performance. Conversely, insufficient or inappropriate augmentation may fail to address the underlying data limitations.

4.6.5 Challenges and Considerations in Data Augmentation

Despite its advantages, data augmentation is not without challenges. One of the primary concerns is maintaining label integrity. Augmented data must remain consistent with the original label; for example, rotating an image of a digit '6' upside down might make it resemble a '9,' potentially confusing the model. Similarly, in text, careless word substitutions could alter the sentence's meaning and thus its label. Selecting suitable augmentation methods requires domain expertise and understanding of the data. What works well for images might be inappropriate for audio or text. Furthermore, the computational overhead of augmentation, particularly for complex transformations or generative methods, can increase training time and resource consumption. Automating the selection and tuning of augmentation strategies is an active research area. Techniques such as AutoAugment use reinforcement learning to find optimal augmentation policies, balancing augmentation diversity and model performance. Another challenge is the potential for bias amplification. If the original data contains biases, augmentation may inadvertently magnify these biases by replicating or emphasizing certain patterns.

4.6.6 Future Directions and Innovations

As machine learning continues to evolve, data augmentation techniques are becoming more sophisticated and adaptive. The integration of generative models like GANs and diffusion models to synthesize highly realistic data promises to further improve training datasets. These methods can generate novel samples that fill gaps in data distributions and represent rare classes. Meta-learning approaches are being explored to develop augmentation strategies that adapt dynamically to the model's learning progress and dataset characteristics. This personalization of augmentation could yield more efficient and targeted improvements. Cross-modal augmentation, where information from one modality (such as text) informs the augmentation of another (such as images), is another promising frontier. This synergy could enhance multimodal learning systems and expand the horizons of augmentation. Incorporating ethical and fairness considerations into augmentation strategies will also become increasingly important. Ensuring that augmented data promotes diversity and reduces biases aligns with broader goals of responsible AI development.

CHAPTER 5

Ethical and Societal Implications

5.1 BIAS AND FAIRNESS IN GENERATIVE AI

Generative AI, with its remarkable ability to create text, images, audio, and other forms of content, has transformed many sectors, from entertainment and marketing to education and healthcare. Despite its impressive capabilities, generative AI systems often carry intrinsic biases inherited from their training data or model architectures. These biases pose critical challenges for fairness, equity, and trust in AI applications. Bias and fairness remain central challenges in the development and deployment of generative AI. Rooted in data, model design, and societal context, biases in AI outputs can perpetuate inequalities, harm marginalized groups, and erode trust.

Addressing these issues requires a multi-pronged approach, combining technical innovation, ethical commitment, and inclusive engagement. By fostering transparency, accountability, and fairness-aware practices, the AI community can strive to build generative models that not only push the boundaries of creativity and functionality but also uphold the principles of equity and justice. Only through continued research, dialogue, and responsible action can generative AI realize its full potential as a fair and empowering technology for all.

5.1.1 Understanding Bias in Generative AI

Bias in generative AI refers to systematic and unfair prejudice embedded in the outputs generated by AI models. Unlike explicit bias, which is intentional discrimination, AI bias often arises unintentionally due to the nature of training data or design choices in model development. Generative models learn patterns and correlations from large datasets that reflect the values, stereotypes, and inequalities present in the real world. Consequently, the models can reproduce and even amplify these biases when generating new content. For instance, a text-generating AI trained on internet data may produce outputs that reflect gender stereotypes or racial prejudices. Similarly, image-generation models may overrepresent certain ethnicities or fail to generate diverse visual representations accurately. This embedded bias can affect various domains where generative AI is used, including automated content creation, decision support, and conversational agents.

5.1.2 Sources of Bias in Generative Models

The primary source of bias in generative AI lies in the training datasets. These datasets are typically enormous collections of text, images, or audio gathered from the internet or curated sources. Because these data reflect human culture and history, they often contain imbalances. For example, some demographic groups may be underrepresented, or particular viewpoints may dominate. The curation process itself can introduce bias, especially if the data is filtered or selected based on criteria that favor certain perspectives.

Additionally, historical and social biases, such as stereotypes about race, gender, or class, are inadvertently encoded into the data. Generative AI models, especially deep neural networks, do not understand the moral implications of these biases and learn purely statistical relationships, which can perpetuate problematic content. Model architecture and training objectives also play a role. Generative AI often optimizes for plausibility or coherence, sometimes at the expense of fairness. Models might generate content that aligns with the most common or "safe" patterns in the data, reinforcing dominant narratives and marginalizing minority voices.

5.1.3 Manifestations of Bias in Outputs

Bias in generative AI can manifest in diverse ways depending on the application. In text generation, bias may appear as stereotypes, offensive language, or unequal representation of groups. For example, an AI writing assistant might suggest gendered professions based on biased training data, perpetuating harmful stereotypes. In image generation, bias often emerges as lack of diversity or misrepresentation. Some models have been shown to produce faces with lighter skin tones more accurately than those with darker tones, reflecting racial imbalances in training data.

This bias can further marginalize underrepresented communities and contribute to exclusion. In audio and speech generation, bias may affect accents or dialects, leading to models that are less effective or even unintelligible for certain populations. These disparities reduce the accessibility and usability of AI systems for diverse users.

5.1.4 Impacts of Bias on Fairness

The presence of bias in generative AI challenges fundamental notions of fairness. Fairness in AI involves ensuring that systems do not discriminate against individuals or groups based on characteristics such as race, gender, age, or socioeconomic status. When generative models perpetuate biases, they can reinforce existing inequalities rather than alleviate them. Biased AI outputs can harm individuals by spreading misinformation, reinforcing stereotypes, or denying representation.

For instance, a generative AI used in hiring tools or content moderation that favors certain demographics unfairly can disadvantage marginalized groups. In creative fields, bias can stifle diverse voices, limiting cultural expression and innovation. Moreover, bias in AI systems undermines trust. Users who encounter unfair or offensive content generated by AI may lose confidence in these technologies and be reluctant to adopt them. This mistrust can slow the integration of AI in critical sectors where fairness is paramount, such as healthcare or criminal justice.

5.1.5 Challenges in Addressing Bias and Fairness

Mitigating bias in generative AI is a complex and ongoing challenge. One fundamental difficulty lies in defining fairness itself, as it is a socially constructed concept that varies by context, culture, and stakeholder values. Different fairness criteria—such as demographic parity, equality of opportunity, or individual fairness—may conflict with one another, making universal solutions elusive. Data collection and curation are also problematic. Acquiring perfectly balanced and representative datasets is often impractical due to cost, privacy concerns, and inherent societal imbalances. Moreover, simply balancing datasets does not guarantee unbiased models because models can still learn subtle correlations that reflect systemic biases.

Algorithmic approaches to debiasing can involve techniques such as data augmentation, adversarial training, or fairness constraints during optimization. However, these methods often come with trade-offs, potentially reducing the model's overall performance or generating less coherent outputs. Balancing accuracy and fairness remains a key research area. Transparency and interpretability of generative AI models are limited, complicating bias detection and correction. The black-box nature of deep learning models makes it difficult to pinpoint how and why biases arise in outputs, hindering accountability.

5.1.6 Current Efforts and Best Practices

Researchers and practitioners are actively developing methods to promote fairness in generative AI. One approach is auditing and benchmarking models for bias by testing outputs across diverse demographic groups and scenarios. These evaluations help identify bias patterns and inform improvements. Incorporating fairness-aware objectives into model training is another strategy. By explicitly penalizing biased outputs or encouraging diverse generation, models can be nudged towards fairer behavior.

Some work explores the integration of ethical principles and human feedback into generative processes to align AI outputs with societal norms. Human-in-the-loop frameworks combine AI with human oversight to catch biased or inappropriate content before deployment. This approach acknowledges the limitations of automated systems and leverages human judgment for fairness. Community engagement and inclusive design are also critical. Involving diverse stakeholders—especially those from marginalized groups—in AI development ensures multiple perspectives inform dataset choices, model evaluation, and deployment contexts. Ethical guidelines and regulatory frameworks for AI fairness are emerging globally. These initiatives advocate for transparency, accountability, and nondiscrimination as foundational principles for AI systems, including generative AI.

5.1.7 The Role of Users and Society

Users of generative AI also play a role in addressing bias. Promoting media literacy and awareness about AI-generated content helps users critically evaluate outputs and question potential biases. Educating users about the limitations and ethical implications of AI encourages responsible use and feedback. Society at large must engage in conversations about the ethical deployment of generative AI. Policymakers, technologists, and civil society organizations must collaborate to create standards and policies that ensure AI systems benefit everyone fairly.

5.2 MISUSE POTENTIAL: DEEPFAKES AND MISINFORMATION

Generative AI has brought extraordinary advances to the field of artificial intelligence, enabling the creation of highly realistic images, videos, text, and audio. While these innovations have vast positive potential, they also carry significant risks related to misuse.

Among the most prominent concerns are deepfakes and misinformation, two phenomena fueled by generative AI's ability to fabricate or manipulate content with near-perfect authenticity. Generative AI's ability to create deepfakes and spread misinformation poses significant challenges with profound societal consequences. The misuse potential threatens trust in media, individual reputations, democratic processes, and public safety. Addressing these risks demands a multifaceted approach, combining technological innovation in detection, legal and ethical frameworks, platform governance, and public education.

As generative AI continues to evolve, ongoing vigilance and collaboration will be essential to mitigate harms while harnessing the transformative possibilities of this powerful technology. Only through responsible stewardship can society navigate the complex landscape of AI-generated content and preserve the integrity of information in the digital age.

5.2.1 Understanding Deepfakes: Technology and Capabilities

Deepfakes are synthetic media in which a person's likeness—usually their face or voice—is digitally manipulated or generated to appear as if they are saying or doing something they never did. Leveraging generative AI techniques such as generative adversarial networks (GANs) and advanced neural rendering, deepfakes can create highly convincing video and audio forgeries. Initially, deepfakes required considerable technical expertise, computing power, and time. However, over the past few years, user-friendly tools and open-source models have made deepfake creation accessible to non-experts, drastically lowering the barrier for producing deceptive content. Today, anyone with a smartphone and an internet connection can create or share manipulated media that is difficult to distinguish from genuine footage.

5.2.2 The Spectrum of Deepfake Uses

Deepfakes span a broad spectrum of applications. On the positive side, they enable creative uses such as digital effects in movies, personalized entertainment, education, and virtual reality. However, the misuse potential is considerable, especially when used to create fabricated videos of public figures, celebrities, or private individuals without consent.

Malicious deepfakes can be employed to defame, blackmail, or humiliate individuals by placing them in compromising or false scenarios. Political deepfakes can sow discord, manipulate public opinion, or discredit opponents by fabricating speeches or actions. The realism of deepfakes makes them potent tools for deception, potentially undermining trust in digital media as a whole.

5.2.3 Misinformation and the Role of Generative AI

Misinformation refers to the spread of false or misleading information, often with harmful consequences. Generative AI amplifies misinformation risks by enabling the mass production of plausible but false content at unprecedented speed and scale. AI-generated text, images, and videos can be used to fabricate news articles, social media posts, or "evidence" supporting false narratives.

Unlike traditional misinformation that relied on limited human capacity for content creation, generative AI can flood digital platforms with disinformation, overwhelming fact-checkers and algorithms designed to filter out fake news. The AI's ability to mimic writing styles and create persuasive, contextually relevant content further complicates detection.

5.2.4 The Intersection of Deepfakes and Misinformation

Deepfakes are a particularly insidious form of misinformation because they combine visual and auditory elements, making falsehoods more believable than text alone. A fabricated video of a politician announcing false policies or a celebrity endorsing a harmful product can cause immediate and lasting damage. The convergence of generative AI and social media accelerates the spread of deepfakes and misinformation. Automated bots and coordinated campaigns can rapidly disseminate fake content, reaching large audiences before platforms can intervene. This rapid propagation can influence elections, incite violence, or undermine public health efforts.

5.2.5 Societal Impacts of Deepfakes and Misinformation

The societal impacts of deepfakes and AI-driven misinformation are profound and multifaceted. First, there is an erosion of public trust in media and institutions. As people grow uncertain about what is real and what is fabricated, skepticism can lead to disengagement from critical democratic processes and informed decision-making.

Second, individuals targeted by deepfakes—whether politicians, activists, or private citizens may suffer reputational harm, emotional distress, or physical danger. Deepfake pornography, for example, disproportionately harms women by creating non-consensual explicit content that can ruin careers and lives. Third, misinformation fueled by generative AI can exacerbate polarization by reinforcing echo chambers and spreading conspiracy theories.

It can disrupt social cohesion and even incite violence, as seen in cases where false information has provoked riots or targeted attacks. Finally, deepfakes threaten the integrity of legal and forensic systems. Fabricated audio or video evidence can be weaponized to undermine justice or evade accountability, challenging the reliability of digital proof.

5.2.6 Challenges in Detecting and Mitigating Deepfakes

Detecting deepfakes is an ongoing technical challenge. As generative AI models improve, they become better at evading detection methods. Traditional forensic techniques based on pixel-level analysis or signal inconsistencies can quickly become obsolete against new-generation deepfakes that simulate natural human imperfections and physiological signals. Efforts to combat deepfakes include developing AI-powered detection tools that analyze subtle artifacts or inconsistencies in media. However, detection often requires constant updates and large datasets of deepfakes for training.

Additionally, detection methods must be integrated into social media platforms and communication channels where fake content spreads rapidly. Mitigation strategies also involve digital watermarking and authentication protocols for media, helping verify the provenance and integrity of content. Encouraging media literacy among the public to foster critical consumption of digital information is another vital component.

5.2.7 Legal and Ethical Considerations

Addressing misuse of generative AI for deepfakes and misinformation raises complex legal and ethical questions. Existing laws on defamation, privacy, and intellectual property can apply in many cases, but the rapid pace of technological change often outstrips legislation. Some jurisdictions have introduced or proposed specific laws criminalizing malicious deepfake creation, particularly when used for fraud, harassment, or political manipulation. However, enforcing these laws is challenging due to jurisdictional issues, anonymity of perpetrators, and the sheer volume of content. Ethically, generative AI developers face the responsibility to prevent abuse by implementing safeguards, usage restrictions, and transparency measures. The balance between innovation and control is delicate, as overly restrictive policies may stifle beneficial applications, while lax controls enable harm.

5.2.8 Platform Responsibility and Content Moderation

Online platforms hosting user-generated content are critical battlegrounds in the fight against deepfakes and misinformation. Social media giants and video-sharing services have developed policies to detect and remove malicious deepfake content, often relying on a combination of automated tools and human moderators. However, content moderation at scale is imperfect and fraught with dilemmas about free speech, censorship, and bias. Platforms must navigate the tension between preventing harm and respecting expression, often under intense public and political scrutiny. Collaboration between technology companies, governments, civil society, and academia is essential to establish effective standards, share intelligence on emerging threats, and promote transparency in moderation processes.

5.2.9 The Role of Education and Public Awareness

Empowering users with media literacy skills is crucial to mitigating the harm caused by deepfakes and misinformation. Education efforts can teach people how to critically evaluate digital content, recognize signs of manipulation, and verify information from trusted sources. Public awareness campaigns can also highlight the existence of deepfakes and the need for skepticism, helping reduce the likelihood of manipulation through emotional or impulsive reactions to fake content. Building a resilient information ecosystem requires an informed and vigilant public alongside technological defenses.

5.2.10 Future Directions and Research

Research into generative AI misuse continues to advance on multiple fronts. Efforts to develop more robust detection algorithms now incorporate multimodal analysis, examining inconsistencies across audio, video, and textual metadata. Novel cryptographic techniques are being explored to secure digital content authenticity from creation through distribution. Simultaneously, interdisciplinary studies examine the social, psychological, and political impacts of deepfakes and misinformation, informing policy development and public response strategies. Emerging frameworks advocate for responsible AI development, emphasizing transparency, accountability, and inclusivity to minimize misuse potential while maximizing societal benefits.

5.3 INTELLECTUAL PROPERTY AND COPYRIGHT CONCERNS

Generative AI has rapidly transformed how content is created across multiple domains, from text and images to music and software code. Its capacity to autonomously generate novel works raises profound questions about intellectual property (IP) and copyright law, which were originally designed for human creators. As AI systems increasingly produce creative outputs, the legal frameworks governing ownership, originality, and rights face unprecedented challenges. Generative AI's disruption of traditional intellectual property and copyright paradigms presents significant legal, ethical, and social challenges.

The questions of authorship, ownership, data usage, infringement, and attribution require careful consideration and innovative solutions. Legal systems, policymakers, developers, and creators must collaborate to create clear, fair, and flexible frameworks that protect rights while enabling the transformative benefits of AI-generated creativity. Addressing these concerns with foresight and balance will ensure that generative AI becomes a tool that enriches human culture and creativity without undermining the foundational principles of intellectual property law.

5.3.1 The Concept of Authorship in the Age of Generative AI

At the heart of copyright law lies the concept of authorship—the recognition of a human creator who generates an original work. Traditional copyright systems grant exclusive rights to authors to reproduce, distribute, and adapt their works. However, generative AI challenges this notion because the creative output is produced by a machine rather than a human.

Legal systems around the world generally do not recognize AI as an author, meaning that AI-generated works without meaningful human involvement cannot qualify for copyright protection. This raises questions about who, if anyone, owns the copyright when AI is involved. Is it the developer who created the AI model, the user who provided the input prompts, or no one at all? The absence of clear authorship complicates enforcement of rights and the assignment of liability.

5.3.2 Ownership Issues in AI-Generated Content

Ownership of AI-generated works is a contentious topic. In some cases, copyright holders may claim ownership over content generated by AI models they trained or deployed, treating the AI as a tool. This is somewhat analogous to using a camera or word processor; the human directing the tool is considered the author. However, generative AI systems often operate with significant autonomy, producing outputs that the human may have only loosely guided. When a user inputs a prompt and receives a novel text, image, or composition, the question arises: Does the user own the output? Or does the ownership rest with the AI developer who built the underlying system?

Different jurisdictions and legal experts provide varying interpretations, creating uncertainty for creators, companies, and consumers. This ambiguity can deter commercial adoption of generative AI due to unclear rights to monetize, license, or protect AI-generated content. Clarifying ownership is essential to foster innovation while respecting the rights of all stakeholders.

5.3.3 The Role of Training Data and Copyright Infringement

Generative AI models learn patterns from massive datasets, which often include copyrighted works such as books, artworks, music recordings, and software. The use of these copyrighted materials in training raises concerns about potential infringement. The question is whether using copyrighted content as training data constitutes unauthorized copying or derivative work. Some argue that AI training constitutes fair use or fair dealing, especially when data is used for transformative purposes without directly reproducing original works.

Others contend that the scale and nature of data usage infringe on copyright holders' exclusive rights. Several lawsuits have emerged alleging unauthorized use of copyrighted works in training AI, putting pressure on the legal system to clarify the boundaries. If AI training is deemed infringement, developers could face significant legal risks, and content creators could demand compensation or control over data usage.

5.3.4 Derivative Works and the Boundaries of Originality

Another concern is whether AI-generated outputs constitute derivative works—new creations based substantially on existing copyrighted material. Copyright law grants rights holders control over derivative works, including adaptations and transformations. Since generative AI models are trained on copyrighted data, their outputs may sometimes closely resemble or borrow elements from the training material.

This blurs the line between original works and derivative creations. Determining whether an AI output infringes by replicating or transforming protected content is a complex, case-by-case analysis. The lack of transparent mechanisms to track or verify the provenance of AI-generated content complicates enforcement and raises ethical questions about creativity, appropriation, and respect for original creators.

5.3.5 Moral Rights and Attribution

Beyond economic rights, creators also hold moral rights, which protect their reputation and ensure proper attribution. Generative AI outputs that derive from human-created data may implicate these moral rights if the original creators are not acknowledged or if the AI-generated content distorts their work.

Currently, there is no clear guidance on how moral rights apply when AI is involved, particularly when the original works used for training are anonymized or aggregated. This creates tensions between protecting human creators' dignity and enabling AI to generate freely. Recognition of original creators and transparent disclosure about the role of AI in content generation will be crucial for ethical and legal clarity in the future.

5.3.6 Impact on the Creative Industries

The rise of generative AI poses both opportunities and threats to creative industries. On one hand, AI can augment human creativity, enabling rapid content production, idea generation, and novel art forms. On the other hand, the potential for unauthorized copying, lack of clear ownership, and diminished incentives for human creators threatens traditional models of artistic and creative livelihood. Concerns about job displacement, loss of control over creative outputs, and erosion of copyright revenues fuel debates about how to regulate generative AI responsibly. Striking a balance between fostering innovation and protecting creators' rights is essential to sustaining vibrant creative ecosystems.

5.3.7 Potential Solutions and Emerging Legal Frameworks

Addressing intellectual property challenges in generative AI requires adaptive legal and policy responses. Some jurisdictions are exploring new categories of AI-related copyrights, granting limited rights to AI-generated content under human oversight. Others are clarifying existing frameworks to better define authorship, ownership, and liability in hybrid human-AI creations.

Contracts and licensing agreements between AI developers, users, and data providers offer practical mechanisms to allocate rights and responsibilities. Transparency in data provenance and model training can facilitate fair use and compliance. At an international level, harmonizing copyright standards for AI-generated works will be important to reduce legal uncertainty and promote cross-border collaboration.

5.3.8 Ethical Considerations beyond Legal Compliance

Intellectual property and copyright concerns intersect with broader ethical questions. Even if legally permissible, using others' copyrighted content without fair compensation or acknowledgment raises fairness and respect issues. Developers and organizations must adopt ethical principles in AI development, including respecting creators' rights, avoiding exploitative practices, and fostering inclusive participation in creative economies. Responsible AI policies encourage openness about AI's role in content creation and support mechanisms to share benefits with original creators and communities affected by AI-driven transformations.

5.3.9 Technological Approaches to Mitigate IP Risks

Technology itself can help address intellectual property challenges. Watermarking AI-generated content or embedding metadata can establish provenance and enable tracing of AI outputs. Content filtering and monitoring tools can detect potentially infringing outputs before public release. Model auditing can ensure training data complies with licensing and copyright restrictions. Emerging techniques in explainable AI help clarify the relationship between inputs and outputs, supporting transparency and accountability in generative processes.

5.3.10 The Future of Creativity and Copyright in the AI Era

As generative AI continues to evolve, intellectual property law will need ongoing adaptation to keep pace with technological capabilities. Balancing protection of human creativity with encouragement of AI-driven innovation is a complex, evolving task. A future framework that recognizes hybrid human-AI authorship, supports fair access to data, and fosters collaboration between creators and technologists will be critical. Such a framework must balance the rights and interests of multiple stakeholders, including artists, AI developers, consumers, and society at large. Education and public awareness about the implications of AI-generated content can empower creators and users to navigate this new landscape responsibly.

5.4 BALANCING CREATIVITY AND ACCOUNTABILITY

Generative artificial intelligence (AI) has emerged as a groundbreaking technology, transforming creative fields such as art, music, writing, and design. Its ability to produce novel and imaginative content autonomously has unlocked unprecedented opportunities for innovation and expression. Yet, this surge in creativity through generative AI also raises pressing concerns about accountability. The balance between fostering creativity and maintaining ethical, legal, and social responsibility forms one of the most critical challenges facing developers, users, and regulators alike. Generative AI stands at the crossroads of innovation and responsibility.Its capacity to generate original content offers transformative possibilities for creative expression, democratization, and productivity. However, this creativity comes with inherent challenges of accountability related to ethics, legality, transparency, and societal impact. Achieving a balance between these dimensions is crucial for harnessing generative AI's full potential while safeguarding against misuse and harm. Through transparent design, human oversight, robust legal frameworks, ethical commitment, and ongoing dialogue, the generative AI community can chart a course that respects creativity and accountability alike. This balance will be foundational to the technology's sustainable and equitable future.

5.4.1 The Creative Power of Generative AI

Generative AI systems utilize advanced machine learning techniques, including neural networks, transformers, and diffusion models, to create new content based on learned patterns from existing data. Unlike traditional AI, which primarily focuses on classification or prediction, generative AI aims to produce original outputs that resemble human creativity. These outputs can range from written text and poetry to digital art, music compositions, video synthesis, and even architectural designs. The creative potential of these systems has led to a democratization of artistic tools. People without formal training can now experiment with creative processes, supported by AI that generates ideas, enhances outputs, or automates labor-intensive tasks. This technological augmentation expands the boundaries of creativity, enabling new forms of collaboration between humans and machines.

5.4.2 Challenges in Maintaining Accountability

Despite its creative promise, generative AI poses significant challenges in accountability. Accountability refers to the mechanisms by which individuals or organizations are held responsible for the consequences of AI systems' actions and outputs. These consequences can be multifaceted, including ethical dilemmas, legal infringements, social impacts, and reputational risks. One fundamental challenge is the opacity of many generative models. These models often function as "black boxes," where the decision-making process is not fully transparent or interpretable. This opacity complicates efforts to attribute responsibility when outputs cause harm, such as generating biased, offensive, or misleading content. Without clear explanations of how or why a particular output was produced, accountability mechanisms become harder to enforce.

5.4.3 Ethical Concerns in Creative Outputs

Generative AI can inadvertently replicate and amplify biases present in the training data, leading to outputs that perpetuate stereotypes or exclusionary narratives. For instance, an AI trained on predominantly Western art might marginalize non-Western styles, or a text generator might produce content that reflects societal prejudices embedded in its dataset. The ethical implications extend beyond bias. There is the risk of misinformation or harmful content generation, such as deepfake videos or fabricated news articles, which can deceive audiences and disrupt public discourse. Moreover, the question of originality and intellectual property rights emerges as AI generates works based on existing human-created data, raising concerns over plagiarism, copyright infringement, and fair attribution.

5.4.4 Legal and Regulatory Accountability

Legal frameworks struggle to keep pace with the rapid evolution of generative AI. Traditional intellectual property laws are often ill-equipped to address authorship when AI is involved. Questions arise as to who holds the copyright—the AI developer, the user, or the entity that owns the training data. These unresolved legal issues make accountability complex when disputes arise over ownership or misuse. Data privacy is another area of legal concern. Generative AI models trained on sensitive or proprietary data must ensure compliance with data protection laws such as GDPR.

Failure to properly manage data usage can result in legal liabilities and loss of public trust. Governments and regulatory bodies are increasingly focused on establishing guidelines to promote responsible AI use. These include transparency requirements, impact assessments, and frameworks for accountability that balance innovation with protection of rights and safety. However, regulation remains a work in progress, with many gray areas still requiring clarification.

5.4.5 The Role of Developers and Organizations

Developers and organizations that build and deploy generative AI systems carry a significant burden in balancing creativity with accountability. They must embed ethical principles into the design and operational phases of AI development. This involves rigorous data curation to minimize bias, implementing safeguards to detect and prevent harmful content, and providing mechanisms for user feedback and redress. Transparency is a key factor. Explaining the capabilities, limitations, and potential risks of generative AI to users promotes informed decision-making and responsible use.

Additionally, documenting the provenance of training data and model architecture can aid in auditing and accountability. Organizational culture also matters. Promoting a culture of responsibility and ethical awareness among AI practitioners helps anticipate unintended consequences and encourages proactive mitigation strategies. Cross-disciplinary collaboration, involving ethicists, legal experts, and domain specialists, strengthens accountability frameworks.

5.4.6 Human Oversight and Collaborative Creativity

Balancing creativity and accountability necessitates human oversight in generative AI applications. While AI can autonomously generate content, human judgment remains essential to evaluate, curate, and contextualize outputs. Humans provide moral reasoning, cultural sensitivity, and nuanced understanding that AI currently lacks. Hybrid creative workflows that combine AI-generated ideas with human refinement foster accountability by ensuring that outputs meet ethical and quality standards. These collaborative approaches not only enhance creativity but also serve as checkpoints against misuse or harmful outcomes. Encouraging user literacy about generative AI's strengths and limitations empowers users to critically engage with AI-generated content. Training and education initiatives can help cultivate responsible use and foster a community committed to ethical creativity.

5.4.7 Technological Solutions to Enhance Accountability

Technological innovations can also support accountability without stifling creativity. Techniques such as explainable AI (XAI) aim to make model decisions more interpretable, helping users understand why a particular output was generated. This transparency facilitates trust and accountability. Watermarking or digital signatures embedded in AI-generated content offer a method to trace origin and detect unauthorized or manipulated outputs. These tools assist in attribution and combating misinformation. Furthermore, robust content moderation systems using a combination of AI and human review can detect and mitigate inappropriate or harmful content before it reaches wider audiences. Continuous monitoring and updating of models in response to feedback ensure ongoing accountability.

5.4.8 Balancing Innovation with Ethical Responsibility

Striking the right balance between encouraging innovation and enforcing accountability requires nuanced policymaking and ethical leadership. Overly restrictive regulations risk stifling creativity and slowing technological progress, while lax oversight can lead to abuse and erosion of public trust. Frameworks that encourage responsible innovation create environments where experimentation is coupled with safeguards. This balance involves setting clear ethical standards, promoting transparency, fostering stakeholder engagement, and establishing consequences for misuse. Engaging diverse voices, including marginalized communities, artists, technologists, and the public, enriches the dialogue around generative AI's creative potential and associated risks. Such inclusiveness enhances accountability by ensuring that AI systems serve a broad spectrum of societal interests.

5.4.9 The Future of Creativity and Accountability in AI

As generative AI evolves, the relationship between creativity and accountability will continue to shape its trajectory. Emerging trends such as decentralized AI, multimodal models, and personalized content generation introduce new complexities and opportunities for accountability frameworks. The future likely involves more adaptive governance models that evolve alongside technology, leveraging continuous feedback loops and real-time monitoring. Responsible AI development will increasingly rely on multi-stakeholder collaboration, combining technical, ethical, legal, and social expertise. Ultimately, balancing creativity and accountability is about fostering AI that not only amazes with its inventive capacities but also aligns with human values and societal well-being. This balance ensures that generative AI contributes positively and sustainably to the creative landscape.

5.5 ENVIRONMENTAL IMPACT OF GENERATIVE AI

Generative artificial intelligence (AI) has seen explosive growth in recent years, powering everything from text generation and image synthesis to complex scientific modeling and creative arts. The transformative potential of generative AI is profound, offering new capabilities across industries and reshaping how humans interact with technology.

However, alongside its remarkable advancements lies a growing concern: the environmental impact of developing, training, and deploying these powerful AI models. As these models become larger and more computationally intensive, the energy consumption and carbon footprint associated with generative AI are attracting increasing scrutiny. Generative AI represents a pinnacle of modern technological achievement, unlocking new creative and functional possibilities. Yet, its environmental impact poses significant challenges that cannot be ignored.

From energy-intensive training and inference to hardware lifecycle effects and data center operations, the ecological footprint of generative AI is multifaceted. Addressing these issues requires coordinated efforts across research, industry, and policy to promote transparency, efficiency, and sustainability. By aligning AI development with environmental stewardship, the generative AI community can foster innovation that respects both human progress and the planet's future.

5.5.1 Energy Consumption in Training Large Models

One of the most significant contributors to the environmental impact of generative AI is the massive energy requirement involved in training state-of-the-art models. Training advanced models such as large-scale Generative Adversarial Networks (GANs), Transformers, or diffusion models involves processing vast datasets through millions or billions of parameters.

These processes require extensive use of high-performance GPUs or specialized hardware like TPUs, often running continuously for days or weeks. The computational intensity of training results in substantial electricity consumption. Studies have shown that training a single large AI model can consume as much energy as multiple households do in a year. This energy usage is especially impactful when powered by electricity generated from fossil fuels, leading to significant carbon emissions. Consequently, the environmental cost of training generative AI models becomes a critical consideration in the broader discussion of AI's sustainability.

5.5.2 Inference and Deployment Energy Costs

While training is the most energy-intensive phase, inference or model deployment also contributes to the environmental footprint. Generative AI models, once trained, are often deployed in cloud-based or edge environments to serve millions of user requests. Each request involves running the model's computations, which, when multiplied by large-scale usage, adds up to significant energy consumption.

For instance, popular text generation models powering chatbots or content creation tools continuously process inputs, consuming electricity and generating heat. Data centers hosting these models require cooling infrastructure that further adds to the overall energy use. Therefore, inference, while less costly per instance compared to training, accumulates a substantial environmental burden due to scale and frequency of use.

5.5.3 Hardware and Resource Demands

The environmental impact of generative AI also stems from the hardware used in both training and deployment. High-performance GPUs and TPUs are critical to efficiently run deep learning models, but manufacturing these components involves mining rare earth metals, complex chemical processes, and significant energy use. The lifecycle environmental costs of hardware, from extraction and production to eventual disposal, contribute to the overall footprint of generative AI systems.

Moreover, as models grow in size and complexity, they demand more powerful and specialized hardware, which can shorten the hardware's useful life and accelerate electronic waste. The frequent need for upgrading infrastructure to accommodate cutting-edge models compounds these issues, highlighting the importance of sustainable hardware design and recycling.

5.5.4 Data Center Efficiency and Location

The environmental footprint of generative AI is closely linked to the efficiency of data centers where training and inference occur. Modern data centers have made strides in improving energy efficiency through advanced cooling technologies, power management, and renewable energy integration.

The design of these facilities plays a crucial role in minimizing the carbon footprint of AI workloads. Geographic location is also pivotal. Data centers powered predominantly by renewable energy sources such as hydroelectric, wind, or solar have significantly lower emissions compared to those relying on coal or natural gas. Some tech companies are actively building data centers in regions with abundant clean energy or investing in carbon offset programs to mitigate their environmental impact.

5.5.5 Trade-Offs Between Model Performance and Sustainability

The drive for ever-more accurate and capable generative models often leads to exponentially larger architectures and longer training times. Researchers and companies face a trade-off between pushing the boundaries of model performance and the sustainability of these endeavors. While larger models can generate more coherent, creative, and useful outputs, the environmental cost of developing them grows considerably. There is growing recognition in the AI community of the need to balance innovation with ecological responsibility. This awareness has sparked interest in developing more efficient training methods, smaller yet powerful models, and techniques that reduce unnecessary computation without sacrificing quality. Such strategies include model pruning, knowledge distillation, and more efficient neural network architectures.

5.5.6 Research into Green AI and Energy-Efficient Algorithms

In response to environmental concerns, a movement called "Green AI" advocates for research focused on energy efficiency and ecological impact. Researchers are actively exploring ways to make generative AI models leaner and less energy-intensive. For example, quantization reduces the precision of model parameters to save computation, while sparsity techniques focus on activating only a fraction of neurons at a time. Other approaches include algorithmic innovations like adaptive learning rates, early stopping in training, and efficient data sampling. These methods help reduce the number of training iterations or computational operations, cutting down energy consumption. Additionally, exploring alternative architectures, such as transformer variants that require fewer resources, is a growing area of study.

5.5.7 Renewable Energy and Carbon Offsetting Initiatives

Several AI companies and research labs have committed to sustainability goals by shifting their infrastructure towards renewable energy. Major cloud providers powering AI workloads increasingly procure clean energy or invest directly in renewable projects. This transition significantly reduces the carbon footprint of training and running generative models. Beyond switching energy sources, some organizations purchase carbon offsets to compensate for emissions generated during AI development. Offsets fund environmental projects such as reforestation or renewable energy development, indirectly balancing the environmental cost. While offsetting is not a perfect solution, it serves as an important step toward more sustainable AI practices.

5.5.8 Transparency and Reporting of Environmental Impact

A critical aspect of addressing the environmental impact of generative AI is transparency. Researchers and organizations are encouraged to report the energy consumption, carbon emissions, and hardware usage involved in training and deploying AI models. Such transparency fosters accountability and allows comparisons across models and approaches. Some academic papers now include "environmental impact statements" alongside performance metrics, highlighting the computational cost involved. This practice promotes informed decisions by the community and motivates the development of energy-conscious AI techniques. However, consistent standards and frameworks for reporting are still evolving.

5.5.9 Ethical Considerations and Societal Responsibility

The environmental consequences of generative AI raise ethical questions about the responsibility of developers, researchers, and corporations. As AI becomes embedded in more aspects of life, the carbon footprint of these systems translates into broader societal costs, including climate change and resource depletion. Balancing AI advancement with ecological stewardship requires a collective effort to prioritize sustainable development. This includes investing in research for efficient algorithms, optimizing infrastructure, choosing renewable energy, and educating stakeholders about environmental impacts. Ethical AI development must encompass environmental sustainability as a core principle.

5.5.10 Future Outlook: Towards Sustainable Generative AI

The future of generative AI must integrate sustainability into its foundation. Advances in hardware efficiency, renewable energy adoption, and green algorithms will continue to reduce the environmental impact. Moreover, innovations such as federated learning and edge computing may decentralize AI workloads, decreasing reliance on large, centralized data centers. The AI community is increasingly aware that environmental sustainability is not only a challenge but an opportunity to drive innovation. By embedding energy efficiency in design and deployment, generative AI can grow responsibly, ensuring that its societal benefits do not come at the cost of planetary health.

CHAPTER

Tools and Platforms for Generative AI

6

6.1 OPEN-SOURCE FRAMEWORKS

6.1.1 TensorFlow and PyTorch for Generative Modeling

Generative modeling has emerged as one of the most exciting fields within artificial intelligence, enabling machines to create new data resembling real-world examples. This includes generating images, text, audio, and even complex 3D objects. Among the tools that have empowered researchers and developers to build such models, TensorFlow and PyTorch stand out as the leading deep learning frameworks. Both offer powerful capabilities tailored for generative modeling, but they come from distinct origins, with unique design philosophies and ecosystems.

TensorFlow and PyTorch have both played transformative roles in the evolution of generative modeling. TensorFlow's emphasis on scalability and production readiness provides a solid foundation for deploying generative AI at scale. In contrast, PyTorch's flexible and intuitive design accelerates innovation and research in new generative architectures. Together, they form complementary pillars that support the full spectrum of generative modeling from experimentation to enterprise deployment. As these frameworks continue to evolve and inspire new applications, they will remain central to the ongoing revolution in machine-generated creativity and intelligence.

Overview of Generative Modeling

Generative modeling refers to the process where AI systems learn the underlying probability distribution of a dataset to produce new, synthetic samples that are statistically similar to the training data. Models such as Generative Adversarial Networks (GANs), Variational Autoencoders (VAEs), and diffusion models exemplify this approach.

These models have revolutionized applications like image synthesis, style transfer, text generation, and more. Developing and training generative models require flexible, efficient, and scalable software frameworks. TensorFlow and PyTorch have risen to meet these demands by providing extensive libraries, GPU acceleration, and modular components for building complex neural networks.

TensorFlow: Stability and Production Readiness

TensorFlow was developed by Google Brain and released in 2015 as an open-source library designed to facilitate large-scale machine learning. Its architecture emphasizes scalability and deployment readiness, which appeals particularly to enterprise environments. TensorFlow supports a wide variety of generative modeling tasks, offering components for building GANs, VAEs, and even custom generative architectures. One of TensorFlow's strengths is its comprehensive ecosystem.

TensorFlow Extended (TFX) supports end-to-end machine learning pipelines, facilitating data ingestion, model training, validation, and deployment. This integrated ecosystem is advantageous for teams aiming to deploy generative models at scale, for instance, in commercial image generation or text synthesis services. TensorFlow originally used static computation graphs, which required users to define the entire computational graph before execution. This approach enhanced optimization and deployment but initially posed challenges in rapid prototyping and debugging, which are critical in research-heavy generative modeling. However, with the introduction of TensorFlow 2.x, eager execution became the default mode, allowing dynamic graph construction. This brought TensorFlow closer to PyTorch's flexibility, making it more user-friendly for experimentation and development of generative models.

The availability of TensorFlow Hub and TensorFlow Model Garden also accelerates generative modeling by providing pre-trained models and implementations of cutting-edge architectures. TensorFlow's tight integration with TPU (Tensor Processing Unit) hardware further boosts performance in training large-scale generative models.

PyTorch: Flexibility and Research Community Focus

PyTorch, developed by Facebook's AI Research lab and released in 2016, quickly gained popularity among researchers due to its intuitive design and dynamic computation graph. This "define-by-run" paradigm allows models to be constructed and modified on the fly, which is ideal for the experimental nature of generative model research. In generative modeling, where architectural innovations and rapid iteration are common, PyTorch's dynamic nature enables users to test novel ideas efficiently. Many seminal papers on GANs, VAEs, and diffusion models have implementations in PyTorch, making it the go-to framework for academia and open-source projects. PyTorch also boasts a rich ecosystem, including libraries such as Torchvision for image processing and PyTorch Lightning, which simplifies training loops while maintaining flexibility. The introduction of tools like Hugging Face Transformers, which is largely built on PyTorch, further fuels its dominance in natural language generation, a key generative AI domain. Moreover, PyTorch's strong community engagement ensures continual contributions of new generative model architectures, optimization techniques, and utilities. The open and accessible nature of PyTorch codebases fosters reproducibility, an important aspect for the iterative development of generative AI.

Comparing TensorFlow and PyTorch for Generative Modeling

While both frameworks can handle the full lifecycle of generative modeling, they differ in certain key aspects that influence user preference depending on the use case. TensorFlow's original strength lay in production-grade deployment. Its static graphs and robust tooling make it suitable for scenarios where models need to be deployed at scale with high efficiency. The integration with Google Cloud and TPUs is also a consideration for enterprises working on very large models.

However, earlier versions' complexity posed a steeper learning curve for researchers. PyTorch's dynamic computation and straightforward API design provide a more natural coding experience for prototyping and experimentation. This flexibility is crucial when designing new generative architectures or customizing training routines. As a result, PyTorch is often the preferred framework in research labs and for open-source projects, where rapid iteration is essential. Both frameworks have closed the gap over time. TensorFlow's eager execution mode enables dynamic model building similar to PyTorch, while PyTorch's growing ecosystem includes tools to simplify deployment and scalability.

Applications and Model Support

In generative modeling, popular architectures like GANs have been extensively implemented in both frameworks. TensorFlow's official tutorials and model garden include implementations of DCGAN, StyleGAN, and CycleGAN, facilitating users to build state-of-the-art image generators.

PyTorch offers similar support through repositories and community contributions, often including the latest variants and experimental models. Variational Autoencoders and their extensions have also been widely realized in both frameworks. TensorFlow's Keras API simplifies VAE construction with modular layers, while PyTorch allows for flexible loss function design and model customization. More recently, diffusion models have gained prominence due to their superior image synthesis quality.

Frameworks like PyTorch have been the primary platforms for open-source diffusion implementations, while TensorFlow is catching up with community-driven projects. Beyond images, both frameworks support text generation tasks. TensorFlow's integration with TensorFlow Text and TFLite for mobile applications complements PyTorch's collaboration with Hugging Face's Transformers library, which powers numerous generative language models.

Performance and Scalability

Performance in generative modeling depends heavily on hardware acceleration and optimization. TensorFlow's mature support for TPUs offers significant speed advantages for training large models, making it suitable for projects requiring massive scale. Its graph optimizations and distributed training capabilities facilitate efficient model parallelism.

PyTorch, while initially more CPU/GPU focused, has made great strides in distributed training support through libraries like DistributedDataParallel. Its seamless integration with NVIDIA GPUs and ease of debugging makes it highly efficient for research-scale projects. Both frameworks support mixed precision training to accelerate computations and reduce memory usage, critical for training resource-intensive generative models. The choice often depends on available hardware and specific project needs.

Community and Ecosystem Influence

The choice between TensorFlow and PyTorch is also influenced by their respective communities. TensorFlow has a strong presence in industry and education, backed by Google's extensive resources. Its comprehensive documentation, tutorials, and enterprise tools cater well to developers building production systems. PyTorch's community thrives in academia and open-source development, where sharing cutting-edge models and fostering innovation is paramount. Platforms like GitHub and forums often feature PyTorch implementations of the newest generative models shortly after publication. The ecosystems complement each other, with many tools and datasets supporting both frameworks. Researchers and practitioners increasingly develop interoperable code, allowing models to be converted or adapted between frameworks.

Challenges and Future Directions

Despite their strengths, both TensorFlow and PyTorch face challenges related to generative modeling. The increasing complexity of models demands continual improvements in ease of use, training speed, and deployment. Handling extremely large models efficiently and managing reproducibility across experiments remain ongoing concerns. Looking forward, both frameworks are investing in enhanced support for multimodal generative models, combining text, images, audio, and video generation capabilities.

Advances in automated model optimization, neural architecture search, and integration with other AI disciplines will further empower generative modeling. Cloud-based services and managed solutions from both communities will lower the barrier for non-experts to leverage generative AI, facilitating wider adoption in creative industries, healthcare, and scientific research.

6.1.2 Hugging Face and OpenAI Tools

The rapid advancement of artificial intelligence has been significantly propelled by the development and accessibility of sophisticated AI tools and platforms. Among the most influential contributors to this ecosystem are Hugging Face and OpenAI, two organizations whose tools have reshaped the landscape of machine learning and natural language processing. Both entities provide state-of-the-art AI models and frameworks, but they approach AI development and deployment with different philosophies, capabilities, and community engagement strategies.

Hugging Face and OpenAI tools have become pillars of modern AI development, each contributing uniquely to the growth and democratization of artificial intelligence. OpenAI's focus on scalable, powerful, and responsibly deployed models has made sophisticated AI accessible to a wide range of users through cloud-based APIs. Meanwhile, Hugging Face's open-source philosophy and vibrant community provide a collaborative environment for innovation, customization, and education. Together, these platforms empower developers, researchers, and organizations to harness the transformative potential of AI, shaping the future of technology and human-computer interaction in profound ways.

Origins and Philosophy

OpenAI was founded in 2015 as a research lab with the mission to ensure that artificial general intelligence benefits all of humanity. It gained early prominence for developing groundbreaking models in natural language understanding and generation, such as the GPT series. OpenAI's philosophy emphasizes the creation of powerful AI systems with a responsible approach to deployment, balancing innovation with ethical considerations. Initially operating as a non-profit, OpenAI transitioned to a capped-profit model to secure investments necessary for large-scale model training.

Hugging Face began as a startup focused on conversational AI but soon pivoted to become a leading open-source platform that fosters community-driven AI development. It is best known for the Transformers library, which provides easy access to numerous pre-trained models for natural language processing, computer vision, and speech tasks. Hugging Face's philosophy centers on openness, collaboration, and accessibility, enabling researchers and developers worldwide to share models, datasets, and code seamlessly.

Core Tools and Offerings

OpenAI's most renowned contributions are its GPT (Generative Pre-trained Transformer) models, including GPT-3 and the latest iterations, which power advanced language understanding and generation capabilities. These models are accessible primarily through OpenAI's API, allowing developers to integrate natural language processing features such as text completion, summarization, translation, and dialogue generation into applications. OpenAI has also developed DALL-E for image generation, Codex for code generation, and CLIP for image-text understanding, broadening the scope beyond text. OpenAI's API is designed for ease of integration, offering a cloud-based service where users send prompts and receive generated content. The platform supports fine-tuning on custom data, enabling tailored solutions for specific business needs. OpenAI also emphasizes safety features, content moderation, and usage policies to prevent misuse of its powerful models.

Hugging Face's flagship offering is the Transformers library, an open-source collection of pre-trained models spanning dozens of architectures such as BERT, RoBERTa, GPT-2, T5, and more. The library supports multiple programming languages and frameworks, including PyTorch and TensorFlow, making it versatile for research and production. Hugging Face's Model Hub is a repository where developers share thousands of models trained on diverse datasets, allowing easy discovery and reuse. Beyond the library, Hugging Face provides the Inference API, which offers hosted endpoints for running models without managing infrastructure. They also offer tools like the Datasets library for accessing and preparing datasets, and the Accelerate library to streamline training on various hardware. The company fosters a strong community through forums, tutorials, and events, encouraging collaboration and innovation.

Community and Ecosystem

One of the defining aspects of Hugging Face is its vibrant and inclusive community. The open-source nature of its tools attracts researchers, developers, and hobbyists who contribute models, code improvements, and educational content. The Model Hub exemplifies this spirit, serving as a marketplace of ideas and resources where cutting-edge models are shared freely. This democratization of AI resources has accelerated experimentation and adoption across academia and industry.

OpenAI, while more centralized in its approach, has also cultivated a broad developer base through its API platform. By offering powerful models as a service, OpenAI has lowered barriers to entry for startups, enterprises, and independent developers who lack resources to train large models themselves. OpenAI actively engages with users through documentation, partnerships, and controlled access to their technologies, balancing openness with responsible governance.

Use Cases and Applications

Both Hugging Face and OpenAI tools have found extensive use across various domains. OpenAI's GPT-3 and Codex models have been adopted in applications ranging from chatbots and virtual assistants to automated content creation and software development aids. Enterprises utilize OpenAI's models for customer support automation, marketing personalization, and data analysis, benefitting from the model's broad general knowledge and contextual understanding. Hugging Face's models are integrated into diverse workflows including sentiment analysis, named entity recognition, machine translation, summarization, and speech recognition.

The availability of specialized models fine-tuned for particular languages, industries, or tasks allows for precise and efficient deployment. Researchers also leverage Hugging Face's ecosystem for rapid prototyping and benchmarking new architectures. Both platforms enable hybrid approaches combining multiple modalities and tasks, such as using CLIP for image-text matching alongside GPT for language generation. This versatility supports cutting-edge applications in multimedia content creation, accessibility tools, and personalized learning.

Technical Strengths and Differences

OpenAI's tools benefit from massive-scale training and proprietary datasets that result in highly sophisticated models with impressive generalization capabilities. Their models often set benchmarks in natural language understanding and generation, handling nuanced queries and creative writing with fluency. The hosted API approach simplifies deployment but depends on internet connectivity and service availability. Hugging Face's open-source framework emphasizes flexibility and extensibility. Developers can inspect, modify, and fine-tune models locally, making it ideal for experimentation and custom projects. The support for multiple frameworks and hardware accelerators provides options for scaling from laptops to large clusters. However, running large models independently can be resource-intensive compared to cloud-hosted services.

Ethical Considerations and Responsible AI

Both organizations recognize the ethical implications of powerful AI models. OpenAI implements usage guidelines, content filters, and monitoring to mitigate risks such as misinformation, bias, and harmful content generation. Their research also explores interpretability and fairness, striving to make AI safer and more transparent. Hugging Face promotes responsible AI through open dialogue and transparency. The community-driven model allows collective scrutiny and improvement, helping identify biases or vulnerabilities. The platform also supports tools for dataset auditing and model evaluation to promote fairness and accountability.

Future Directions and Innovations

Looking ahead, OpenAI is investing in building more capable and aligned AI systems, aiming to advance toward artificial general intelligence while ensuring safety and ethical use. They continue to expand the scope of their models to multimodal inputs and outputs, integrating vision, language, and code. Hugging Face plans to deepen its ecosystem with improved tools for model training efficiency, dataset management, and deployment automation. The company is also focusing on democratizing access to AI by lowering hardware requirements and fostering education. Both platforms are expected to play complementary roles in the AI landscape: OpenAI pushing the frontier with large-scale, cutting-edge models accessible via APIs, and Hugging Face nurturing the community-driven, open-source innovation that fuels research and diverse applications.

6.2 PROPRIETARY GENERATIVE AI PLATFORMS

6.2.1 MidJourney, DALL-E, and Stable Diffusion for Visuals

The domain of generative AI has seen remarkable progress in recent years, particularly in the generation of visual content. Among the forefront of this revolution are three prominent platforms: MidJourney, DALL-E, and Stable Diffusion. Each of these tools leverages cutting-edge deep learning models to transform textual prompts into vivid and creative images, thereby expanding the possibilities for artists, designers, and businesses alike.

MidJourney, DALL-E, and Stable Diffusion represent three pillars in the burgeoning field of AI-powered text-to-image generation. Each platform brings unique strengths and philosophies, contributing to a rich ecosystem that empowers users to create compelling visuals from simple language prompts. Their impact extends beyond art and design, influencing commerce, education, and entertainment. While challenges related to ethics, legality, and accessibility persist, ongoing innovation and community engagement continue to shape the future of AI-generated imagery. Together, these tools highlight the transformative potential of generative AI in reimagining how humans create and communicate visually.

The Rise of Text-to-Image Generation

Text-to-image generation is a specialized area within generative AI focused on creating images from natural language descriptions. The concept itself is rooted in bridging language and vision, two modalities of human cognition that AI aims to emulate. Early attempts involved rule-based systems and simpler generative models, but recent advancements in deep neural networks, especially those using transformer architectures and diffusion models, have enabled much more realistic and contextually rich image synthesis. MidJourney, DALL-E, and Stable Diffusion exemplify this progress by offering platforms that generate high-quality visuals based on user-provided text prompts. These systems interpret semantic cues from language and synthesize corresponding imagery that often showcases impressive creativity, detail, and coherence.

DALL-E: Pioneering Creativity with Language-Driven Imagery

DALL-E, developed by OpenAI, is one of the earliest and most influential text-to-image generation models. Released initially in 2021, DALL-E built on the GPT transformer architecture to generate images from textual descriptions. Its name cleverly combines the surrealist artist Salvador Dalí and Pixar's robot character WALL·E, reflecting its mission to blend art and artificial intelligence. What makes DALL-E particularly notable is its ability to generate highly imaginative and novel images that go beyond simple photo-realism. For example, it can produce images of "an armchair in the shape of an avocado" or "a baby daikon radish in a tutu walking a dog," demonstrating a nuanced understanding of objects, styles, and contexts.

This capability arises from its training on vast datasets of image-text pairs, enabling it to model complex relationships between linguistic concepts and visual features. OpenAI's follow-up, DALL-E 2, improved upon the original by producing images with higher resolution, better realism, and more consistent adherence to the input prompt. The model introduced new techniques such as CLIP (Contrastive Language–Image Pre-training) to enhance alignment between text and images. DALL-E's release as a commercial API allowed artists, developers, and companies to integrate its capabilities into applications ranging from advertising to entertainment and education.

MidJourney: A Community-Driven Artistic Tool

MidJourney is a more recent entrant into the text-to-image space, emphasizing creativity and artistic expression. Launched in 2022, MidJourney quickly gained popularity for its distinct style and the way it encourages experimentation. Unlike DALL-E, which aims for a wide range of realistic images, MidJourney often generates artwork with painterly textures, surreal elements, and a dreamlike aesthetic that resonates with digital artists and creatives.

The platform operates primarily through a Discord-based interface where users submit text prompts and receive generated images. This community-centric approach fosters collaboration, feedback, and sharing among users, cultivating a vibrant ecosystem of visual experimentation. MidJourney's appeal lies not just in its outputs but also in how it democratizes art creation. Users without formal training in drawing or design can produce complex, visually striking compositions simply by describing their ideas. This lowers barriers to entry for creative expression and opens new avenues for storytelling, concept art, and digital illustration.

Stable Diffusion: Open-Source Innovation and Accessibility

Stable Diffusion stands apart as an open-source text-to-image model that has significantly expanded access to advanced image generation technology. Developed by Stability AI in collaboration with academic and industry partners, Stable Diffusion was released publicly in 2022, allowing anyone with sufficient computational resources to run the model locally or in customized cloud environments. The model is based on diffusion processes, a generative technique where images are created by iteratively denoising random noise until a coherent picture emerges, guided by the text prompt. This approach contrasts with autoregressive or GAN-based methods and has proven effective for producing detailed and diverse images. The open-source nature of Stable Diffusion has spurred a wide range of innovations and derivative projects. Artists, developers, and researchers have fine-tuned the model for various styles, integrated it into creative tools, and used it for novel applications such as animation, style transfer, and image editing. Its availability has accelerated experimentation and lowered costs, enabling widespread adoption across hobbyist and professional domains.

Comparing the Three Platforms

Though MidJourney, DALL-E, and Stable Diffusion share the core objective of generating images from text, they differ significantly in design philosophy, accessibility, and output characteristics. DALL-E's strength lies in its advanced alignment of text and image semantics, producing images that can be highly imaginative yet grounded in coherent visual logic. Its closed-source, commercial nature ensures controlled deployment and quality but limits direct modification by users. MidJourney focuses on artistic style and community engagement. It serves as a creative playground where aesthetics and experimentation take precedence over strict realism. Its platform design encourages collaboration and iterative creativity. Stable Diffusion offers unparalleled openness and flexibility, empowering users to modify, fine-tune, and deploy models freely. This has resulted in a diverse ecosystem of derivative tools and applications, though it requires more technical knowledge to harness fully.

Applications across Creative and Commercial Domains

The practical uses of these platforms span creative arts, marketing, entertainment, education, and more. Artists use these tools to generate concept art, storyboards, and inspiration for projects. Graphic designers employ them to rapidly prototype visuals or create unique assets for branding and advertising. In entertainment, game developers and filmmakers leverage text-to-image models for world-building, character design, and visual effects, reducing production timelines and costs. Educators use these models to create engaging illustrations or visual aids, enhancing learning experiences. Brands integrate these platforms into marketing campaigns to generate personalized content at scale. Automated image generation helps produce customized visuals tailored to customer segments or social media trends, boosting engagement and conversion.

Ethical and Practical Considerations

The rise of these powerful visual generation tools brings forth ethical and practical challenges. Issues of copyright and ownership arise when AI generates images based on datasets that include copyrighted material. Determining the provenance and originality of AI-generated art remains a complex legal frontier. There are also concerns regarding bias and representation in training data, which can affect the inclusivity and fairness of generated images. Content moderation is necessary to prevent the creation of harmful, offensive, or misleading visuals. From a practical standpoint, users must consider computational resource requirements, especially for Stable Diffusion's local deployment, which demands GPUs with substantial memory. Cloud services for DALL-E and MidJourney offer ease of use but may incur ongoing costs and raise data privacy questions.

The Future of AI-Driven Visual Creation

Looking forward, text-to-image generation platforms are likely to evolve towards even more interactive, multimodal, and context-aware systems. Integration with video and 3D modeling could enable dynamic storytelling and immersive experiences. Improvements in model efficiency will make high-quality image generation accessible on lower-powered devices, broadening user bases. Hybrid systems combining AI creativity with human curation and editing will enhance control and quality, fostering new art forms and workflows. Ethical frameworks and standards will mature, providing clearer guidelines for responsible use and intellectual property management. As these technologies become more embedded in daily creative practices, they promise to democratize visual expression, amplify human imagination, and unlock novel possibilities across industries.

6.2.2 Commercial Text Generation Platforms

The emergence of commercial text generation platforms marks a significant milestone in the advancement of natural language processing and artificial intelligence. These platforms leverage sophisticated generative AI models to produce coherent, contextually relevant, and high-quality text for a wide range of applications. From automating customer support to generating marketing copy, drafting legal documents, or assisting in creative writing, commercial text generation tools have transformed how businesses and individuals create and interact with textual content.

Commercial text generation platforms represent a transformative technology reshaping the landscape of content creation and digital communication. By providing accessible, scalable, and customizable AI-driven text generation, these platforms empower businesses and individuals to automate routine writing tasks, generate creative content, and enhance user interactions. While challenges remain in ensuring accuracy, fairness, and ethical usage, ongoing advancements and responsible practices are paving the way for broader adoption and more sophisticated capabilities. As these platforms continue to evolve, they will play an increasingly central role in how society creates, consumes, and interacts with text in the digital age.

Evolution of Commercial Text Generation

Text generation has its roots in early rule-based systems and template-based natural language generation, which were limited by rigid structures and manual effort. The breakthrough came with the rise of machine learning and neural networks, particularly with the development of transformer architectures such as the Transformer model introduced by Vaswani et al. in 2017.

These models enabled unprecedented capabilities in understanding and generating human-like text. Commercial platforms emerged by harnessing these advancements, offering text generation as accessible cloud-based services or APIs. Companies like OpenAI, Google, Microsoft, and others have developed models such as GPT series, BERT-based generators, and T5, integrating them into platforms that cater to diverse business needs. These commercial platforms have democratized access to powerful language models, enabling organizations without extensive AI expertise or infrastructure to benefit from cutting-edge text generation.

Core Features of Commercial Text Generation Platforms

Commercial text generation platforms typically offer a suite of features designed to maximize usability, customization, and integration. One fundamental feature is API access, which allows developers to incorporate text generation capabilities into applications, websites, or workflows seamlessly.

This abstraction removes the need to build and maintain large models locally, shifting the computational burden to cloud infrastructure. These platforms also provide pre-trained models fine-tuned on various domains, enabling more relevant and accurate text output tailored to specific industries such as finance, healthcare, or legal sectors. Fine-tuning capabilities allow users to customize models further by training on proprietary data, enhancing performance for niche use cases.

Another key feature is prompt engineering support, where users can design and optimize input prompts to guide the model's behavior effectively. Some platforms incorporate tools that assist in crafting prompts or provide templates for common tasks such as summarization, translation, or question answering. Quality controls and moderation tools are often integrated to ensure the generated text adheres to ethical standards, avoids harmful content, and aligns with regulatory requirements. This is particularly important in sensitive applications involving user-generated content or public-facing communications.

Use Cases across Industries

Commercial text generation platforms find applications across a broad spectrum of industries, driving efficiency and innovation. In customer service, AI-powered chatbots and virtual assistants generate responses to user queries, providing 24/7 support and freeing human agents to focus on complex issues. These systems improve response time, consistency, and customer satisfaction. Marketing and advertising sectors leverage text generation to create compelling copy, social media posts, and email campaigns. Automated content creation reduces time-to-market and allows for rapid A/B testing of messaging, optimizing engagement and conversion rates. In journalism and media, platforms assist in drafting news articles, summarizing reports, and generating headlines.

This speeds up content production and helps journalists focus on investigative or analytical aspects. Legal firms use text generation for drafting contracts, summarizing case law, and automating routine documentation, increasing accuracy and reducing manual labor. Education and e-learning benefit from personalized content generation, such as automated essay feedback, question generation, and tutoring systems that adapt to individual learning needs. Creative industries, including gaming and entertainment, use text generation to produce dialogues, narratives, and scripts, enriching user experiences with dynamic content.

Integration and Customization

A vital aspect of commercial text generation platforms is their ability to integrate with existing enterprise systems and workflows. Through robust APIs and SDKs, these platforms connect with CRM tools, content management systems, customer support software, and analytics platforms, creating seamless pipelines for content creation and deployment. Customization options empower organizations to align the generated text with brand voice, tone, and style guidelines.

This is achieved through fine-tuning models on company-specific data or by using adjustable parameters that control creativity, formality, and length of outputs. Such flexibility is crucial for maintaining consistency and professionalism in automated communications. Some platforms offer interactive interfaces and no-code tools that allow non-technical users to harness text generation capabilities. These interfaces often include features like drag-and-drop prompt builders, template libraries, and real-time previews, enabling wider adoption across teams beyond data scientists or developers.

Challenges and Limitations

Despite their impressive capabilities, commercial text generation platforms face several challenges and limitations. One major concern is the risk of generating inaccurate, biased, or misleading content. Since models learn from large datasets that may contain inherent biases or errors, outputs can reflect or amplify these issues, posing ethical and reputational risks. Ensuring the factual correctness of generated content remains a significant hurdle, particularly in domains like healthcare or legal where errors can have serious consequences. While ongoing research aims to improve factual grounding and verification, users must exercise caution and implement human-in-the-loop review processes. Data privacy and security are also critical considerations, especially when dealing with sensitive or proprietary information. Commercial platforms must comply with regulations like GDPR and HIPAA, and customers often require guarantees regarding data handling, storage, and model access. Cost and computational resources can be a limitation for small businesses or individual users, as large-scale models consume substantial compute power and incur ongoing expenses. Platform providers address this by offering tiered pricing and optimizing inference efficiency, but accessibility remains an area for improvement.

Ethical and Regulatory Considerations

The use of commercial text generation platforms raises important ethical questions around transparency, accountability, and content ownership. Users and providers must clarify the role of AI in content creation, disclosing when text is machine-generated to maintain trust. Efforts are underway to develop guidelines and standards for responsible AI usage, including fairness audits, content moderation policies, and mechanisms for addressing harmful or inappropriate outputs. Regulators are increasingly scrutinizing AI-generated content, prompting platforms to implement safeguards and reporting features. Moreover, intellectual property concerns arise when AI generates text that may resemble copyrighted materials. Platforms often include terms of service outlining usage rights, but the legal landscape is still evolving, requiring vigilance from both users and providers.

Future Trends and Innovations

Looking forward, commercial text generation platforms are poised to become more powerful, versatile, and user-friendly. Advances in few-shot and zero-shot learning will reduce dependence on large labeled datasets and fine-tuning, enabling more adaptable models that perform well across diverse tasks with minimal customization. Multimodal integration, combining text with images, audio, and video, will open new creative possibilities and richer user experiences. Enhanced explainability and interpretability features will help users understand how and why models generate specific outputs, fostering trust and enabling better control. Real-time generation and interactive applications will expand, supported by edge computing and optimized model architectures, facilitating personalized and context-aware text generation in everyday devices. Collaboration between human creativity and AI will deepen, with platforms offering co-writing tools, suggestion engines, and content ideation assistants that enhance productivity and innovation rather than replace human input.

6.3 WORKFLOW MANAGEMENT AND DEPLOYMENT TOOLS

The rapid advancement of generative AI has opened vast opportunities across industries, from creative content generation to scientific research and automated software development. However, harnessing the full potential of generative AI requires robust workflow management and deployment frameworks. These tools and platforms play a crucial role in organizing the complex lifecycle of generative AI systems — including data preparation, model training, evaluation, optimization, and production deployment.

Managing this lifecycle efficiently ensures reproducibility, scalability, collaboration, and operational reliability, all of which are essential for both research and commercial applications. Workflow management and deployment tools are foundational to the success and scalability of generative AI systems. By automating and orchestrating complex pipelines, these platforms enable reproducible experimentation, efficient resource use, collaborative development, and reliable production services. While challenges remain around scalability, privacy, and output variability, ongoing innovations in tools and platforms are steadily addressing these issues. As generative AI continues to expand its impact across domains, robust workflow and deployment ecosystems will be essential to unlocking its full potential and delivering transformative applications at scale.

6.3.1 The Need for Workflow Management in Generative AI

Generative AI models, especially large-scale ones, involve multiple stages that demand careful orchestration. Initially, vast datasets must be curated and preprocessed, ensuring quality and relevance. Following data preparation, models are trained on computationally intensive hardware, often in distributed or cloud environments. Training requires not only substantial computing resources but also efficient scheduling, monitoring, and logging mechanisms to track performance metrics and debug issues. Post-training, models undergo evaluation using specialized metrics to assess quality, diversity, and fidelity of generated outputs.

Iterative cycles of hyperparameter tuning and retraining are common to achieve optimal performance. Finally, models need to be deployed into production environments where they serve real-time or batch generation tasks, requiring scalability, latency guarantees, and fault tolerance. Without workflow management tools, these processes can become error prone, fragmented, and difficult to reproduce. Workflow management platforms help by providing automated pipelines, version control for code and data, resource allocation, and collaboration support, enabling teams to focus more on innovation and less on manual overhead.

6.3.2 Popular Workflow Management Platforms

Several workflow management frameworks have emerged to address these needs, offering varying degrees of specialization for AI workloads. Apache Airflow is widely used for orchestrating complex data workflows and ETL pipelines. While originally designed for general data engineering tasks, Airflow's modularity and extensibility make it suitable for AI workflows where data ingestion and preprocessing form critical initial steps. For AI-specific pipelines, tools like Kubeflow have gained prominence. Kubeflow is an open-source project designed to run machine learning workflows on Kubernetes clusters, combining container orchestration with ML-specific components such as Jupyter notebooks, hyperparameter tuning, and model serving. Kubeflow's pipeline framework allows users to define workflows as code, enabling reproducibility and scalability for training generative AI models.

MLflow is another popular platform focused on experiment tracking, model versioning, and lifecycle management. It facilitates recording model parameters, metrics, and artifacts, making it easier to compare different runs and manage model deployments. Its integration with various ML libraries and cloud services makes MLflow a versatile tool for managing generative AI experiments. Weights & Biases (W&B) offers a cloud-based platform that emphasizes collaboration and visualization. It supports real-time tracking of training progress, performance metrics, and dataset versions, which is particularly useful when iterating on complex generative models requiring fine-tuning and debugging.

6.3.3 Tools for Data and Model Versioning

Version control is a fundamental aspect of managing AI workflows, ensuring traceability and reproducibility. Unlike traditional software, AI workflows must track changes in data, model architectures, and hyperparameters. Tools such as DVC (Data Version Control) extend Git-like versioning to datasets and models, enabling teams to track dataset versions alongside code.

This is critical in generative AI where subtle changes in training data can drastically affect model outputs. Additionally, platforms like Pachyderm offer data lineage tracking combined with scalable pipeline execution. Pachyderm treats data as code, providing reproducible workflows with automatic versioning and rollback capabilities. This transparency helps identify causes of mode collapse or degraded performance in generative models by linking training outcomes to specific data or code versions.

6.3.4 Deployment Platforms for Generative AI

Once a generative AI model is trained and validated, deployment is the next critical step. Deployment platforms provide infrastructure to host models, manage inference requests, and scale resources dynamically based on demand. Cloud providers such as AWS, Google Cloud Platform, and Microsoft Azure offer managed services tailored to AI model deployment. Amazon SageMaker, Google AI Platform, and Azure Machine Learning enable users to deploy generative AI models as REST APIs, manage endpoints, and automate scaling. These platforms often integrate seamlessly with workflow tools and support containerization technologies like Docker and Kubernetes, facilitating portability and reproducibility.

For latency-sensitive applications, edge deployment solutions allow generative AI models to run on devices closer to the user, such as smartphones or IoT devices. Frameworks like TensorFlow Lite and NVIDIA Jetson provide tools to optimize and deploy models on constrained hardware, enabling real-time generation without dependence on cloud connectivity. Open-source serving tools such as TorchServe and TensorFlow Serving simplify model deployment by providing scalable, production-ready inference servers. These servers support batching, model versioning, and A/B testing, which are vital for maintaining and updating generative AI services.

6.3.5 Integration of Workflow and Deployment

A key trend in generative AI development is the integration of workflow management and deployment platforms into cohesive end-to-end solutions. This integration streamlines the journey from experimentation to production, ensuring that improvements in model design, data quality, or training parameters translate rapidly into deployed services. For instance, Kubeflow Pipelines can orchestrate the entire process from data ingestion to training and deployment on Kubernetes clusters.

This unified approach reduces friction between teams, promotes continuous delivery of AI models, and facilitates monitoring and retraining based on real-world feedback. Similarly, managed AI platforms from cloud providers increasingly offer integrated pipelines combining experiment tracking, model registry, deployment, and monitoring. These all-in-one solutions simplify operational complexity and accelerate the time-to-market for generative AI applications.

6.3.6 Challenges in Workflow and Deployment

Despite these advances, managing workflows and deployments for generative AI is not without challenges. The large scale and complexity of models strain compute and storage resources, demanding sophisticated scheduling and resource management to optimize costs and performance. Data privacy and compliance concerns add another layer of complexity. Ensuring secure handling of training data and generated content requires integration of governance policies into the workflow and deployment stages. The non-deterministic nature of generative AI outputs complicates testing and validation during deployment. Unlike traditional software where outputs are predictable, generative models can produce varied results, making quality assurance and anomaly detection more difficult. Finally, the rapid pace of research and experimentation means that workflows and deployment pipelines must be flexible and adaptable. Teams need platforms that support easy experimentation without sacrificing reliability or reproducibility.

6.3.7 Future Directions

Looking ahead, workflow management and deployment tools for generative AI are evolving towards greater automation and intelligence. AutoML and meta-learning techniques promise to automate hyperparameter tuning and model selection within pipelines, reducing manual effort. Federated learning frameworks may be integrated into workflows to allow training on distributed, privacy-sensitive data without centralizing datasets. This will be especially relevant for generative AI applications in healthcare or finance. Explainability and monitoring tools tailored to generative models will become more sophisticated, providing insights into model behavior and output quality in production. This will improve trust and enable proactive detection of mode collapse or bias. Finally, the convergence of cloud, edge, and hybrid deployment strategies will enable generative AI systems to serve diverse use cases, from centralized content creation platforms to personalized on-device assistants.

CHAPTER 7

Challenges in Generative AI

7.1 MODE COLLAPSE IN GANS

Generative Adversarial Networks, commonly known as GANs, have revolutionized generative modeling by enabling the creation of remarkably realistic images, videos, and other forms of synthetic data. Since their introduction by Ian Goodfellow and colleagues in 2014, GANs have been a cornerstone of research in generative AI. Despite their success, GANs face significant training challenges, one of the most notorious being mode collapse. Mode collapse remains one of the defining challenges in the development and deployment of Generative Adversarial Networks. Its impact on diversity and the quality of generated outputs limits the practical usefulness of GANs, especially in applications demanding rich variability.

Understanding mode collapse requires a deep appreciation of the adversarial training dynamics and the complex interplay between generator and discriminator. While significant progress has been made through improved architectures, loss functions, and training strategies, mode collapse persists as a nuanced and multifaceted problem. Continued research into more robust, stable, and interpretable GAN models, along with hybrid generative frameworks, will be essential in overcoming this challenge and realizing the full potential of generative AI.

7.1.1 Understanding Mode Collapse

Mode collapse occurs when a GAN's generator produces a limited variety of outputs regardless of the diversity present in the input noise or latent space. Essentially, instead of generating a broad spectrum of realistic samples, the generator "collapses" to producing only a few modes or even a single mode of the data distribution repeatedly.

This phenomenon leads to a lack of diversity in generated samples, which defeats the purpose of generative modeling — to synthesize novel, varied data points that mimic the real-world data distribution. In the context of image generation, for example, mode collapse might mean that the generator produces multiple copies or slight variations of the same image rather than capturing the rich variety seen in the training dataset. This not only reduces the usefulness of the GAN for practical applications but also signals a failure of the underlying training dynamics.

7.1.2 Why Mode Collapse Happens

Mode collapse is fundamentally linked to the adversarial nature of GAN training. A GAN consists of two neural networks — the generator and the discriminator — that compete in a zero-sum game. The generator aims to produce samples that fool the discriminator, while the discriminator tries to distinguish real data from generated samples.

The equilibrium of this game should ideally result in the generator producing outputs indistinguishable from real data, capturing all modes of the distribution. However, this balance is notoriously difficult to achieve. Mode collapse often arises when the generator discovers a small set of samples that successfully fool the discriminator, and then repeatedly produces these "safe" outputs. Because these outputs yield a strong discriminator response, the generator has little incentive to explore other regions of the data distribution, leading to collapse.

This problem is exacerbated by the highly non-convex and unstable optimization landscape inherent in GAN training. The adversarial objective does not guarantee convergence to a global optimum, and gradient signals can become weak, noisy, or misleading. Without sufficient guidance or regularization, the generator's parameters may settle into local optima corresponding to limited modes.

7.1.3 Types and Degrees of Mode Collapse

Mode collapse is not an all-or-nothing phenomenon; it can manifest in varying degrees and forms. In some cases, partial mode collapse occurs, where the generator covers only a subset of the data distribution's modes. For example, a GAN trained on a dataset of animals might only generate images of dogs, ignoring other animals like cats or birds.

In more severe cases, total mode collapse happens, where the generator outputs essentially the same image regardless of the input noise. This is the most detrimental form, as it completely loses the generative diversity that defines GANs. Additionally, mode collapse can be transient or persistent. Sometimes, mode collapse may appear early in training but be resolved as the GAN continues to improve. Other times, it persists throughout training, requiring intervention through architectural changes or training modifications.

7.1.4 Detecting Mode Collapse

Detecting mode collapse is critical for monitoring GAN training and ensuring quality outputs. Visual inspection of generated samples is often the first step, as researchers look for diversity and realism. However, this qualitative approach is subjective and impractical for large-scale or automated evaluation. Quantitative metrics have been developed to assess mode collapse more objectively. Metrics like the Inception Score (IS) and Fréchet Inception Distance (FID) provide indirect measures of sample quality and diversity but have limitations. More specialized metrics, such as Precision and Recall for generative models, aim to quantify fidelity and diversity separately. Recall, in particular, is useful for detecting mode collapse, as low recall indicates poor coverage of the real data distribution. Other approaches involve analyzing the latent space mapping to see if different noise inputs produce distinct outputs. If multiple inputs result in similar or identical samples, this suggests mode collapse.

7.1.5 Strategies to Mitigate Mode Collapse

Over the years, researchers have proposed numerous strategies to combat mode collapse, focusing on modifying the GAN architecture, improving the training procedure, or introducing regularization techniques. One foundational approach is the design of alternative loss functions and objective formulations. For instance, the Wasserstein GAN (WGAN) introduced a different loss metric based on the Earth Mover's Distance, which provides smoother gradients and improves training stability.

This smoother gradient flow helps the generator explore the latent space more effectively, reducing the likelihood of mode collapse. Another approach involves architectural changes such as minibatch discrimination, which encourages the discriminator to assess batches of generated samples collectively rather than independently. This technique forces the generator to produce varied samples within a batch to avoid detection, promoting diversity. Techniques like feature matching modify the generator's objective to minimize the difference between statistics of real and generated samples rather than fooling the discriminator directly.

This encourages the generator to replicate the overall distribution more faithfully. Regularization methods such as gradient penalty, introduced in WGAN-GP, improve training stability by penalizing large gradients, which reduces sudden jumps in the generator's behavior that can trigger mode collapse. Furthermore, recent work on training schedules and normalization techniques, including spectral normalization, have improved GAN convergence and reduced collapse instances.

7.1.6 The Role of Latent Space Exploration

A crucial element in avoiding mode collapse is ensuring that the generator meaningfully uses the input noise or latent variables. When the latent space is poorly explored or poorly mapped to outputs, the generator can ignore parts of the latent distribution, leading to collapse. Encouraging latent space disentanglement and ensuring that different latent vectors produce diverse outputs helps maintain mode coverage. Some models integrate explicit latent space regularizers or incorporate encoders that map data back to latent codes, promoting a more structured and comprehensive exploration of modes.

7.1.7 Challenges That Remain

Despite significant progress, mode collapse remains a persistent challenge, especially as GANs grow more complex and are applied to higher-dimensional, more varied datasets. Ensuring stable training across diverse domains requires careful hyperparameter tuning, architecture selection, and dataset preparation. Moreover, the subtlety of partial mode collapse makes it difficult to detect and address in some applications. For example, in text or audio generation, where diversity and quality are harder to quantify visually, mode collapse can silently degrade model usefulness. The interplay between mode collapse and other GAN issues like vanishing gradients, non-convergence, and sensitivity to initialization means that a holistic understanding and approach are needed rather than isolated fixes.

7.1.8 Future Directions

Looking forward, several promising directions may further reduce mode collapse in GANs. One such direction is the integration of hybrid models combining GANs with other generative frameworks like VAEs or diffusion models. These hybrids can leverage the strengths of multiple approaches to improve diversity and stability. Self-supervised learning and contrastive learning techniques applied to the discriminator can enhance its ability to recognize subtle differences between modes, providing better feedback to the generator.

Meta-learning approaches that adapt training dynamics on-the-fly may help GANs escape local optima associated with mode collapse by dynamically adjusting learning rates or loss functions. Additionally, advances in explainability and interpretability may offer new insights into why mode collapse occurs and how to preempt it through model introspection.

7.2 SCALABILITY AND COMPUTATIONAL COSTS

Generative AI represents one of the most transformative developments in artificial intelligence, enabling machines to autonomously create complex content such as images, text, audio, and more. However, as these models have grown more sophisticated, so have the challenges related to scalability and computational costs. These issues have become critical bottlenecks in the development, deployment, and adoption of generative AI systems. Scalability and computational costs represent some of the most pressing challenges in the advancement of generative AI.

The growing complexity of models, the massive hardware and infrastructure requirements, the environmental and economic impacts, and the need for efficient algorithms collectively shape a multifaceted problem. Overcoming these obstacles is essential to democratize access, enable real-time deployment, and ensure sustainable growth in generative AI capabilities. Innovations across hardware design, algorithmic efficiency, data management, and deployment strategies hold the key to unlocking the full potential of generative AI while managing its computational footprint. As the field continues to evolve rapidly, balancing ambition with practicality will determine the future trajectory of generative AI technologies.

7.2.1 The Increasing Complexity of Generative Models

One of the foremost contributors to scalability challenges in generative AI is the dramatic increase in model complexity. Early generative models were relatively small and computationally manageable, but contemporary state-of-the-art models, such as large-scale transformer-based architectures or diffusion models, often comprise billions of parameters. These enormous networks require extensive computational resources for training, including thousands of GPUs or specialized hardware over weeks or months. Training such models involves iterating over massive datasets to optimize millions of parameters, which translates into significant demand for memory, processing power, and storage. As the scale of models grows, the computational complexity increases not linearly but often exponentially, pushing the boundaries of current hardware and software capabilities. This makes scaling generative AI an inherently difficult problem that necessitates advances in both algorithmic efficiency and system-level engineering.

7.2.2 Hardware Limitations and Infrastructure Demands

The hardware infrastructure needed to train and deploy generative AI at scale is immense. High-performance GPUs, TPUs, and custom AI accelerators form the backbone of modern AI computation. However, these devices are expensive, power-hungry, and require sophisticated cooling and maintenance systems. Data centers that host such hardware must be designed to handle continuous heavy loads, resulting in high capital and operational expenditures. Moreover, the communication overhead among distributed computing nodes during training further complicates scaling. Large models are typically trained in parallel across multiple devices and machines, which introduces challenges in synchronizing gradients, managing data flow, and minimizing latency. Efficient distributed training requires specialized frameworks and algorithms designed to optimize resource utilization and reduce bottlenecks. Even beyond training, inference—the process of generating outputs from a trained model—can be computationally intensive, especially when deployed at scale to serve millions of users in real time.

Ensuring low-latency, high-throughput responses demands robust infrastructure, optimized software stacks, and often hardware acceleration.

7.2.3 Energy Consumption and Environmental Impact

Scalability in generative AI is not only a matter of technical feasibility but also a growing concern due to its energy consumption and environmental footprint. Training large generative models can consume enormous amounts of electricity, sometimes equivalent to the annual energy consumption of several households or even small cities. This has raised alarms about the sustainability of current AI research practices and the potential environmental costs of continued scaling.

The carbon footprint associated with AI training and deployment has prompted calls for more energy-efficient algorithms, hardware, and data center operations. Strategies such as utilizing renewable energy, improving cooling efficiency, and developing low-power AI accelerators are being explored to mitigate these impacts. However, balancing the computational demands of generative AI with sustainability remains a significant challenge.

7.2.4 Economic Costs and Access Inequality

The financial burden of scaling generative AI systems presents another major obstacle. The costs of procuring, maintaining, and operating large-scale AI infrastructure can reach millions of dollars, limiting access primarily to well-funded corporations and research institutions. This creates a disparity in who can develop and benefit from cutting-edge generative AI technologies.

Smaller organizations, startups, and researchers in less wealthy regions may struggle to compete, potentially slowing innovation and diversity in the field. Cloud-based AI services have partially democratized access by offering pay-as-you-go resources, but the most computationally intensive tasks remain expensive and sometimes prohibitive. Addressing these economic challenges involves developing more cost-effective training methods, such as model compression, knowledge distillation, and transfer learning, which enable smaller or more efficient models without sacrificing performance.

7.2.5 Algorithmic Efficiency and Model Compression

To overcome scalability challenges, researchers have increasingly focused on improving the algorithmic efficiency of generative models. Techniques like pruning, quantization, and knowledge distillation reduce the number of parameters or the precision of computations, decreasing the computational and memory footprint. Model pruning removes redundant or less important weights in a network, while quantization converts high-precision weights into lower-precision representations, both reducing resource requirements. Knowledge distillation transfers knowledge from a large "teacher" model to a smaller "student" model that can achieve similar performance with fewer resources. While these approaches help make generative models more manageable, they often involve trade-offs between efficiency and accuracy or creativity. Finding optimal balances remains an active area of research, essential for enabling broader adoption and deployment.

7.2.6 Challenges in Data Handling and Storage

Scalability is also closely tied to the volume and complexity of training data. Generative AI models require vast and diverse datasets to learn rich representations, which in turn demand significant storage capacity and data processing capabilities. Managing such data at scale involves challenges in collection, cleaning, annotation, and retrieval. Moreover, data throughput during training can become a bottleneck if storage and input/output (I/O) systems are not optimized. High-speed storage solutions, efficient data pipelines, and caching mechanisms are necessary to ensure that GPUs and other accelerators remain fully utilized rather than idling due to data access delays. As datasets grow, the costs and logistics of maintaining and updating them also increase, adding another dimension to scalability challenges.

7.2.7 Scalability in Deployment and Real-Time Inference

Deploying generative AI models at scale for real-world applications introduces additional complexities. Many applications, such as conversational agents, real-time image generation, or personalized content creation, require rapid inference to serve user requests with minimal delay. Running large generative models in production environments can strain server resources, especially when handling concurrent requests. Techniques such as model partitioning, caching, and approximate inference can help mitigate these issues but add complexity to system design. Edge deployment, where generative models run on devices like smartphones or embedded systems, presents even greater scalability challenges due to limited computational resources and energy constraints. Developing lightweight models that maintain acceptable performance is critical for expanding generative AI to decentralized environments.

7.2.8 Security and Privacy Concerns at Scale

Scaling generative AI systems also raises security and privacy issues. Large-scale models trained on sensitive data must ensure data confidentiality and comply with privacy regulations. Distributed training and cloud deployments increase exposure to potential breaches or misuse. Furthermore, as generative models scale, the risk of generating harmful, biased, or malicious content also increases. Implementing safeguards and monitoring systems at scale is resource-intensive but essential to maintain trust and prevent misuse.

7.2.9 Future Directions for Scalability and Cost Reduction

Addressing the challenges of scalability and computational costs in generative AI requires concerted efforts across hardware, software, and algorithmic domains. Research into more efficient model architectures, such as sparse networks or modular designs, promises to reduce computational overhead without sacrificing generative quality. Advancements in hardware, including next-generation GPUs, AI-specific accelerators, and neuromorphic computing, aim to provide more power-efficient computation tailored to generative workloads. Software frameworks that better exploit parallelism, optimize memory usage, and streamline distributed training also play a critical role. On the algorithmic side, meta-learning, transfer learning, and few-shot learning approaches strive to reduce training data and computational demands by leveraging prior knowledge.

Hybrid models that combine symbolic reasoning with generative AI may offer more efficient pathways to complex generation. Collaborative efforts between academia, industry, and policymakers will be crucial in developing standards, sharing infrastructure, and incentivizing sustainable AI research practices.

7.3 EVALUATION METRICS FOR GENERATIVE MODELS

Generative AI models have transformed the landscape of artificial intelligence by enabling machines to create content that closely resembles human-generated data. From text and images to audio and complex simulations, generative models such as GANs (Generative Adversarial Networks), VAEs (Variational Autoencoders), and diffusion models have showcased remarkable abilities.

However, evaluating these models remains one of the most significant challenges in the field. Unlike traditional discriminative models where accuracy or error rates provide straightforward metrics, generative models produce outputs that are often subjective, multi-dimensional, and context-dependent. Evaluation metrics for generative models remain a profound challenge in generative AI, shaped by the intrinsic complexity, subjectivity, and diversity of the generation task. While existing quantitative metrics provide valuable insights, their limitations highlight the need for multi-faceted, interpretable, and context-aware evaluation frameworks. Human evaluation continues to play a critical role but must be complemented by scalable automated methods.

As generative AI applications grow in scope and sophistication, addressing the challenges in evaluation metrics will be central to building reliable, trustworthy, and effective generative systems that can be confidently deployed across domains. Continued innovation in metric design, interdisciplinary collaboration, and human-centered evaluation practices will shape the future of generative AI's impact on society.

7.3.1 The Complexity of Generative Model Evaluation

The fundamental challenge in evaluating generative AI lies in the nature of the task itself. Generative models aim to produce new samples that resemble real-world data distributions. Unlike classification or regression, where a correct label or value can be clearly defined, generative tasks involve creativity, variation, and subtle semantic attributes. For instance, when a model generates an image, there is no single "correct" answer, but rather an entire space of plausible outputs. Similarly, in natural language generation, the quality of text is assessed not only on grammar or coherence but also on creativity, relevance, style, and emotional tone. This intrinsic ambiguity complicates metric design because evaluation must capture multiple facets of generation quality simultaneously.

Metrics must measure fidelity—the closeness of generated samples to real data distribution—while also capturing diversity to avoid mode collapse, where models produce limited or repetitive outputs. Moreover, generative models must be evaluated for their ability to generalize beyond training data without simply memorizing or replicating existing samples. Balancing these sometimes competing criteria is a major challenge.

7.3.2 Quantitative Metrics and Their Limitations

Several quantitative metrics have been proposed and widely adopted to evaluate generative models, particularly in the domain of image synthesis. The Inception Score (IS) was among the earliest and most popular metrics, using a pretrained classifier to measure the clarity and diversity of generated images. A high inception score indicates that generated images are both meaningful (the classifier confidently assigns a class) and varied (class distribution is diverse). Despite its popularity, IS has several limitations, including sensitivity to the choice of pretrained model and inability to detect mode collapse properly. The Fréchet Inception Distance (FID) emerged as an improvement over IS by comparing the statistics (mean and covariance) of feature embeddings between real and generated images.

FID measures the distance between two multivariate Gaussian distributions and provides a better approximation of the overall quality and diversity of generated samples. Nonetheless, FID assumes Gaussian distributions of features, which may not always hold, and is also susceptible to biases based on the pretrained model used for feature extraction. Other metrics like Precision and Recall for generative models have been proposed to separately evaluate the fidelity and diversity of samples. Precision measures the proportion of generated samples that lie close to the real data distribution, while recall measures how well the model covers the real data distribution. These metrics provide more granular insights but require careful calibration and can be computationally intensive. In text generation, metrics such as BLEU, ROUGE, and METEOR, originally designed for machine translation and summarization, are commonly used. They assess the overlap between generated text and reference samples by comparing n-grams or word sequences. While useful for some tasks, these metrics often fail to capture semantic coherence, creativity, or fluency, making them insufficient for open-ended text generation tasks. Recently, learned metrics based on neural networks trained to predict human judgments have gained traction, but their generalizability and interpretability remain concerns.

7.3.3 The Role of Human Evaluation

Due to the limitations of automated metrics, human evaluation remains a gold standard for assessing generative AI outputs. Humans can judge qualities like creativity, coherence, emotional impact, and appropriateness more holistically than algorithms. For example, in conversational AI, human raters evaluate dialogue naturalness, relevance, and engagement, aspects difficult to quantify otherwise. However, human evaluation is costly, time-consuming, and can suffer from subjectivity and inconsistency.

Different raters may have varied standards or preferences, and large-scale evaluation requires careful design of guidelines and inter-rater reliability checks. Moreover, human evaluation is impractical for frequent iterative model training cycles or real-time feedback, limiting its scalability. Thus, a major challenge is integrating human insights into automated evaluation frameworks that approximate human judgment but remain objective and reproducible. Techniques like crowd-sourcing, user studies, and expert panels are often combined with quantitative metrics to achieve balanced assessment.

7.3.4 Challenges in Multimodal and Complex Generative Tasks

As generative models extend beyond images and text to more complex and multimodal domains, evaluation challenges multiply. For example, models generating videos must be assessed for spatial and temporal consistency, realistic motion, and narrative coherence. Similarly, in audio synthesis, metrics must evaluate sound quality, timbre, rhythm, and intelligibility. Multimodal generative models that integrate text, images, and audio simultaneously require metrics capable of assessing cross-modal coherence and alignment.

For example, an AI generating an image based on a textual description must be evaluated not only for image quality but also for how well the image matches the input prompt. Traditional single-modality metrics fail to capture such dependencies, necessitating novel evaluation frameworks. Moreover, as generative AI expands into domains like drug discovery or scientific simulations, evaluation criteria become domain-specific and often require expert knowledge. Validating generated molecular structures or experimental predictions involves complex benchmarks beyond standard machine learning metrics, adding layers of difficulty.

7.3.5 Trade-offs Between Fidelity, Diversity, and Novelty

One of the nuanced challenges in generative model evaluation is balancing fidelity with diversity and novelty. Fidelity refers to how realistic or accurate generated samples are, while diversity indicates the variety within generated outputs. Novelty measures the extent to which generated data introduces new, unseen features beyond the training set. High fidelity with low diversity might indicate that a model is overfitting or memorizing training data, producing repetitive outputs. Conversely, high diversity with low fidelity may generate unrealistic or nonsensical samples. Evaluating these dimensions simultaneously is complex because improvement in one area may degrade another. Metrics like FID implicitly combine fidelity and diversity, but separating these factors for diagnostic purposes is difficult. Furthermore, novelty is often neglected in standard metrics, though it is critical for creative applications. Developing metrics that can disentangle and measure these qualities precisely remains an active research challenge.

7.3.6 Robustness and Generalization in Evaluation

Another challenge lies in assessing the robustness and generalization capabilities of generative models. A good generative model should not only replicate training data but also generate plausible samples in new or slightly different contexts. Evaluating how well models generalize to out-of-distribution inputs or novel combinations is essential but often overlooked. Robustness also pertains to the model's behavior under adversarial or noisy conditions. For example, small perturbations in input prompts should not cause drastically different or erroneous outputs. Incorporating robustness tests into evaluation pipelines adds complexity but is crucial for reliable deployment.

7.3.7 Interpretability and Explainability in Evaluation Metrics

Evaluation metrics themselves must be interpretable and meaningful to practitioners and stakeholders. A metric that produces a single scalar score is easier to communicate but may obscure important details about model behavior. Conversely, multi-dimensional metrics provide richer insights but complicate decision-making. Transparent evaluation frameworks that explain what aspects of generation are being measured, their limitations, and how scores relate to real-world quality are essential. This interpretability enables better benchmarking, model comparison, and targeted improvement efforts.

7.3.8 Emerging Directions and Future Prospects

To address the evaluation challenges, researchers are exploring several promising directions. One approach is the development of learned evaluation metrics that use neural networks trained on large datasets annotated with human judgments. These models aim to predict human preferences more accurately than heuristic metrics. Another direction involves task-specific and user-centric evaluation, where metrics are tailored to the intended application and end-user needs. For example, generative models for education might be evaluated differently than those for entertainment or scientific research. Hybrid evaluation frameworks combining quantitative metrics, human feedback, and domain-specific benchmarks are becoming more common. These frameworks offer a more holistic assessment while balancing scalability and rigor. Advances in explainable AI may also enhance evaluation by providing insight into model uncertainty, confidence, and failure modes, enabling more nuanced interpretations of output quality.

7.4 TRANSPARENCY AND INTERPRETABILITY IN OUTPUTS

Generative AI has rapidly advanced over recent years, reshaping numerous domains by enabling the creation of highly sophisticated outputs such as text, images, music, and even complex simulations. Despite its remarkable capabilities, one of the critical challenges facing generative AI today is the issue of transparency and interpretability. Unlike traditional software programs, where the logic and decision pathways are explicit and understandable, generative AI models often operate as "black boxes." Transparency and interpretability in generative AI outputs present formidable challenges that stem from the complexity, scale, and probabilistic nature of current models. These challenges affect trust, accountability, ethical deployment, and practical usability. While progress is being made through visualization techniques, surrogate models, and user-centered design, much work remains to ensure that generative AI systems are not only powerful but also understandable and responsible. Addressing these issues is essential to realizing the full promise of generative AI while safeguarding against unintended consequences and fostering greater human-AI collaboration.

7.4.1 The Importance of Transparency in Generative AI

Transparency in generative AI refers to the degree to which the internal workings of the model, its decision-making processes, and the sources of its outputs can be made understandable and accessible to humans. This is essential for building user trust, diagnosing errors, mitigating biases, and ensuring ethical use. As generative models become more embedded in applications such as healthcare diagnosis, legal advice, or creative content generation, stakeholders demand clear explanations of how models arrive at their conclusions or creations. Transparency also plays a crucial role in regulatory compliance. With increasing scrutiny from governments and institutions, AI systems must often meet standards for explainability to ensure they do not inadvertently cause harm or discrimination. Without adequate transparency, models risk becoming inscrutable tools that generate outputs without accountability, making it difficult to contest or audit decisions made based on their results.

7.4.2 Interpretability: Understanding the Outputs

Interpretability complements transparency by focusing on making the outputs of generative AI understandable to users. Given the complexity of these models, interpretability often involves simplifying or visualizing the rationale behind a particular generated sample, whether it is a piece of text, an image, or an audio segment. The goal is to provide insights into which input features or internal representations influenced the final output. For example, in a text generation system, interpretability might involve identifying which parts of the input prompt or training data the model relied on to produce a given sentence. In image synthesis, it could mean visualizing how certain latent variables or layers in the model contributed to specific visual features. These explanations help users assess the reliability, relevance, and potential biases in the outputs, improving decision-making and human-AI collaboration.

7.4.3 Challenges in Achieving Transparency

Despite its importance, achieving transparency in generative AI models is extraordinarily difficult. One core reason is the inherent complexity of the architectures used, such as large-scale transformer networks or deep convolutional neural networks. These models consist of millions or even billions of parameters, making it infeasible for humans to inspect every weight or activation directly. Moreover, generative models do not operate with explicit rules or symbolic reasoning that can be easily followed. Instead, they learn statistical patterns from vast datasets, encoding relationships in highly distributed and abstract ways. This lack of a straightforward mapping between inputs, internal states, and outputs complicates attempts to trace the decision process. Another factor is the use of latent variables and probabilistic sampling in generative models. Outputs often result from stochastic processes, meaning the same input can yield different outputs on different runs. This variability, while beneficial for creativity and diversity, hinders clear interpretation and reproducibility.

7.4.4 Interpreting High-Dimensional Latent Spaces

Generative AI systems frequently rely on latent spaces—abstract multidimensional representations learned during training that capture essential features of the input data. While these latent spaces enable powerful generation capabilities, they are often inscrutable to human intuition. Understanding how movement within these spaces affects the generated outputs is a non-trivial task. Techniques such as latent space traversal and visualization have been developed to gain insight, but they only scratch the surface. Latent variables might encode complex entangled factors that do not correspond to any single interpretable attribute, making it difficult to link changes in latent space to concrete, understandable modifications in the output. This entanglement impedes transparency and interpretability, especially for end-users who are not AI experts.

7.4.5 Bias and Ethical Concerns Linked to Opacity

The opaque nature of generative AI also exacerbates issues of bias and fairness. Because these models learn from large datasets that often reflect historical and societal prejudices, their outputs may inadvertently perpetuate or amplify harmful stereotypes. Without transparent mechanisms to diagnose and explain these biases, developers and users struggle to detect and mitigate them. For example, a generative text model trained on internet data might produce gender-biased or racially insensitive language, while an image generation system might overrepresent certain demographics or aesthetics. Without interpretability tools to highlight the source and nature of such biases, ethical concerns remain unaddressed, undermining public trust and potentially causing harm.

7.4.6 Explainability versus Performance Trade-Off

Another challenge is the frequent trade-off between model performance and explainability. Often, the most accurate and flexible generative models are also the most complex and least interpretable. Simplifying models or adding interpretability constraints can reduce their generative capabilities or lead to less natural outputs. Balancing this trade-off remains an ongoing research challenge, as stakeholders require both high-quality outputs and sufficient transparency. Some efforts to address this involve post-hoc explanation methods that analyze model behavior after training. However, these methods may only provide partial insights and can sometimes be misleading or inconsistent. Ideally, interpretability should be built into the model design from the outset, but this requires novel architectures and training approaches that are still under development.

7.4.7 Tools and Methods for Improving Transparency

To tackle these challenges, researchers have proposed a range of tools and methods. Attention visualization is one popular approach, showing which parts of the input data the model "attends" to when generating output. While helpful, attention maps do not always correspond to causal explanations and can be difficult to interpret in highly complex models. Another technique involves probing or analyzing intermediate layers to uncover what information is represented and how it influences output. This can identify which neurons or features are responsible for certain behaviors, offering a window into the model's reasoning. Explainable AI frameworks also promote the use of surrogate models—simpler, interpretable models trained to approximate the behavior of a complex generative system locally. Although these surrogates cannot capture all nuances, they provide practical explanations that users can understand. Transparency can also be enhanced through rigorous documentation practices, including model cards and data sheets, which detail training data, model capabilities, limitations, and potential biases. This meta-information supports better governance and responsible deployment.

7.4.8 The Human Factor: User-Centered Interpretability

Interpretability is not only a technical challenge but also a human-centered design problem. Different users have different needs for explanations depending on their expertise, goals, and context. A data scientist may require detailed, technical insights into model internals, whereas an end-user or regulator might need simpler, actionable explanations. Designing interfaces that communicate the right level of interpretability, and that are intuitive and accessible, is vital. Interactive tools allowing users to query the model, explore alternative outputs, or test counterfactual scenarios can empower more informed interactions. Moreover, transparency efforts must account for cognitive biases and limitations. Clear communication should avoid overwhelming users with technical jargon or spurious details that reduce trust rather than enhance it.

7.4.9 Future Directions and the Path Ahead

Looking forward, the quest for transparency and interpretability in generative AI remains one of the most pressing and vibrant areas of research. Advances in inherently interpretable model architectures, causal modeling techniques, and hybrid symbolic-neural methods hold promise for making generative AI more understandable. Multidisciplinary collaboration between AI researchers, ethicists, cognitive scientists, and domain experts is critical for developing frameworks that ensure transparency does not come at the cost of utility or innovation. Standards and best practices for model auditing, fairness assessment, and user education will also be essential as generative AI becomes increasingly widespread. Ultimately, transparency and interpretability are not just technical desiderata—they are foundational to building AI systems that society can trust, embrace, and use responsibly. As generative AI continues to push the boundaries of creativity and automation, addressing these challenges head-on will determine how successfully these powerful tools can be integrated into human life.

CHAPTER 8

Future Trends and Research Directions

8.1 GENERATIVE AI IN MULTIMODAL SYSTEMS

Generative AI in multimodal systems represents a significant breakthrough in artificial intelligence, allowing machines to process and generate data across multiple sensory modalities. Unlike traditional AI models that operate within a single data format—be it text, images, or audio—multimodal generative systems are designed to understand, integrate, and synthesize information from different sources simultaneously. This shift has opened up new possibilities for more intuitive human-computer interaction, advanced content creation, and intelligent automation.

Generative AI in multimodal systems marks a transformative leap in artificial intelligence, bringing machines closer to the richness and complexity of human perception and communication. By integrating diverse data modalities into cohesive and intelligent outputs, these systems unlock new possibilities in creativity, education, healthcare, and beyond. While challenges remain in data integration, interpretability, and ethics, the trajectory of innovation is clear. Multimodal generative AI is not just an extension of what machines can do—it is a reimagining of how they can understand, collaborate with, and empower human beings in an increasingly interconnected world.

8.1.1 Understanding Multimodal Generative AI

At its core, a multimodal generative AI system leverages different types of data modalities—such as visual, textual, auditory, and sometimes even haptic or olfactory signals—to generate outputs that are coherent across these modalities. For instance, a system may generate a realistic video from a textual prompt, or synthesize spoken dialogue based on an image description. The key challenge and innovation in multimodal generative AI lies in the integration of heterogeneous data into a unified representation that can be effectively modeled and reproduced. This involves several stages of processing. First, the system must encode each modality in a way that retains the meaningful semantic features of the input. Then, these representations must be aligned or fused within a shared latent space. Finally, the generative component must decode this fused representation to produce outputs in one or more modalities. Technologies such as transformers, variational autoencoders, and diffusion models have played crucial roles in facilitating this process, thanks to their flexibility and power in modeling complex data structures.

8.1.2 Architectural Foundations and Advances

Multimodal generative AI systems are often built upon advanced neural architectures that are capable of handling diverse data types. Transformer-based models have become the backbone of many such systems due to their ability to capture long-range dependencies and manage sequential data effectively. Models like CLIP (Contrastive Language-Image Pretraining) and DALL·E from OpenAI exemplify the synergy between visual and textual data. CLIP learns joint representations of images and text, enabling it to perform zero-shot classification tasks with impressive accuracy, while DALL·E demonstrates the capacity to generate high-quality images from natural language descriptions.

More recent models such as GPT-4 and Gemini have extended these capabilities even further by incorporating a wider range of modalities and exhibiting strong performance across diverse generative tasks. These models often use cross-attention mechanisms to allow information from one modality to inform the generation in another, ensuring contextual consistency and semantic alignment. Training such models requires massive datasets that pair information from multiple sources, as well as computationally intensive infrastructure.

8.1.3 Applications across Industries

The application potential of multimodal generative AI is vast and spans numerous industries. In the field of content creation, artists and designers use these systems to generate illustrations, animations, and storyboards from textual or audio prompts, drastically reducing production time and expanding creative possibilities. For example, tools that generate concept art from narrative scripts allow writers and filmmakers to visualize their ideas more vividly and iteratively. In the education sector, multimodal AI can create personalized learning materials that include synchronized video, narration, and textual explanations tailored to a student's level of understanding. This enhances engagement and accommodates different learning styles, making education more inclusive and effective.

Healthcare is another domain that benefits significantly from multimodal generative AI. Systems can integrate medical imaging data, patient history, and genomic information to assist in diagnosis and treatment planning. A radiologist might receive an AI-generated report that interprets an MRI scan in the context of patient symptoms and lab results, offering a more comprehensive view than any single data source could provide. In customer service and virtual assistance, multimodal systems enhance the naturalness and utility of AI agents. By analyzing both spoken queries and visual cues, such as uploaded images or real-time video, AI assistants can respond more accurately and contextually. This creates more human-like and effective interactions, particularly in technical support, retail, and travel industries.

8.1.4 Challenges in Multimodal Generative AI

Despite its promise, multimodal generative AI faces several challenges. One of the foremost is data alignment and availability. Training effective multimodal models requires large datasets that include well-aligned samples across modalities. For example, pairing textual captions with images or transcriptions with video can be resource-intensive and may suffer from noise or inconsistencies. Ensuring data quality and diversity is crucial for model generalization and fairness. Another significant challenge is the complexity of modeling across modalities with differing structures and temporal characteristics. Audio and video, for instance, are time-dependent and continuous, whereas text and images are often discrete and static. Building architectures that can reconcile these differences without sacrificing fidelity or coherence is a central research problem.

Interpretability is also a concern. As models become more complex and capable, understanding how and why they produce specific outputs becomes more difficult. This is particularly problematic in sensitive applications such as healthcare or legal decision-making, where transparency is crucial. Researchers are exploring various techniques, such as attention visualization and modular architectures, to enhance model explainability. Ethical concerns are magnified in multimodal generative systems. The ability to generate highly realistic but synthetic media raises the risk of misinformation, deepfakes, and manipulation. Ensuring that these tools are used responsibly requires robust watermarking, detection tools, and policy frameworks. Moreover, bias in multimodal datasets can propagate into model behavior, leading to outputs that reinforce stereotypes or marginalize certain groups.

8.1.5 Future Directions and Innovations

Looking ahead, the future of generative AI in multimodal systems is poised for further innovation and integration. One promising direction is the development of unified models capable of handling an even broader spectrum of modalities. These models would not only combine vision, text, and audio but also integrate signals such as touch, temperature, and even emotion, potentially enabling new forms of embodied AI in robotics and assistive technology.

Another important trajectory is the move toward real-time generation and interaction. Advances in hardware acceleration and efficient model design are making it increasingly feasible to deploy multimodal generative models in real-time applications, such as virtual reality, gaming, and live broadcasting. These systems could respond dynamically to user input across modalities, creating more immersive and interactive experiences. Personalization is also expected to become a central feature of future systems. By integrating user preferences, context, and prior interactions, multimodal generative AI can tailor its outputs more precisely to individual users. This could lead to highly adaptive virtual tutors, companions, or creative collaborators that understand and respond to users on multiple sensory levels. Finally, as multimodal AI systems become more prevalent, interdisciplinary collaboration will be essential. Advances will depend not only on machine learning techniques but also on insights from linguistics, cognitive science, neuroscience, and human-computer interaction. Ensuring these systems serve human needs and values requires a concerted effort across technical, ethical, and social dimensions.

8.2 CAUSAL GENERATIVE AI MODELS

Causal generative AI models represent a powerful fusion of two transformative branches of machine learning: generative modeling and causal inference. These models aim to go beyond traditional statistical correlations and attempt to model the underlying causal relationships that govern data generation. While conventional generative models like variational autoencoders (VAEs), generative adversarial networks (GANs), and diffusion models focus on learning data distributions, causal generative models introduce a deeper layer of understanding by incorporating the cause-and-effect structure within those distributions.

8.2.1 Understanding the Concept of Causality in AI

At the heart of causal generative AI lies the concept of causality. Unlike mere correlation, which captures associations between variables, causality aims to understand how one variable influences another. In other words, causal models seek to answer "what-if" questions, also known as counterfactuals. For instance, in a healthcare setting, a causal model might predict how a patient's outcome would change if a different treatment were administered. This capacity to reason about interventions and alternate realities makes causal models particularly powerful. Traditional AI systems often rely heavily on large datasets and pattern recognition to make predictions. However, such predictions may falter when applied in new contexts or environments due to confounding variables or data shifts. Causal models attempt to overcome this limitation by modeling the data generation process in a structured, interpretable manner. This not only improves robustness and generalizability but also enhances transparency, as the causal pathways can be visualized and understood.

8.2.2 Integrating Causality into Generative Models

Incorporating causal reasoning into generative models involves combining structural causal models (SCMs) with probabilistic modeling frameworks. Structural causal models use directed acyclic graphs (DAGs) to represent cause-effect relationships between variables. Each node in the graph corresponds to a variable, and the edges denote causal influence. Once a causal graph is established, it can be used to simulate data by sampling from the root causes and propagating the effects through the network. By aligning generative modeling with SCMs, it becomes possible to generate synthetic data that obeys known or hypothesized causal relationships. This has significant implications for simulations, counterfactual analysis, and domain adaptation.

For example, if a generative model knows that a variable like income causally affects education level and not the other way around, it can produce more realistic and policy-relevant data samples. One way this integration is realized is through causal VAEs, where the latent variables are structured to reflect a causal graph. These models learn disentangled representations where each latent variable corresponds to a specific cause in the data-generating process. This allows the model to perform interventions, such as fixing one latent cause and observing the effect on generated outputs. Such capabilities move generative AI beyond superficial pattern matching and toward genuine reasoning about the world.

8.2.3 Benefits of Causal Generative AI Models

Causal generative models offer several compelling benefits over traditional generative approaches. First and foremost is interpretability. Because these models are grounded in explicit causal structures, their behavior is often easier to understand and explain. This is especially important in high-stakes domains such as medicine or law, where trust and accountability are essential. Another key advantage is robustness to distributional shifts.

Traditional models trained on one data distribution may perform poorly when deployed in a different setting. Causal models, however, can adapt more effectively because they separate stable causal mechanisms from context-dependent associations. This makes them particularly valuable in transfer learning and domain generalization tasks, where models must maintain performance across varying environments. Moreover, causal models can generate counterfactuals, which are essential for personalized decision-making.

In clinical settings, for instance, doctors often want to know how a patient would respond to an alternative treatment. A causal generative model can simulate such scenarios and provide actionable insights that go beyond average-case predictions. This counterfactual reasoning can also inform fairness audits, by showing how outcomes would differ under alternative, potentially fairer conditions.

8.2.4 Applications across Disciplines

The potential applications of causal generative AI models are vast and interdisciplinary. In healthcare, they can help simulate patient outcomes under different treatment protocols, enabling more personalized and effective care strategies. For example, a causal generative model trained on electronic health records might simulate how a patient's recovery would change with a different medication regimen, helping clinicians make informed decisions. In economics and social science, these models are used to assess the impact of policy changes.

Governments can simulate the effects of tax reforms or educational interventions before implementing them, ensuring more data-driven and equitable decisions. By modeling the causal mechanisms of social systems, generative AI can provide policymakers with nuanced simulations that traditional statistical tools cannot offer. In the domain of climate science, causal generative models are used to explore the consequences of various environmental policies. Scientists can simulate the effects of carbon tax policies or deforestation measures on long-term climate patterns. This helps create more grounded and actionable insights in the fight against global warming. In marketing and business strategy, causal models help optimize customer engagement by revealing which variables—like price, product quality, or ad placement—truly drive sales. Marketers can test hypothetical campaigns in a simulated environment before investing resources, reducing risk and increasing return on investment.

8.2.5 Challenges in Building Causal Generative Models

Despite their promise, causal generative models face several challenges. One of the most significant is the difficulty of establishing a valid causal graph. In many real-world situations, the true causal relationships among variables are unknown or only partially understood. Inferring these relationships from data requires strong assumptions and domain expertise, and incorrect assumptions can lead to misleading conclusions. Another challenge is computational complexity. Modeling and simulating causal structures—especially in high-dimensional data—can be resource-intensive. Learning disentangled and interpretable latent variables that map onto real-world causes is a non-trivial task that requires sophisticated training regimes and large, high-quality datasets.

Moreover, causal inference is fundamentally constrained by the problem of confounding, where hidden variables influence both the cause and the effect. While techniques like instrumental variables and front-door/back-door criteria help mitigate confounding, they are not always applicable or sufficient. This introduces uncertainty into the conclusions drawn from causal generative models, highlighting the need for cautious interpretation and validation. Ethical concerns also arise when simulating counterfactuals, especially in sensitive areas like criminal justice or employment. Decisions based on hypothetical scenarios must be scrutinized for fairness, bias, and potential harms. Transparency in how causal relationships are modeled and how interventions are simulated is essential for maintaining public trust and avoiding unintended consequences.

8.2.6 Future Directions and the Path Forward

Looking ahead, the field of causal generative AI is poised for significant growth. Advances in automated causal discovery, combined with improved deep learning architectures, promise to make these models more scalable and user-friendly. Integration with large language models and multimodal systems could allow for causal reasoning across diverse data types, from text and images to time-series and structured data. Interdisciplinary collaboration will be key to realizing the full potential of causal generative AI. Domain experts must work closely with machine learning researchers to construct meaningful causal models that are grounded in real-world knowledge. This collaboration can yield tools that not only mimic human creativity but also reason like human experts. As AI becomes more embedded in decision-making processes across society, the ability to model and reason about cause and effect will be increasingly important. Causal generative AI offers a promising pathway to build more reliable, explainable, and ethical AI systems that do not merely reflect patterns in data but understand the mechanisms that shape our world. In this sense, causal generative models are not just a technical innovation—they represent a philosophical advancement in how machines can engage with the complexities of human life.

8.3 HUMAN-AI COLLABORATION IN CREATIVITY

The intersection of artificial intelligence and human creativity marks a transformative era in the evolution of art, literature, music, design, and countless other creative disciplines. Human-AI collaboration in creativity is not simply about automation or outsourcing imaginative work to machines; it represents a symbiotic relationship where technology acts as a partner that can extend, augment, and reframe human expression. In this evolving landscape, AI is being integrated as a co-creator, offering suggestions, generating variations, and enabling individuals to explore novel creative spaces that may have previously been inaccessible.

8.3.1 The Evolution of Creativity and the Emergence of AI Tools

Creativity has historically been seen as a deeply human trait, driven by emotion, intuition, and cultural context. However, the development of generative AI models capable of producing music, visual art, poetry, and narrative has challenged this long-held belief. Early AI-assisted creative tools, such as computer-aided design software and algorithmic music composition programs, functioned more like advanced calculators or aids. They allowed artists to refine and structure their ideas but did not actively contribute original content. With the rise of machine learning and especially deep learning, however, the creative capabilities of AI have expanded significantly. Models like GPT for text, DALL·E for images, and MuseNet for music now offer interactive platforms that can co-create with humans in real-time. These tools can ingest prompts, learn from style inputs, and generate content that either imitates or innovates upon established norms. For instance, a writer might use a language model to brainstorm dialogue or plot developments, while a visual artist might use image generators to explore new aesthetics based on a few keywords or a rough sketch. This shift from passive tool to active collaborator marks a fundamental change in how creativity is conceived and executed.

8.3.2 Reframing the Role of the Human Artist

One of the most significant impacts of AI in creative collaboration is the redefinition of the human artist's role. In a traditional context, the artist is the sole originator of an idea and is responsible for translating that idea into a tangible form. In an AI-assisted context, the human becomes more of a curator, director, or editor. The artist provides the vision, prompts, and refinement, while the AI generates a multitude of potential outputs based on those inputs.

This partnership can be empowering because it reduces the cognitive load associated with exploring creative alternatives. A musician can instantly hear how a melody might sound in a different genre. A filmmaker can generate storyboards or scripts in minutes. An architect can visualize multiple structural designs based on abstract criteria. The speed and flexibility of AI allow creators to iterate faster, fail more safely, and ultimately achieve greater creative depth than they might have alone. However, this collaborative model also raises questions about authorship and originality.

When an AI contributes significantly to a creative work, how much credit should it receive? How do we evaluate the authenticity or emotional depth of a piece created in part by a machine? These are philosophical and ethical dilemmas that will continue to evolve alongside the technology.

8.3.3 Enhancing Accessibility and Democratizing Creativity

Another profound impact of human-AI collaboration is its potential to democratize access to creative tools and processes. Traditionally, expertise in creative fields required years of training, specialized knowledge, and access to expensive resources. AI changes that dynamic by lowering the entry barriers to high-quality creative output. An amateur poet can use a language model to refine their verses. A non-musician can generate a symphony.

A person with no design background can produce stunning visuals using AI-based platforms. This democratization opens up creative expression to more people, allowing diverse voices and perspectives to be heard. It also fosters cross-disciplinary innovation, where people from different fields—such as science, engineering, or education—can engage with creative processes more fluidly. By serving as a catalyst for experimentation, AI encourages a broader spectrum of society to participate in cultural production and storytelling. Moreover, AI tools can serve as aids for individuals with disabilities, offering voice-to-text capabilities, visual enhancements, or assistive composition technologies that enable creative work that might otherwise be difficult or impossible. In this way, AI becomes not just a creative collaborator, but a powerful agent of inclusion.

8.3.4 Inspiration, Iteration, and Creative Serendipity

One of the most exciting aspects of working with AI in a creative context is the capacity for serendipity. AI systems often produce results that are unexpected, surprising, or even unintentionally profound. These generative "mistakes" can open up new directions for creative exploration. A poet might be inspired by an AI-generated metaphor they would not have conceived of themselves.

A visual artist might integrate a pattern or texture that the model produced randomly. These moments of serendipity resemble the flashes of inspiration that artists often describe as central to their creative process. Furthermore, AI accelerates the process of iteration, allowing creators to quickly test variations, explore alternatives, and refine their work. This ability to move rapidly through cycles of generation and revision fosters an environment where creativity is more fluid and dynamic. It encourages risk-taking and unconventional thinking, as the cost of failure is reduced and the speed of feedback is increased. This shift in process encourages a more experimental and playful approach to creativity, where ideas can be explored without the fear of wasted effort.

8.3.5 Limitations and Challenges in AI-Creative Partnerships

Despite its many benefits, human-AI collaboration in creativity is not without challenges. One of the primary limitations is that AI, while powerful, lacks genuine understanding, emotion, and cultural context. It can mimic styles and patterns, but it does not experience the world, and thus its outputs can sometimes feel hollow or inauthentic. Without careful human guidance, the outputs generated by AI can be cliché, ethically problematic, or creatively uninspired. There is also the risk of over-reliance, where creators begin to defer too heavily to AI outputs, potentially dulling their own creative instincts. Maintaining a balance where AI serves to augment rather than replace human creativity is essential.

Moreover, concerns about plagiarism and data provenance have emerged, particularly as many generative models are trained on large datasets that include copyrighted material. Ensuring transparency and ethical use of training data remains a critical issue in AI-generated content. Additionally, biases present in training data can influence the outputs of generative models, sometimes reinforcing harmful stereotypes or excluding marginalized perspectives. Human creators must remain vigilant and critical, curating and editing AI-generated content to align with ethical and inclusive standards.

8.3.6 Looking Ahead: The Future of Co-Creation

As generative AI models become more advanced, we are likely to see even more seamless and intuitive forms of human-AI collaboration. Future systems may be able to interpret visual cues, emotional tones, or even brain signals to co-create in ways that feel more like true collaboration than command-response. The integration of AI into virtual and augmented reality environments will further blur the line between creator and tool, enabling immersive, real-time co-creation experiences. Education systems may begin incorporating AI co-creators into creative curricula, training students not only in artistic skills but also in how to critically and ethically engage with AI tools.

Professional industries in advertising, entertainment, and design will increasingly rely on AI collaborators to manage the complexity and speed demanded by modern audiences. Ultimately, the goal is not to replace human creativity but to expand its horizons. By embracing AI as a collaborator, artists and creators can push the boundaries of imagination, innovate across disciplines, and tell richer, more diverse stories than ever before. The fusion of human emotion and AI computation promises a new chapter in the history of creativity—one defined not by competition, but by cooperation.

8.4 GENERATIVE AI FOR PERSONALIZED EXPERIENCES

Generative AI is transforming the way digital systems interact with individuals by offering personalized experiences that go far beyond traditional recommendation systems. As this technology continues to evolve, it enables dynamic content creation tailored specifically to user preferences, behaviors, and contexts. Whether it's generating custom music playlists, crafting personalized marketing messages, curating individualized learning content, or even composing entire conversations, generative AI has redefined the standard for user engagement.

Personalized experiences powered by AI are not just about adjusting what content users see, but about dynamically generating new content that feels uniquely relevant to each person. Generative AI has unlocked new frontiers in personalized digital experiences, offering capabilities that were once thought to be the domain of human creativity and intuition. From marketing and education to healthcare and entertainment, AI systems are now able to create content and interactions that are not only relevant but also emotionally resonant. As these technologies mature, the challenge will be to harness their power responsibly, ensuring that personalization serves to enhance rather than exploit the user experience. With careful attention to ethical considerations, user empowerment, and continual innovation, generative AI promises to redefine the way individuals engage with the digital world in deeply personal and meaningful ways.

8.4.1 The Shift from Static to Dynamic Personalization

In the early stages of digital personalization, static rule-based systems were the norm. These systems relied on user segmentation and predefined rules to deliver content. For example, a user might be shown a specific advertisement based on their age, location, or past purchases. While this form of personalization had its merits, it lacked the depth and flexibility required to adapt to the nuances of individual users in real-time.

The rise of machine learning allowed for more data-driven personalization, yet even this approach typically focused on selecting existing content from a pool rather than creating new content. Generative AI marks a significant departure from these earlier systems by enabling dynamic personalization. Instead of selecting from pre-existing options, the AI generates new outputs—be it text, images, music, or even code—based on a user's unique input and interaction history. This real-time generation capability enables a much more fluid and adaptable personalization model, which can evolve as the user's behavior changes or as new data becomes available. This flexibility is key to building deeper and more meaningful digital experiences.

8.4.2 Generative AI in Personalized Content Creation

One of the most direct applications of generative AI in personalization is in content creation. For example, in the domain of marketing, generative AI can craft personalized email campaigns that reflect a recipient's interests, browsing history, and previous interactions with a brand. Instead of sending a generic message to all users, businesses can use AI-generated content to tailor subject lines, product recommendations, and body text that resonate more effectively with each individual. This increases the likelihood of engagement and conversion, as the content feels more relevant and less intrusive.

Similarly, in media and entertainment, generative AI is used to create personalized narratives in video games, where storylines can evolve based on a player's choices and style of play. AI can generate dialogue, quests, and even visual environments that are unique to each user. This capability is also being explored in streaming platforms, where generative models help curate content and even generate trailers or highlight reels that align with a viewer's preferences. Personalized content creation does not stop at entertainment—it extends to news, education, and even healthcare, where AI-generated content can be customized to match a reader's language level, learning style, or health condition.

8.4.3 Personalized Education through Generative AI

Education is another field experiencing a revolution through generative AI, with systems that can adapt teaching materials to suit the learning needs of individual students. Instead of presenting all learners with the same material, generative models can create explanations, examples, quizzes, and feedback tailored to a student's proficiency, interests, and progress. For instance, if a student struggles with a particular mathematical concept, the AI can generate alternative explanations or practice problems that target their specific area of difficulty.

These adaptive learning systems can also change the pace of content delivery, ensuring that students are neither overwhelmed nor under-challenged. Generative AI can identify gaps in understanding and generate supplemental materials to address them. This approach not only enhances learning outcomes but also improves student motivation and confidence, as the instruction feels more supportive and personalized. Moreover, generative models can be integrated into virtual tutors and chatbots, providing real-time help and feedback in a conversational manner.

8.4.4 Healthcare and Wellness Personalization

In the healthcare domain, generative AI is making strides in personalizing patient care and wellness guidance. AI systems can generate individualized health reports, treatment plans, or diet recommendations based on a patient's medical history, genetic information, and lifestyle data. This enables a more nuanced and effective approach to preventive care and chronic disease management.

For mental health, AI-driven chatbots use natural language generation to engage in personalized therapeutic conversations, offering coping strategies and emotional support that reflect a user's specific experiences and mental state. Generative AI also facilitates the personalization of wellness content, such as meditation scripts, fitness routines, or nutritional advice. Instead of providing generic plans, AI can synthesize user data to create routines that align with individual goals, preferences, and physical conditions. This level of personalization encourages adherence and engagement, making wellness interventions more effective.

8.4.5 Retail and E-Commerce Experience Enhancement

In retail and e-commerce, generative AI personalizes the shopping experience by generating product descriptions, styling suggestions, and chatbot conversations that cater to individual tastes. Rather than showing a standard product listing, an AI system can tailor the text and visuals to reflect a user's browsing habits and brand affinities. This helps customers feel more understood and valued, enhancing their overall experience with the platform. Additionally, AI-powered virtual assistants in online stores can generate conversational responses to customer queries that reflect their purchase history, preferences, and current needs. This mimics the experience of interacting with a highly knowledgeable in-store assistant. By creating a sense of human-like interaction and deep understanding, generative AI contributes to greater customer satisfaction and loyalty.

8.4.6 Balancing Personalization with Privacy and Ethics

While the benefits of generative AI for personalized experiences are substantial, they also raise important questions about privacy and ethical use of data. Personalization depends on collecting and analyzing large amounts of user data, which can include sensitive information. Ensuring that this data is handled responsibly and with user consent is critical to maintaining trust. Transparent data practices, secure data storage, and mechanisms for users to control their data are essential components of ethical personalization strategies. Furthermore, developers must be cautious of over-personalization, which can lead to filter bubbles or reinforce harmful biases. For instance, if an AI system only generates content that aligns with a user's existing beliefs or behaviors, it can limit exposure to diverse perspectives and new ideas. Striking the right balance between personalization and diversity is crucial to creating enriching and equitable user experiences.

8.4.7 Future Directions for Personalized Generative AI

The future of generative AI in personalization will likely involve deeper integration of multimodal data and more context-aware systems. As AI models gain the ability to process and generate content across different modalities—text, image, audio, and video—they can deliver even richer and more cohesive experiences. For example, a virtual assistant could not only understand spoken queries but also generate visual presentations or schedule recommendations tailored to the user's preferences and calendar. Real-time personalization will also become more sophisticated, with systems that adapt on the fly to subtle cues such as emotional tone, facial expressions, or interaction patterns. These advancements will depend on improved models, more powerful hardware, and thoughtful design to ensure responsiveness without compromising privacy.

CHAPTER 9

Best Practices for Developing Generative AI Systems

9.1 DATA CURATION AND PREPROCESSING

Data curation and preprocessing form the bedrock of effective generative AI system development. These steps are often underestimated in terms of their complexity and importance, yet they play a decisive role in shaping the capabilities, safety, and trustworthiness of generative models. The quality, structure, balance, and relevance of training data directly influence the model's ability to learn nuanced patterns and produce coherent, creative, or contextually appropriate outputs.

Generative AI systems, whether designed to produce text, images, music, or code, depend heavily on robust datasets that capture the richness and diversity of human expression while avoiding noise, bias, and redundancy. Data curation and preprocessing are foundational pillars in the development of generative AI systems. The process involves meticulous sourcing, cleaning, labeling, normalization, augmentation, and monitoring to ensure that the data not only trains the model effectively but also reflects ethical and operational standards. Given that generative models learn to imitate their training data, flaws or biases in the dataset can directly translate into harmful outputs.

By implementing best practices in data curation, developers can build systems that are more robust, fair, transparent, and aligned with human values. As the field continues to evolve, the emphasis on responsible data practices will only become more central to the success and societal acceptance of generative AI.

9.1.1 Understanding the Role of Data in Generative AI

Unlike traditional AI systems that primarily focus on classification or prediction tasks, generative AI systems require data not just as a source of labels but as a blueprint for creative synthesis. The data must exemplify the kind of output the model is expected to produce, from stylistically rich language for large language models to diverse image samples for generative adversarial networks or diffusion models. This amplifies the importance of data selection and cleanliness.

In generative modeling, the system does not merely learn from the data but attempts to emulate its distributions, structures, and styles. Therefore, imperfections, biases, and inconsistencies in the dataset can be directly mirrored in the outputs, often with amplified consequences.

9.1.2 Sourcing High-Quality and Ethical Data

The first step in the curation process is identifying trustworthy and representative data sources. High-quality data must be accurate, complete, and contextually relevant to the problem domain. For text generation tasks, data might be sourced from books, articles, conversation transcripts, or code repositories, while for image generation, curated image libraries, medical scans, or user-generated content might be used. Ethical sourcing involves ensuring data is collected with proper permissions, adheres to intellectual property rights, and protects the privacy of individuals whose content may be included. As generative AI becomes increasingly public-facing, the legal and reputational risks of using copyrighted or sensitive material have grown, making ethical considerations integral to the curation strategy. Data also needs to reflect diversity and inclusiveness, particularly in applications that interact with a wide range of users.

A language model trained exclusively on Western literature, for instance, may fail to recognize or generate content that reflects global cultural perspectives. Similarly, image models trained on datasets lacking representation across skin tones, ages, or geographic regions may yield biased outputs. Addressing these issues begins with ensuring the dataset contains varied and balanced samples that capture a broad range of human experiences.

9.1.3 Cleaning and Filtering for Accuracy and Safety

Once data has been collected, it must undergo rigorous cleaning to remove irrelevant, erroneous, or harmful content. In text-based models, this can include stripping out formatting issues, correcting grammar mistakes, removing offensive or hateful language, and eliminating boilerplate content that adds little value. For image data, preprocessing might involve removing corrupted files, filtering inappropriate or low-resolution images, and standardizing formats. One of the challenges in cleaning generative datasets is determining the threshold for what constitutes noise or offensive content, especially in domains involving user-generated or web-crawled data. Automated filtering techniques, including regular expressions, keyword lists, and machine learning classifiers, can aid in this process but may also require human review to validate effectiveness. Establishing content moderation guidelines, using multi-stage filtering, and maintaining audit logs of removed data are best practices that help ensure a clean and accountable dataset.

9.1.4 Data Labeling and Annotation for Supervised Guidance

In many generative tasks, data must be annotated with metadata, tags, or labels that guide conditional generation or structured learning. For example, in image-to-text or text-to-image models, labels linking captions to visual elements are essential. In music generation, tags indicating genre, tempo, or instrumentation may be used to control outputs. Manual labeling, while accurate, can be time-consuming and costly, especially at large scales. Semi-supervised and crowdsourced annotation methods, as well as the use of pretrained classifiers for auto-labeling, can offer practical alternatives. Ensuring label consistency and avoiding annotation bias are key to maintaining dataset quality.

Labeling standards and documentation, such as data sheets or model cards, provide transparency into how labels were applied and interpreted. Regular auditing of labeled datasets helps identify systemic errors or biases, which can then be addressed through retraining or relabeling strategies.

9.1.5 Normalization and Standardization across Modalities

Once labeled and cleaned, data must be normalized to ensure uniformity across the dataset. For text, this can include converting characters to lowercase, removing stop words, and applying tokenization or subword encoding. In image data, normalization might involve scaling pixel values, aligning image dimensions, or applying color corrections. Audio and video data require synchronized sampling rates and encoding formats to facilitate downstream modeling.

Normalization ensures that the model receives inputs in a consistent format, reducing the learning burden and improving convergence rates during training. It also helps prevent the model from being unduly influenced by variations in formatting or scale. While aggressive normalization can sometimes strip data of subtle features, careful calibration of preprocessing parameters—guided by domain knowledge—helps preserve relevant information while maintaining consistency.

9.1.6 Data Augmentation for Robustness and Generalization

Data augmentation is another essential preprocessing step that enhances model robustness and generalization. By synthetically expanding the dataset through transformations, it becomes possible to expose the model to variations it may encounter during deployment. In image tasks, augmentations can include flipping, rotating, cropping, or adding noise. For text, paraphrasing, back-translation, and synonym substitution are common techniques.

In music and audio, pitch shifting, speed variation, and background noise injection serve similar purposes. Augmentation not only increases the effective size of the training set but also helps the model develop invariance to superficial changes in input. This leads to better generalization and less overfitting. However, augmentations must be applied in a way that preserves the semantic integrity of the data. For instance, aggressive paraphrasing in text could distort the intended meaning, just as random cropping in images might remove key visual elements. Thoughtful selection and validation of augmentation strategies are essential to ensure their utility.

9.1.7 Building Scalable and Reproducible Data Pipelines

The complexity of modern generative AI models necessitates scalable and reproducible data pipelines. These pipelines automate the ingestion, cleaning, transformation, and formatting of data, ensuring that preprocessing steps can be repeated and audited across development cycles. Tools such as Apache Airflow, TensorFlow Data, or PyTorch DataLoaders provide infrastructure for creating modular and efficient data workflows. Version control systems like DVC or data lake solutions further enhance the traceability and maintainability of large datasets.

Reproducibility is especially critical in regulated or high-stakes domains, where the ability to trace the provenance and transformation of data can impact certification or audit requirements. Best practices include logging all preprocessing scripts, capturing checksums of data files, and documenting preprocessing parameters. Implementing automated validation checks at each stage of the pipeline helps catch data drift, corruption, or unexpected anomalies early in the process.

9.1.8 Monitoring and Updating the Dataset Over Time

Data curation is not a one-time effort but an ongoing process. As new data becomes available, user needs evolve, or model shortcomings are identified, it is essential to update the dataset periodically. Continuous integration of fresh, high-quality data ensures the model remains relevant and responsive to changing contexts.

Likewise, feedback from deployed systems—such as user interactions, failure cases, or output reviews—can guide refinements in the dataset. Monitoring tools can track dataset characteristics over time, flagging shifts in distribution, increased duplication, or imbalances that may affect model performance.

Periodic audits and dataset retraining cycles maintain alignment between the data and the model's intended purpose. Governance structures that oversee dataset updates, including data stewards or ethical review boards, further enhance accountability and transparency.

9.2 CHOOSING THE RIGHT MODEL ARCHITECTURE

In the development of generative AI systems, selecting the appropriate model architecture is one of the most crucial decisions that determines the success, scalability, and adaptability of the system. With a growing number of architectural frameworks ranging from recurrent neural networks to transformers, variational autoencoders, and diffusion models, the choice of architecture is no longer a matter of technical preference but a strategic alignment with project goals, data characteristics, resource constraints, and deployment environments. Model architecture influences not only how data is processed and learned but also how effectively and efficiently the system generates novel outputs across text, images, audio, or code. Choosing the right model architecture is a foundational aspect of building successful generative AI systems. It requires a holistic assessment of the generative task, data availability, resource constraints, deployment environment, and ethical considerations.

By understanding the strengths and limitations of various architectures—such as transformers, VAEs, GANs, and diffusion models—developers can make informed decisions that optimize performance, scalability, and usability. The best practices in architecture selection include aligning with task-specific goals, balancing complexity with interpretability, optimizing for training and deployment conditions, and anticipating future adaptability. As generative AI continues to evolve, a thoughtful and strategic approach to architecture selection will remain a critical determinant of system success.

9.2.1 Understanding the Nature of the Generative Task

The first and most fundamental step in choosing the right architecture is to clearly define the generative task and understand its domain-specific requirements. Different tasks—such as text completion, image synthesis, music generation, or code creation—demand different modeling capabilities. For instance, text generation benefits from architectures that handle long-range dependencies and preserve grammar, coherence, and context. This makes transformer-based models particularly suitable due to their attention mechanisms and scalability.

Conversely, for tasks such as image-to-image translation or style transfer, convolutional neural networks or U-Nets often provide better performance by leveraging local spatial structures. The nature of the output also matters. Some generative tasks require discrete outputs, while others involve continuous data. Text and code are inherently symbolic and sequential, which makes autoregressive models more appropriate. Images and audio, on the other hand, require models that can handle high-dimensional, continuous-valued data, thus benefiting from architectures like GANs, VAEs, or diffusion models. Understanding these distinctions helps align the architecture with the requirements of fidelity, creativity, and control.

9.2.2 Evaluating Data Availability and Quality

The success of generative models is deeply tied to the availability and quality of data. Architectures such as deep transformers, which include hundreds of billions of parameters, typically require large, diverse, and well-structured datasets to learn meaningful patterns. If only limited data is available, simpler models or architectures that can perform transfer learning or few-shot learning may be more appropriate. For instance, variational autoencoders can be effective in low-data regimes when combined with domain-specific priors, while pre-trained transformer models like GPT or BERT variants can be fine-tuned on smaller datasets to achieve competitive results.

The diversity, balance, and representativeness of the data also affect model choice. In multimodal generative tasks involving combinations of text, images, and audio, hybrid architectures or encoder-decoder frameworks capable of handling different data types simultaneously are essential. For example, CLIP-like models that align vision and language or diffusion transformers that can generate high-fidelity images from textual prompts require specifically designed cross-modal interfaces.

9.2.3 Balancing Complexity, Interpretability, and Performance

Model architecture influences not only performance but also interpretability and operational complexity. Deep and complex architectures like large-scale transformers and GANs offer high accuracy and expressiveness but are often harder to interpret, train, and debug. On the other hand, simpler architectures such as RNNs or traditional autoencoders might offer greater transparency and ease of deployment but may fall short in performance for more demanding tasks.

When interpretability is a critical concern—such as in healthcare or finance—choosing architectures that support explanation mechanisms, such as attention-based models or disentangled representations, becomes important. Moreover, simpler models may be preferable in environments with strict computational or regulatory constraints. The trade-off between architectural complexity and interpretability should be evaluated carefully, keeping in mind both the end-user requirements and the system's operational context.

9.2.4 Considering Training Efficiency and Resource Constraints

Training generative models can be highly resource-intensive, particularly when using architectures like GANs or large transformer models. The selection of architecture must therefore consider available computational resources, including GPU or TPU availability, memory limits, and training time constraints. While diffusion models and transformers have achieved state-of-the-art results, they also demand significant infrastructure, often necessitating specialized hardware and distributed training. For organizations with limited resources, optimizing for efficiency may involve using distilled or pruned versions of large models, leveraging pre-trained checkpoints, or selecting architectures known for their speed and efficiency.

Transformer variants like ALBERT, DistilBERT, and T5 can reduce computational demands while maintaining acceptable performance. Additionally, model parallelism, gradient checkpointing, and mixed-precision training are techniques that can be employed to manage large architectures efficiently, but they may also influence the choice of architecture based on their compatibility.

9.2.5 Adapting to Deployment Environment and Latency Requirements

Deployment conditions strongly influence model architecture choices. Generative AI systems deployed in real-time environments, such as chatbots or creative applications, need low-latency response times and lightweight inference. Architectures that support fast decoding and efficient memory usage are better suited for such scenarios.

For instance, autoregressive models may suffer from slower inference due to token-by-token generation, while non-autoregressive or parallelizable architectures can offer faster results, albeit sometimes at the cost of reduced fluency or accuracy. In contrast, batch-oriented or asynchronous systems, such as recommendation engines or image stylization tools, can afford more complex and slower models that are optimized for quality over speed. Edge deployment adds another layer of constraint, requiring compact models that can run efficiently on mobile devices or embedded systems.

Techniques such as quantization, weight sharing, and model compression can help adapt larger architectures to constrained environments, but these often necessitate an initial selection of an architecture that is amenable to such transformations.

9.2.6 Incorporating Flexibility and Transferability

Given the fast-evolving landscape of generative AI, choosing an architecture that supports future flexibility and transferability is increasingly important. Models that can be extended to handle new tasks, adapt to new data, or support additional modalities offer long-term value. Transformer-based architectures, due to their modularity and attention mechanisms, have proven particularly versatile and have become foundational in large-scale generative systems. The ability to fine-tune, retrain, or expand a model without starting from scratch supports rapid iteration and adaptation.

Architectures that are open-sourced and well-supported by the research community provide additional benefits in terms of available tooling, pretrained weights, and compatibility with existing infrastructure. Using architectures that support plug-and-play modules, such as encoder-decoder interfaces, helps decouple components for independent development and maintenance.

9.2.7 Integrating Ethical and Societal Considerations

Model architecture also has implications for ethical and societal impacts. Some architectures, due to their tendency to memorize training data or amplify biases, pose higher risks than others. For example, large language models trained on unfiltered internet data can produce outputs that are biased, offensive, or harmful. In such cases, architectural choices must include provisions for mitigation, such as incorporating safety layers, filtering mechanisms, or human-in-the-loop systems. Choosing architectures that support controllability and interpretability can help mitigate these risks.

VAEs, for instance, provide a latent space that can be manipulated to produce specific types of outputs. Conditional generation architectures allow developers to guide outputs based on explicit parameters or constraints. These design choices not only improve usability but also support transparency and accountability.

9.3 OPTIMIZING TRAINING AND DEPLOYMENT PIPELINES

The development of generative AI systems involves a complex interplay between model architecture design, data processing, training methodologies, and deployment strategies. As these systems scale in both capability and impact, optimizing the training and deployment pipelines becomes critical. Poorly optimized processes not only increase the cost of development but also lead to models that underperform or are difficult to maintain in real-world applications.

Optimizing training and deployment pipelines for generative AI systems is an ongoing process that demands technical rigor, strategic planning, and ethical foresight. By adopting best practices across data preparation, model training, evaluation, deployment, and maintenance, teams can develop scalable and high-performing generative models. These models not only deliver impressive outputs but also serve users reliably, responsibly, and transparently. As generative AI continues to evolve, so too must the practices and tools that underpin its development, ensuring that innovation is matched by accountability and excellence.

9.3.1 Establishing a Clear Problem Definition and System Goals

Optimization begins before a single line of code is written or data is collected. Clearly defining the problem that the generative AI system is meant to solve sets the direction for all subsequent decisions. Whether the goal is to generate realistic images, compose music, or write coherent text, the objectives must be measurable and aligned with user needs.

Teams should consider questions like what types of outputs are desired, what constitutes success, and what constraints the system must operate under. This helps guide the choice of model architecture, data requirements, and evaluation criteria, forming the foundation for a streamlined pipeline.

9.3.2 Designing Scalable and Modular Data Pipelines

Data is the cornerstone of any AI system, and for generative models, the quality and diversity of training data are especially important. A well-optimized pipeline begins with scalable and modular data ingestion processes that can handle large volumes of data from heterogeneous sources. Data must be cleaned, labeled where necessary, and preprocessed consistently to ensure compatibility with model input requirements. Modular data pipelines allow teams to reuse components for different tasks, apply updates easily, and test changes without disrupting the entire workflow. These pipelines often include stages for deduplication, tokenization, normalization, and filtering. For text models, preprocessing might involve handling rare tokens, punctuation, or multi-language inputs. For image and audio models, tasks may include resolution standardization, augmentation, or spectrogram generation. Automating these steps reduces manual errors and increases reproducibility across training runs.

9.3.3 Efficient Use of Compute Resources

Training generative AI models is computationally expensive, often requiring vast GPU or TPU resources over extended periods. To optimize training efficiency, developers must make strategic decisions regarding hardware utilization, distributed training frameworks, and checkpointing strategies. Selecting the right batch size, learning rate schedule, and mixed precision settings can significantly reduce training time without sacrificing performance. Frameworks like PyTorch and TensorFlow provide support for data parallelism, model parallelism, and gradient accumulation, which enable training large models across multiple devices.

Tools such as DeepSpeed, Horovod, and Ray help manage distributed environments, ensuring efficient communication and fault tolerance. Checkpointing models regularly allows teams to resume training after interruptions and experiment with hyperparameters without starting from scratch. Another key consideration is the use of pretraining followed by fine-tuning. Rather than training from scratch, many generative models are initially trained on general-purpose corpora and later fine-tuned for specific tasks or domains. This approach saves time and resources while producing more adaptable and context-aware systems.

9.3.4 Monitoring Training Metrics and Model Behavior

Continuous monitoring during training is essential for identifying issues like overfitting, mode collapse, or vanishing gradients. Tracking loss curves, perplexity, and other performance metrics helps diagnose problems early and adjust training configurations accordingly.

In generative models, qualitative evaluation of outputs during training can provide additional insights, especially when quantitative metrics do not capture nuances in creativity, coherence, or realism. Logging frameworks such as TensorBoard, Weights & Biases, and MLflow offer visualization tools to help monitor experiments, compare configurations, and share findings across teams. Incorporating early stopping criteria, learning rate schedulers, and validation checkpoints can further refine training efficiency and model performance.

9.3.5 Robust Evaluation and Testing Procedures

Evaluating generative models requires a combination of automated metrics and human-in-the-loop assessments. While metrics like BLEU, ROUGE, FID, and IS provide quantifiable indicators of quality, they often fall short in capturing subjective or context-specific aspects of generation. Human evaluations, user studies, or expert reviews are often necessary to validate the model's practical utility and adherence to expectations.

Testing should include edge cases, stress tests, and adversarial scenarios to assess the robustness of the system. This is especially important in applications involving safety, bias, or fairness. Implementing unit tests and integration tests within the machine learning pipeline ensures that data transformations, model components, and output handlers work as expected.

9.3.6 Optimizing Deployment Strategies for Real-World Use

Once a generative model is trained and validated, deploying it into production presents a new set of challenges. Deployment optimization focuses on reducing latency, minimizing resource usage, and maintaining reliability under variable load conditions. Depending on the use case, models can be deployed on-premises, in the cloud, or at the edge.

Each option requires different considerations in terms of scalability, cost, and data security. Model compression techniques such as pruning, quantization, and knowledge distillation can significantly reduce the model size and computational load without severely affecting output quality. These methods enable faster inference and lower memory requirements, making it possible to run generative models on mobile devices or in constrained environments. Using containerization tools like Docker and orchestration platforms such as Kubernetes ensures consistent deployment across different systems and environments.

Serving frameworks like TorchServe, TensorFlow Serving, or Triton Inference Server streamline model APIs and manage inference requests efficiently. For models with large token-level outputs, optimizing tokenizer libraries and batching requests can reduce latency and improve throughput.

9.3.7 Monitoring and Maintaining Deployed Systems

Deployment is not the end of the pipeline. Continuous monitoring of deployed generative systems is vital to ensure sustained performance, detect drift, and respond to unexpected behaviors. Logging inputs and outputs, tracking system load, and analyzing user interactions help identify issues and inform future improvements. A robust feedback loop enables the system to learn from real-world usage. This might involve collecting user corrections, analyzing failure cases, or identifying new content domains that require adaptation. Incorporating these insights into future training cycles enhances model relevance and longevity. Security and privacy considerations are also central to maintenance. Generative AI models must be protected against prompt injection, data leakage, and adversarial exploitation. Regular updates, access control policies, and audit logs are necessary components of a secure deployment pipeline.

9.3.8 Facilitating Collaboration and Documentation

Optimizing training and deployment pipelines also means building a collaborative and transparent development culture. Teams should maintain comprehensive documentation of datasets, model architectures, training runs, and deployment processes. This facilitates onboarding, debugging, and knowledge transfer. Version control for models, data, and code ensures traceability and reproducibility. Tools like Git, DVC, and model registries help manage the lifecycle of experiments and provide checkpoints for rollbacks or comparisons. Cross-functional collaboration between data scientists, software engineers, designers, and business stakeholders ensures that the system meets both technical standards and user expectations.

9.3.9 Ethical Considerations and Responsible AI Practices

Generative AI systems can generate misinformation, offensive content, or biased outputs if not carefully managed. Embedding ethical review into the development pipeline helps mitigate these risks. This includes curating high-quality, diverse training data, applying filters to block harmful outputs, and involving ethicists or domain experts in review cycles. Transparency tools like model cards and data statements help communicate the limitations and intended uses of the system. Providing users with disclaimers, content controls, or report buttons can empower them to engage responsibly with AI outputs.

9.4 ENGAGING STAKEHOLDERS IN MODEL DEVELOPMENT

The development of generative AI systems is a multidisciplinary and complex process that requires not only technical expertise but also strategic collaboration with a broad range of stakeholders. As generative AI technologies such as large language models, image generators, and audio synthesizers become increasingly integrated into products, services, and decision-making processes, the role of stakeholders—ranging from users and domain experts to ethicists and regulators—becomes essential. Stakeholder engagement ensures that generative AI systems are aligned with societal values, meet the needs of users, and adhere to ethical and legal standards. Engaging stakeholders effectively is not just a matter of gathering feedback; it is about embedding inclusive perspectives throughout the AI lifecycle to foster transparency, trust, and innovation. Engaging stakeholders in the development of generative AI systems is no longer optional; it is a best practice that underpins responsible and effective innovation. By involving diverse voices early and continuously, developers can ensure that generative AI systems are aligned with user needs, ethical standards, and societal values.

Best practices include early design involvement, continuous collaboration, transparent communication, ethical alignment, inclusive participation, co-creation, and iterative feedback mechanisms. These principles not only mitigate risks but also enhance the creativity, utility, and trustworthiness of generative AI. As these technologies continue to reshape how we communicate, create, and make decisions, stakeholder engagement will remain a vital pillar of sustainable and inclusive AI development.

9.4.1 Understanding the Importance of Stakeholder Engagement

Stakeholders in generative AI development can include end-users, clients, business leaders, domain experts, data scientists, legal professionals, civil society groups, and policy makers. Each group brings unique insights into the potential uses, benefits, and risks of generative AI systems. For example, while developers might focus on optimizing model performance, legal experts can highlight compliance risks, and users can identify usability challenges. Engaging these diverse perspectives early and continuously helps prevent blind spots that may arise from a purely technical approach. Stakeholder engagement also enhances accountability.

By including voices beyond the core development team, organizations can demonstrate their commitment to responsible innovation. It fosters trust among users and the public, especially when dealing with sensitive content or high-stakes applications. Moreover, such engagement supports the identification of real-world needs and ensures that the system is developed with relevance, inclusiveness, and fairness in mind.

9.4.2 Involving Stakeholders Early in the Design Process

One of the best practices in generative AI development is to involve stakeholders from the earliest stages of the design process. This phase is critical because it sets the foundation for the system's objectives, use cases, and design principles. Early engagement helps clarify what the model is supposed to do, who will use it, and in what contexts. It also provides an opportunity to identify potential ethical, social, or legal concerns before significant resources are invested.

For instance, if a generative AI system is being developed for medical applications, involving healthcare professionals and patients can help define appropriate constraints and ensure that the outputs are medically accurate and ethically sound. Similarly, in educational applications, engaging teachers and students can highlight the importance of age-appropriate content and effective pedagogical strategies. Early consultation allows developers to define success metrics that go beyond accuracy or fluency and instead include user satisfaction, fairness, and contextual relevance.

9.4.3 Continuous Collaboration throughout the Development Lifecycle

Engagement should not be a one-time event but a continuous process integrated into every phase of development. From data collection and preprocessing to model training, evaluation, deployment, and maintenance, stakeholder feedback plays a crucial role in shaping outcomes. Continuous collaboration can be facilitated through regular meetings, participatory workshops, surveys, user testing, and public consultations. During data collection and preprocessing, stakeholders can help assess the quality, relevance, and biases in the data.

In the training phase, transparency about modeling decisions can allow external reviewers or domain experts to suggest alternative strategies or flag issues. Evaluation metrics should be co-developed with stakeholders to ensure that they reflect practical and ethical dimensions of model performance. When the system is deployed, mechanisms should be in place to capture user feedback, monitor for unintended consequences, and iterate on the model accordingly.

9.4.4 Designing for Transparency and Explainability

One of the key concerns for stakeholders, especially those in regulatory, legal, or high-stakes environments, is the explainability of AI systems. Generative models, particularly those based on deep learning, are often viewed as black boxes, making it difficult for non-experts to understand how decisions are made or outputs are generated. This opacity can hinder trust and raise concerns about accountability.

To address this, developers should prioritize transparency in both model design and communication. This includes documenting datasets, model architectures, training procedures, and known limitations. Techniques such as model cards, data sheets, and interpretability tools can help communicate this information clearly to different stakeholder groups.

Moreover, providing interpretable outputs or post-hoc explanations—such as highlighting which training examples influenced a generated text or image—can further support user understanding and trust.

9.4.5 Aligning with Ethical and Regulatory Standards

Engaging ethicists, legal professionals, and compliance officers is essential for ensuring that generative AI systems meet ethical and regulatory standards. These stakeholders help identify potential harms such as bias, discrimination, misinformation, or misuse, and advise on frameworks for risk mitigation. For example, when developing a language model, legal experts might flag the risk of generating defamatory content or plagiarized text, while ethicists might raise concerns about reinforcing stereotypes or producing harmful language. To operationalize ethical principles, organizations should establish clear guidelines for model development, conduct regular ethical audits, and implement human-in-the-loop systems where appropriate.

Regulatory bodies are increasingly interested in setting standards for AI transparency, safety, and fairness, so engaging with policymakers and staying informed about evolving laws is vital. Proactive collaboration with regulators can also help shape responsible innovation and reduce future compliance burdens.

9.4.6 Facilitating Inclusive and Equitable Participation

Inclusivity is a cornerstone of effective stakeholder engagement. It is important to ensure that marginalized, underrepresented, or vulnerable groups have a voice in the development of generative AI systems, especially those that may impact them disproportionately. Inclusion involves not just inviting diverse perspectives, but actively creating spaces where those perspectives are respected and valued.

Developers should take care to engage with communities that are typically excluded from tech development, such as non-native language speakers, people with disabilities, or those with limited digital access. This may require adjusting engagement methods to be culturally sensitive, linguistically accessible, or accommodating of different communication styles. Doing so not only enriches the development process but also leads to more equitable and effective AI systems.

9.4.7 Enabling Stakeholder Empowerment and Co-Creation

Beyond consultation, empowering stakeholders to co-create with developers enhances the legitimacy and usefulness of generative AI systems. Co-creation means involving stakeholders as active participants in the design, prototyping, and testing of the technology. It fosters a sense of ownership and accountability and often leads to innovations that developers might not have envisioned alone.

For example, artists working with AI image generators can provide iterative feedback to refine stylistic elements or enhance creative control. In journalism, editors can work alongside language models to fine-tune content generation tools for specific editorial standards. Such collaborations blur the boundary between user and developer, turning generative AI systems into dynamic platforms for shared creativity and problem-solving.

9.4.8 Establishing Feedback Loops and Iterative Improvement

Effective stakeholder engagement requires robust feedback mechanisms that are responsive and adaptable. Feedback loops should be designed to capture both qualitative and quantitative data from stakeholders, including satisfaction, usability, error reports, and ethical concerns. This data should be integrated into agile development cycles, allowing teams to update models, improve documentation, and refine user interfaces. In high-stakes applications, feedback loops may also include red-teaming exercises, external audits, or community reviews. Transparency in how feedback is acted upon builds trust and signals a commitment to continuous improvement. Moreover, publishing the outcomes of stakeholder engagement—such as revised design goals or mitigation strategies—can further enhance credibility and accountability.

Glossary of Key Terms

Attention Mechanism: A neural network component that allows the model to focus on relevant parts of the input data.

Autoencoder: A neural network that learns to compress and then reconstruct data; used in some generative architectures.

Backpropagation: The method by which neural networks update weights based on loss gradients.

Bias in AI: Systematic errors in AI outputs due to prejudices in training data or model design.

Carbon Footprint of AI: The environmental impact caused by the energy consumption of AI training and deployment.

Computational Cost: The resources (like time and energy) required to train or run AI models.

Conditioning: Modifying model behavior based on specific inputs or constraints, such as prompts or class labels.

Content Filtering: Mechanisms used to remove or block inappropriate or harmful AI-generated content.

Data Augmentation: Techniques to expand training datasets by generating modified or synthetic examples.

Decoder: A neural network that transforms latent representations back into data or predictions.

Deepfake: A synthetic media format created using AI, often to replicate real human appearances or voices.

Diffusion Model: A generative model that starts with noise and gradually transforms it into data through a learned denoising process.

Discriminative Model: A model that distinguishes between different classes or categories rather than generating new samples.

Encoder: A component of neural networks that transforms input data into a latent representation.

Ethical AI: The practice of developing AI systems that align with societal values and norms.

Explainability: The degree to which a model's decision-making process can be understood by humans.

Few-Shot Learning: A capability of a model to perform tasks with very limited examples provided at inference time.

Fine-Tuning: The process of adapting a pre-trained model to a specific task or domain with additional training data.

GAN (Generative Adversarial Network): A type of generative model consisting of a generator and a discriminator trained in opposition to produce realistic outputs.

Generative AI: A branch of artificial intelligence focused on creating new content such as text, images, audio, and data patterns based on training data.

Generative Model: A type of machine learning model that learns the underlying distribution of data to generate new data instances.

GPT (Generative Pre-trained Transformer): A series of large language models developed by OpenAI that generate human-like text.

Human-in-the-Loop: A framework where human input and oversight are integrated into AI system development and deployment.

Hyperparameter: Tunable settings in model architecture or training, like learning rate or batch size.

Inference: The phase where a trained model generates or predicts output from new input data.

Interpretability: The extent to which internal mechanics of an AI system can be discerned and explained.

Knowledge Distillation: The technique of transferring knowledge from a large model to a smaller, efficient one.

Latent Space: A compressed, abstract representation of data where generative models explore variations to produce new outputs.

Loss Function: A mathematical expression used to quantify the error during model training.

Mode Collapse: A problem in GANs where the generator produces limited diversity in outputs.

Model Drift: The degradation of model performance over time due to changing data distributions.

Multimodal AI: AI systems that can process and generate multiple types of data, such as text, image, and audio.

Noise Vector: Random input used in generative models (especially GANs) to seed the generation process.

Open Source Models: AI models whose code and weights are publicly available for study and use.

Overfitting: A scenario where a model learns training data too well, leading to poor generalization on new data.

Perplexity: A measurement of how well a language model predicts a sequence, indicating its fluency.

Pretraining: Initial model training on a large, general dataset before fine-tuning on a specific task.

Prompt Engineering: The process of crafting inputs (prompts) to effectively guide the outputs of generative AI models.

Reinforcement Learning: A type of learning where models learn by receiving feedback from their actions in an environment.

Sampling: The method of generating outputs from a probabilistic model using learned distributions.

Self-Supervised Learning: A technique where the model generates its own labels or tasks during training, often used in language models.

Synthetic Data: Artificial data generated by AI models to augment training datasets or protect privacy.

Text-to-Image Generation: The use of generative AI to create images from natural language descriptions.

Tokenization: The process of converting text into smaller units (tokens) for processing by language models.

Training Data: The dataset used to teach generative models how to understand and replicate the patterns of real-world data.

Transfer Learning: Applying knowledge from one domain or task to another, often by fine-tuning a pre-trained model.

Transformer: A neural network architecture that uses self-attention mechanisms and is foundational in many generative AI models like GPT.

Unsupervised Learning: A learning paradigm where models find patterns in data without labeled outputs, common in generative AI.

VAE (Variational Autoencoder): A generative model that encodes input data into a probabilistic latent space and decodes it to reconstruct data.

Zero-Shot Learning: The ability of a model to perform a task it has not been explicitly trained on, using general knowledge.

Reference

AI For Beginners 2025: A Hands-On Guide to AI Automation Spencer V. Webster; Independently Published, 2025

AI Made Simple: A Beginner's Guide to Generative Intelligence Rajeev Kapur; Independently Published, 2023

Artificial Intelligence: A Modern Approach Authors: Stuart Russell and Peter Norvig Publisher: Pearson Publication Year: 2020 (4th Edition)

Artificial Intelligence: A New Synthesis Author: Nils J. Nilsson Publisher: Morgan Kaufmann Publication Year: 1998

Artificial Intelligence: Foundations of Computational Agents Authors: David L. Poole and Alan K. Mackworth Publisher: Cambridge University Press Publication Year: 2010

Artificial Intelligence: Structures and Strategies for Complex Problem Solving Author: Ge orge F. Luger Publisher: Pearson Publication Year: 2008 (6th Edition)

Artificial Intelligence: A Guide for Thinking Humans Author: Melanie Mitchell Publisher: Farrar, Straus and Giroux Publication Year: 2019

Artificial Intelligence: A Guide to Intelligent Systems Author: Michael Negnevitsky Publisher: Pearson Publication Year: 2005

Artificial Intelligence: A Systems Approach Author: M. Tim Jones Publisher: Jones & Bartlett Learning Publication Year: 2008

Artifi c ial Intelligence: A Very Short Introduction Author: Margaret A. Boden Publisher: Oxford University Press Publication Year: 2018

Artifi cial Intelligence: The Basics Author: Kevin Warwick Publisher: Routledge Publication Year: 2012

Artificial Intelligence: What Everyone Needs to Know Author: Jerry Kaplan Publisher: Oxford University Press Publication Year: 2016

Atlas of AI: Power, Politics, and the Planetary Costs of Artificial Intelligence Kate Crawford; Yale University Press, 2021

Biomedical Data Analysis and Processing Using Explainable (XAI) and Responsive Artificial Intelligence (RAI) Publisher: Springer Publication Year: 2022

Co-Intelligence: Living and Working with AI Ethan Mollick; Independently Published, *2024*

Computer Vision: Algorithms and Applications Author: Richard Szeliski Publisher: Springer Publication Year: 2010

Deep Learning Authors: Ian Goodfellow, Yoshua Bengio, and Aaron Courville Publisher: MIT Press Publication Year: 2016

Explainable AI Recipes: Implement Solutions to Model Interpretability with Python Publisher: Apress Publication Year: 2021

Explainable AI with Python: Interpretability and Explainability of Machine Learning Models and Deep Learning Neural Networks Publisher: Springer Publication Year: 2021

Explainable AI: Interpreting, Explaining and Visualizing Deep Learning Publisher: Springer Publication Year: 2019

Explainable Artificial Intelligence: An Introduction to Interpretable Machine Learning Publisher: Springer Publication Year: 2021

Explainable Artificial Intelligence: First World Conference, xAI 2023, Lisbon, Portugal, July 26–28, 2023, Proceedings, Part I Publisher: Springer Publication Year: 2023

Explainable Artificial Intelligence: Second World Conference, xAI 2024, Valletta, Malta, July 17–19, 2024, Proceedings, Part I Publisher: Springer Publication Year: 2024

Generative AI and Libraries: Claiming Our Place in the Center of a Changing World American Library Association; ALA Editions, 2024

Generative AI in Action Amit Bahree; Manning Publications, 2024

Generative AI on AWS: Building Context-Aware Multimodal Reasoning Applications Chris Fregly, Antje Barth, Shelbee Eigenbrode; Packt Publishing, 2023

Generative AI with LangChain: Build Large Language Model (LLM) Apps with Python, ChatGPT, and other LLMs Ben Auffarth; Packt Publishing, 2023

Generative AI with Local LLM Leanpub; 2024 19. Generative AI for Beginners Made Easy ModernMind Publications; Independently Published, 2023

Generative AI with Python and TensorFlow 2: Create Images, Text, and Music with VAEs, GANs, LSTMs, Transformer Models Joseph Babcock, Raghav Bali; Packt Publishing, 2021

Generative AI: The Insights You Need from Harvard Business Review Harvard Business Review Press, 2024

Generative Artificial Intelligence: What Everyone Needs to Know Jerry Kaplan; Oxford University Press, 2024

Generative Deep Learning: Teaching Machines to Paint, Write, Compose, and Play David Foster, Karl Friston; O'Reilly Media, 2019

Introduction to Generative AI Numa Dhamani, Maggie Engler; Independently Published, 2023

Introduction to LLMs for Business Leaders: Responsible AI Strategy Beyond Fear and Hype I. Almeida; Independently Published, 2023

Life 3.0: Being Human in the Age of Artificial Intelligence Max Tegmark; Knopf, 2017

Machine Learning: A Probabilistic Perspective Author: Kevin P. Murphy Publisher: MIT Press Publication Year: 2012

Natural Language Processing with Python Authors: Steven Bird, Ewan Klein, and Edward Loper Publisher: O'Reilly Media Publication Year: 2009

Pattern Recognition and Machine Learning Author: Christopher M. Bishop Publisher: Springer Publication Year: 2006

Probabilistic Graphical Models: Principles and Techniques Author: Daphne Koller and Nir Friedman Publisher: MIT Press Publication Year: 2009

Prompt Engineering for Generative AI: Future-Proof Inputs for Reliable AI Outputs James Phoenix, Mike Taylor; Independently Published, 2024

Reinforcement Learning: An Introduction Authors: Richard S. Sutton and Andrew G. Barto Publisher: MIT Press Publication Year: 2018 (2nd Edition)

Robust Explainable AI Publisher: Springer Publication Year: 2023

Speech and Language Processing Authors: Daniel Jurafsky and James H. Martin Publisher: Pearson Publication Year: 2008 (2nd Edition)

Superintelligence: Paths, Dangers, Strategies Author: Nick Bostrom Publisher: Oxford University Press Publication Year: 2014

Supremacy: AI, ChatGPT and the Race That Will Change the World Parmy Olson; St. Martin's Press, 2024

The Quest for Artificial Intelligence: A History of Ideas and Achievements Author: Nils J. Nilsson Publisher: Cambridge University Press Publication Year: 2009

The Singularity Is Nearer: When We Merge with AI Ray Kurzweil; Penguin Books, 2024

Index

www.ingramcontent.com/pod-product-compliance
Lightning Source LLC
LaVergne TN
LVHW081938200926
848484LV00009B/2457